Retirement Portfolios

Retirement Portfolios

Theory, Construction, and Management

MICHAEL J. ZWECHER

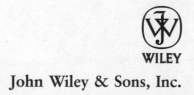

John Wiley & Sons, Inc.

Published by John Wiley & Sons, Inc., Hoboken, New Jersey.
Published simultaneously in Canada.

For general information on our other products and services or for technical support, please
contact our Customer Care Department within the United States at (800) 762-2974, outside
the United States at (317) 572-3993 or fax (317) 572-4002.

Wiley also publishes its books in a variety of electronic formats. Some content that appears
in print may not be available in electronic books. For more information about Wiley
products, visit our web site at www.wiley.com.

Library of Congress Cataloging-in-Publication Data:

Zwecher, Michael J., 1957–
    Retirement portfolios : theory, construction, and management / Michael J. Zwecher.
        p. cm.—(Wiley finance series)
    Includes bibliographical references and index.
    ISBN 978-0-470-55681-8 (cloth)
    1. Retirement income–Planning. 2. Portfolio management. I. Title.
    HG179.Z94 2010
    332.024′014–dc22

                                                                              2009031706

Printed in the United States of America.

10 9 8 7 6 5 4 3 2 1

This book is dedicated to my daughters, Olivia, Maia, and Zoe, three children who make every day the best day ever but guarantee that I will never be able to retire.

Contents

Preface

Life in 2009 and Beyond

"What was I paying you for?"

Whether asked in a civil or angry tone, that is the question that many advisers hear explicitly or implicitly from their clients. It's a valid question. The business model of retail financial services has been based around creating high expectations but devoid of defined milestones or goals; in the jargon of the MBA, the business model has been built around selling hope without offering the client any explicit deliverables.

For nearly 25 years, beginning in 1981, selling based on expectations and hopes was enough to build a business. As the affluent classes expanded, portfolios were created and markets boomed. Retail advisers could sell expectations and the market generally delivered the outcomes for accumulators and retirees alike. The few storm clouds and squalls that did appear could all be managed—and the manageability of those small storms seemed to justify a business model with expected performance as its linchpin. As in any business model an arms race inevitably develops around the selling linchpin. In financial markets expectations of performance begat expectations of outperformance. Built around raised expectations of performance rather than delivery of outcomes, this business model left clients—and the model itself—vulnerable to the financial hurricane.

The first dark clouds appeared with an unexpected mortgage write-down by HSBC Holdings in early 2007. The clouds were followed in June with the lightning bolt forced liquidation of two Bear Stearns hedge funds. Credit markets soon began to blow apart leaving corporate borrowers unable to roll debts, particularly those funded with short-term paper. Asset-backed commercial paper, auction rate securities, variable rate debt obligations, and the entire repo market foundered. The Fed cut rates and injected liquidity, yet Bear Stearns and AIG still failed. Lehman failed, Merrill almost failed. Morgan Stanley looked to be in a death spiral.

The events of 2007–2009 were a double blow. The softening of the housing market was impacting the balance sheets of clients and putting a drag on the economy, but the failures within the financial system nearly sent the economy over a cliff. Not only did the markets for all asset classes deflate with suddenness and violence as if it were a case of financial "Ebola," many of the mainstay firms that proffered advice to retail clients were destroyed. They were largely responsible for the debacle, inept at handling the crisis, and unconcerned about the damage wrought. It is hard to sell your advice as wise when your firm is blowing itself to kingdom come and the CEO is mismanaging nearly every utterance, including public testimony before Congress. For clients, it meant that plans, built on thrift and deferred consumption were destroyed. For advisers, the impact has been, and is being, felt at both the personal and career levels.

In the aftermath of the panic, with its damage to both client portfolios and client relationships, some have been quick to declare the retail model dead. Selling based on expectations and fair-weather investing may not be dead, but it will certainly be tempered for a while, perhaps even for a generation. Clients are reevaluating their strategies and tactics for building portfolios, which means that the business model will, if nothing else, evolve.

Selling expectation-based portfolios based on concepts promising risk-free enhancement of yield such as alpha[1] are great for raising client's expectations of higher return per unit of risk. Unfortunately, what was often sold as alpha was really either just a liquidity premium or a premium for non-linear risk; in normal markets these premiums accrued to the holder. In markets such as the one of 2008, however, illiquidity acted as a lead weight on a struggling swimmer and events that previously seemed like remote possibilities came to pass. For the most part, alpha-promising products are great for selling on aspiration but poor for resiliency in meeting future needs. Advisers need to have a business model that allows them to sell based on expectations that meet both client's aspirations and future needs.

In spite of all that has happened, the news is mostly good. Portfolios can be constructed to withstand market turmoil, and they can be constructed out of familiar components. The "sleeves" might feel a little different, but the feel is familiar. For many people, this means keeping the type of portfolio that they know and are comfortable holding. For the adviser, the change in business model is substantial, but the change in day-to-day operations will feel natural. To be sure, there are some things to think about and do differently. For most people there's no need to take a "sledgehammer" approach. Saving for retirement doesn't become any easier, but you can build portfolios that are sensible, robust enough against market cycles to protect lifestyle and still provide opportunities for aspiration to a better lifestyle.

Clients defer consumption and save their money for a reason. A portfolio is not a flower garden designed for purely aesthetic value, but a means to prepare for future needs. While willing to take risk, clients maintain an expectation that *enough* of the money will be there when it is required to meet future needs. For the adviser, it means that creating outcomes is important. It doesn't mean, or have to mean, risk avoidance. But it will mean that alert risk monitoring will be required for some and risk compartmentalization for others.

This is a good time to reflect on what advisers can do that is both viable in a business sense and valued by their shell-shocked clients. Advisers offer more than market knowledge, product knowledge, transactions, and advice. Advisers have a comparative advantage as service providers for clients. This book focuses on helping advisers—and individual clients—utilize that advantage and ensure value-additive portfolio creation and proper management.

In the traditional model, advisers combine product and market knowledge with sales acumen to create a book of business. Here we show how to extend beyond the simple lens of risk-return to create a scalable business model that allows for most of what you are used to doing but simultaneously meets the customized needs of clients. We also cover other ways an adviser adds value, particularly as a *delegate:* Someone who can take action without the conflicted passions of trying to manage one's own emotions and portfolio simultaneously. Whether the relationship allows for discretion or not, the adviser's monitoring of markets means that the adviser can act faster and without waffling when conditions are met (nondiscretionary) or deemed warranted (discretionary).

Retirement is the most opaque, costly, and angst ridden part of financial planning that most people face. The good news is that it doesn't have to be that way. The bad news is that, as of 2008, only a small percentage of financial advisers describe themselves as competent when it comes to creating portfolios designed to meet retirement needs. Clients can't look to 401(k) administrators for solutions; they'll probably receive a nice pamphlet with lots of bromides for the "average" retiree, but it will be next to useless for your client. For the most part, they are neither properly registered to be allowed to offer investment advice nor, as plan administrators, able to provide tailored advice; asking for information about something not on the menu would be a complete waste of time. For some, the last two sentences are a problem, for you and for me they're an opportunity.

When properly explained, understanding how to structure portfolios for retirement income is an easier problem than most advisers realize. Saving for retirement may be difficult, but, with the proper understanding, you can analyze the circumstances of your clients and from there show them what to do without feeling lost yourself. By knowing where they are, and where they want to be, you will better understand how you can take actions to improve outcomes.

Much of what advisers and clients need to know is straightforward and intuitive—its stuff that makes sense. Most of the material is geared for the financial professional; if you're an individual whose goals are simply to understand what needs to be done and be able to converse intelligently with your adviser you may want to skim the more technical sections. Each chapter is designed to (1) enhance understanding, (2) enhance competence, and (3) enhance expertise. At the very least, you should finish this book with a better understanding of what needs to be done, even if you skip the sections on how to do it or how to do it really well.

Most parts of the book are not technical but expository. However, some parts will require—and reward—those with patience and concentration. There is a workbook accompanying this book for those who want to implement the portfolios discussed here. I make no apologies for the segments on allocations and active risk management being technical in nature. On balance, I've attempted to minimize the abstract and maximize concrete examples. Most of the mathematical concepts are found in the accompanying workbook or moved to the appendix of this one. There are a few background areas where I get into the assumptions and theory underlying the methods used, but I keep those for exposition that will be of most use to those who want to implement some of the ideas discussed in the book for a varied client base.

In reading this book, you will spend most of your time learning how to reframe your existing practice to provide more value to clients. Much will focus on what to ask and how to act to protect your client's retirement *and* aspirations. You'll also be given a menu of alternatives that you can undertake in concert with your clients. All of the alternatives presented here conform to best practices. Your job will be to understand your client's preferences and pick which alternative works best for him or her. For an individual, you can choose between going it alone or conveying what you want your financial adviser to do on your behalf.

In writing this book I have received no funding or payment from any firm. It is not my intention to sell anything but rather educate so that you can do the selling. For that reason, this book is aimed at helping professionals understand how to manage a portfolio of assets to protect a lifestyle without changing the desirable features of current practice and bridging them to the emerging thought on best practices. Some intrepid individuals may find this book useful, but it is not meant as a simple guide for average readers. For professionals, I have sought to provide a framework of solutions that can be scaled across their client base. These professionals can be:

- Transaction-oriented salespeople
- Asset gatherers
- Portfolio managers
- Insurance planners
- Financial planners

PART ONE: FRAMING THE PROBLEM

Part One (Chapters 1–5) provides the setup, the thematic underpinning for viewing retirement income needs. These first chapters are designed to focus your attention on framing the retirement portfolio problem in a way that can be solved. If you think back to your days of doing word problems, Part One is designed to help you understand the important aspects of the portfolio problem and set up the problem to be solved in Parts Two through Four.

Chapter 1, Portfolio Focus and Stage of Life, shows you how tools and techniques used in the accumulation phase of your client's life don't work well or are inappropriate for both planning for and living in retirement.

Chapter 2, The Top-Down View: A Short Primer on Economic Models of Retirement Income, provides a capsule summary of the last 40 years of economists' work in the areas of consumption planning and lifetime portfolio selection relating to retirement. This provides a useful way of framing the issues and splitting up the problem into two parts: meeting your client's lifestyle needs and meeting your client's need to aspire. Our focus for the remainder of Part One is on the lifestyle needs and we defer the aspirational needs to Parts Two through Four, where we discuss allocations, portfolios, and risk management for retirement.

Chapter 3, The Importance of Lifestyle Flooring, is all about understanding lifestyle (flooring) needs and the classifications of product types that help to safeguard lifestyle during retirement. We delve a little deeper to see how what is considered a need will be funded. By matching needs against resources, and the options available for securing lifestyle needs.

Chapter 4, Monetizing Mortality: Annuities and Longevity Insurance, looks at risk pooling, how longevity-based products work, and an individual's ability to monetize one's own mortality. Roughly 15 percent of all retirement assets are held in insurance-related retirement products such as annuities. For many, it is the only retirement product that they own. There are many classes of these insurance-related products and most individual products seem difficult to understand. The goal of Chapter 4 is to simplify the understanding of insurance products and, when coupled with Chapter 3, help your clients decide if insurance products are right for them.

Chapter 5, Flooring with Capital Markets Products, is a brief look at using capital markets products to help secure a floor under a lifestyle. It is not meant as a comprehensive guide, but in tandem with Chapter 4, meant to provide a perspective on the possibilities for creating lifestyle security with standard products such as stocks and bonds that can be used to construct a retirement income portfolio. When coupled with Chapter 3, Chapter 5 helps to crystallize the notions of a protected floor.

PART TWO: ADAPTING PORTFOLIOS
FOR RETIREMENT INCOME

Part Two is designed to move you from understanding to action. The theme is to start with the subtle changes that make big differences. This part is dedicated to taking your ingredients and combining them in a recipe to meet outcome-oriented goals. In Part Two, we start with some simple retirement income constructs that dovetail with traditional accumulation portfolios. The objectives are twofold. Our first objective is to show advisers and individuals that there are straightforward ways to prepare for the act of retirement, naturally transitioning from an accumulation to a retirement income focus. Our second objective is to show that the changes to portfolios are not drastic; conceptually, they make sense to clients and they are as scalable as traditional constructs.

Chapter 6, Building Retirement Income Portfolios, walks through the basic portfolio construction for retirement income. For those still working or in the preretirement accumulation phase, this chapter offers simple construction types for building retirement income portfolios. The portfolio constructs offered are straightforward for individuals and scalable for professionals to offer to multiple clients. The last section of Chapter 6 offers a list of 11 common pitfalls regarding the use of taxable versus tax-advantaged accounts for assets. To paraphrase Nigel Tufnel, most books only offer 10 pitfalls, but this book has 11.

Chapter 7, Creating Allocations for Constructing Practical Portfolios by Age and Lifestyle Needs, provides some information and examples of functional asset allocation useful for conceiving complete retirement income portfolios. This chapter provides guidance on allocations to lifestyle security, longevity risk, precautionary needs, and risky assets. We also discuss the impact of having lifestyle security on an individual's risk tolerance. Chapter 7 helps to clarify the line between those who are more natural candidates for insurance products versus standard capital-markets products like bonds.

PART THREE: MANAGING PORTFOLIOS
FOR RETIREMENT INCOME

All portfolios need to be monitored and occasionally they need attention. This is as true of a passive portfolio as an actively managed one. For passively managed portfolios, the goal is to keep the portfolio on a predetermined track. For actively risk-managed portfolios, the goal is to seek the higher returns that come with higher risk without letting the risk threaten to endanger lifestyle.

Chapter 8, Rebalancing Retirement Income Portfolios—even if you set up a passive portfolio for retirement income, it requires periodic rebalancing to raise what it provides for the client's lifestyle and to avoid increases in risk. There is a difference between rebalancing as used in the normal context of accumulation portfolios and portfolios that are set up to protect a lifestyle. In our case, rebalancing is a more delicate, but not more difficult, problem. There is a role for traditional rebalancing within the aspirational segment of the portfolio that is also discussed.

Chapter 9, Active Risk Management for Retirement Income Portfolios, shows how to actively risk manage around a lifestyle floor, without ever losing sight of the need to maintain the floor. We show how portfolios can be set up to take a little more risk, attempting to gain higher return, and be prudent at the same time. Remarkably, using historical returns we see that a little risk can go a long way in helping to raise lifestyles. Fortunately, historical returns also teach us that taking a lot of risk, even if coupled with diligent risk management, can pay off but is more likely to lead to no net gain in lifestyle.

PART FOUR: MAKING IT HAPPEN

By the time you get to Part Four, you should have a solid understanding about the important considerations for retirement portfolios, the methods for constructing retirement portfolios, and the techniques for managing the portfolios. What comes next? This part is about adapting a traditional business to encompass retirement portfolios. The emphasis here is on having a process that is backward compatible with your existing business model. To that end, we emphasize making the transition feel natural, working within current infrastructure, understanding the subtle changes in client segmentation, and how product sets fit into our framework. We cover a large number of examples that can be considered as outlines of portfolios targeted for the different segments. Information that speaks directly to clients is included in Chapter 14. The last chapter of the book is focused on final thoughts about myths and fallacies that are dangerous for portfolios and some helpful ways to rehabilitate the still viable portfolios that may have suffered a setback.

Chapter 10, The Transition Phase, moves from a focus on accumulation of assets to a focus on lifestyle protection. The goal of this chapter is to have the transition fit the natural evolution of a portfolio so that clients feel comfortable in the undertaking. This chapter shows the best time to begin the transition and constructs that make the transition natural.

Chapter 11, Putting Together the Proposal, combines the ideas of the book and focuses on putting it all together for a proposal to a (new) client.

Here we show how to take an ordinary accumulation portfolio and provide a makeover to create a retirement income portfolio—all in an intuitive and straightforward manner.

Chapter 12, Market Segmentation, synthesizes the material of earlier chapters regarding the segmentation of clients. As you will see, there are subtle but profound differences between traditional segmentation and effective segmentation for retirement income. The goal is to show how producers, marketers, and investment managers can create offerings targeting relevant market segments.

Chapter 13, Products and Example Portfolios, provides several case studies and sample portfolios that can be used for various client types. Though there are no specific product "endorsements," these portfolios are meant not as theoretical constructs but as prototypes.

Chapter 14, Preparing Your Client for a Retirement Income Portfolio, helps you provide something to the client and with the client in mind. It is designed as a tool to help you frame the issues to clients in a way that they can understand.

Chapter 15, Salvage Operations, Mistakes, and Fallacies, is meant to provide guidance for climbing out of the hole that has swallowed so many client portfolios. As a prelude, we first discuss common mistakes and fallacies in retirement income planning. We then move on to salvaging what is left in 2009 and the more general problem of helping clients who suffer a financial setback.

APPENDIXES

This book also includes two appendixes. Appendix A, History of Theoretical Developments in Life-Cycle Planning, features the more technical aspects of the material covered in Chapter 2. It is more technical and goes a little deeper into the material than the main text while still being accessible to nonacademics.

Appendix B, How Professionals Can Maximize the Usefulness of this Book, answers this question, whether your business model is transaction based or fee based, institutional or retail. This appendix explains the relevancy to maximizing the usefulness of retirement portfolios in your business.

Acknowledgments

This book was written between September 2008 and July 2009. For most of that period, it was a good time to be focused on something other than the day-to-day spasms in financial markets. But out of the mix doesn't mean that I worked alone, in a vacuum, or without the generous help of others.

Many people contributed to the book intellectually, thematically, and stylistically. Many contributed to helping research, frame, or tighten the arguments that appear within. Still others helped provide impetus to write this book.

Much helpfulness came from members and affiliates of the Retirement Income Industry Association (RIIA), including François Gadenne (Chair, RIIA), Steve Mitchell (COO, RIIA), Bob Powell (Editor, *Marketwatch*), Elvin Turner (Turner Consulting, LLC), Greg Cherry (RIIA Research Committee, Chair), and Rick Miller (Sensible Financial).

Among those whose contributions were the most insightful and interesting were Zvi Bodie (Boston University), Ravindra Koneru (Endowment of the Institute for Advanced Study, Princeton), Larry Kotlikoff (Boston University), John Lambert (Bank of America), Fong Liu (Barclays), Annamaria Lusardi (Dartmouth University), Moshe Milevsky (York University), Armando Rico (Merrill Lynch), and Nevenka Vrdoljak (Bank of America).

In helping to hone and frame the arguments to fit within the body of practice of financial advisers were John Carl (Retirement Learning Center), Elizabeth Chen (Merrill Lynch), Keith Heyen (Wells Fargo), Michael Higuchi (Merrill Lynch), Tom Latta (Merrill Lynch), David Musto (JPMorgan), Keith Piken (Bank of America), Bob Rafter (Retirement Learning Center), Jim Russell (Merrill Lynch), George Wilbanks (Russell Reynolds), Bruce Wolfe (Allianz), Joe Zidle (Merrill Lynch), and Jeff Zorn (Northwestern Mutual).

Many others helped to push me along in writing the book including Kazi Ariff (Bank of America), Harvey "Skip" Brandt (Starwood), Glenn Worman (Morgan Stanley), Jim Gatheral (Merrill Lynch), Laura DiFraia (Wachovia), Doug Manchester (Goldman Sachs), Gloria Nelson (Afton Marketing), Stacy Schaus (Pimco), Bob Triest (Federal Reserve Bank of Boston), Dabin Wang (Barclay's), and Lainie Zwecher.

I also want to mention the people at John Wiley & Sons who were very helpful in taking this book from concept to reality, including Pamela van Giessen, Emilie Herman, Kevin Holm, and Kate Wood.

Framing the Problem

Portfolio Focus and Stage of Life

Objectives

Why retirement income planning differs from accumulation

The danger of drawdown plans

In the same way that saving for a child's wedding is different from actually planning the wedding, planning to live *in* retirement is different from planning for the far-off act of retiring. Every few years a new financial panic ushers in a series of stories about retirees and those nearing retirement having their fears raised and their hopes dashed because their portfolios are not set up to protect their lifestyle during retirement. The goal of this book is to help you transition and manage your client's (or your own) portfolio from a generic retirement fund to a portfolio that will see them through to the end. So let's get to it.

For most of your clients, retirement isn't just another stage in the evolution of their portfolios. It is a main reason why they saved part of their incomes and created their portfolios. The point of this brief chapter is to introduce you to some of the reasons for rethinking the construction of such portfolios so that they meet this objective and other objectives your clients desire. At some point, the client's priorities will begin to shift from accumulation of assets to maintenance of lifestyle. As you will see, switching the focus of the portfolio may utilize familiar products but requires changes in portfolio management. In later chapters, we'll discuss methods for transitioning clients and building "normal" looking portfolios designed for maintenance of lifestyle without foregoing aspiration. In this chapter, we focus on reasons that retirement requires a different approach from that of shifting the accumulation portfolio into reverse.

In this first chapter, we walk through examples to sow the idea of why a "balanced" portfolio may not last through retirement; how retirement saving differs from creating retirement income; how fixing the spending level (variable weights) of a typical portfolio can leave the client vulnerable to running out of money too soon; how fixing the depletion weights (variable spending) in a typical portfolio can lead to undesirable swings in the client's lifestyle; a section on retiring at the wrong time—which I call the Murphy's Law of timing retirement.

We also discuss the production industry's tendency to focus on single products that are supposed to act as magic bullets but usually only appeal to a narrow segment of the client base. In brief, we will contrast products with solutions. Clients want solutions, products may enable or be part of solutions, but it is rare that a product is the solution.

A "BALANCED" PORTFOLIO APPROACH MAY NOT LAST THROUGH RETIREMENT

Balanced portfolios are great for accumulating wealth within one's comfort level, but eventually collecting assets must give way to deploying assets. Much of the inadequacy of maintaining balance as the goal will be fleshed out in later chapters. What I mean by this section's provocative heading is that most of *Modern Portfolio Theory* (MPT), and the portfolio advice that flows from it, is geared toward an arbitrary accumulation portfolio. An accumulation portfolio is unconstrained by the need for meeting drawdown cash-flow needs. For an accumulation portfolio, the main concern is maintaining a portfolio's balance of risky and safe assets to let the portfolio grow at a rate and risk level at which the client is comfortable. In accumulation, the problem is how to make the client's portfolio grow while letting both of you sleep at night. In retirement, the game is to enable the client to meet or exceed lifestyle needs each and every year, while making sure that the money and aspirational goals will survive. Sports metaphor: Saving for retirement is largely an offensive game and retirement income planning is a combination offensive–defensive game.[1] We show you how to implement both static and active accumulation plans and provide you with the means to defend them not just for the average retirement, but for every retirement.

In retirement, the problem is to maintain a lifestyle; a lifestyle that must be funded and defended. It can be funded partially from Social Security and defined benefit pensions, but also from the client's portfolio. The idea of risk versus return is not wrong; however, in retirement, the probability of outliving one's money becomes a very serious issue, especially when markets are stressed. Drawdown plans are very sensitive to down-market conditions early in retirement. Defending a lifestyle against unforeseen liabilities such as health or personal injury problems will be discussed, but the focus of this book is on things within your control as a financial adviser and having flexibility designed into the portfolio for the things that are out of your or your client's control.

Fixed Spending Levels (Variable Weights) and Shortfall Risk

Why worry so much about the defensive game? If the market tanks right before or just after retirement (as in 1973, 2000, or 2008), then your client may end up in a big hole and forced to eat "seed corn" in order to maintain lifestyle. On the other side, if the defensive stance is too rigid, you will be unable to adjust for contingencies and opportunities. To harp on the downside for a moment: Depending on how and how fast the market and portfolios recover determines whether eating the seed corn was merely a dangerous or a fatal mistake. Improperly defended, your client risks what is termed a *shortfall*. Shortfall risk can become an existential problem once your client stops generating outside income.

Consider the lucky, the unlucky retiree, and the average retiree who each need the money to last for 20 years (Table 1.1). A string of positive returns during the first 10 years of retirement means that this lucky individual is able to withdraw $50,000 per year without running out of money.

Table 1.1 shows the lucky retiree who gets a ride on a bull market early and is able to make the money last with plenty of room to spare. Note that in the remaining amount, after taking a withdrawal at the end of the year, is the amount with which you begin the next year. Table 1.2 shows the unlucky retiree who attempts the same drawdown strategy but retires into the teeth of a bear market. Here, a string of negative returns at the beginning of retirement means that this unlucky individual runs out of money after 11 years. This performance is worse than having put the money in a mattress. It begs the question that if keeping cash would work with certainty, what would it take to secure the lifestyle but keep open the opportunity for upside?

In both cases (Table 1.1 and Table 1.2), the average return was zero and only the ordering of the returns differed. In a later chapter, we'll return to this individual who started with $1 million and needed $50,000 per year for 20 years. We will show that this individual's retirement was fully funded and that making it work should have been a no brainer.

Suppose now we consider the "average" retiree. For this person, we assume that the rate of return is always the average return. In this case, with an average rate of return of 0 percent, starting at $1 million and taking out $50,000 per year will last exactly 20 years. Although the returns data are contrived, these examples demonstrate clearly that a standard drawdown strategy has potentially large risks for a retiree. In any drawdown

TABLE 1.1 The Lucky Retiree Whose Funds Will Last

Period	Beginning Amount	Lucky Return	End of Period	Withdrawal	Remaining
1	$1,000,000	10%	$1,100,000	$50,000	$1,050,000
2	$1,050,000	10%	$1,155,000	$50,000	$1,105,000
3	$1,105,000	10%	$1,215,500	$50,000	$1,165,500
4	$1,165,500	10%	$1,282,050	$50,000	$1,232,050
5	$1,232,050	10%	$1,355,255	$50,000	$1,305,255
6	$1,305,255	10%	$1,435,781	$50,000	$1,385,781
7	$1,385,781	10%	$1,524,359	$50,000	$1,474,359
8	$1,474,359	10%	$1,621,794	$50,000	$1,571,794
9	$1,571,794	10%	$1,728,974	$50,000	$1,678,974
10	$1,678,974	10%	$1,846,871	$50,000	$1,796,871
11	$1,796,871	−10%	$1,617,184	$50,000	$1,567,184
12	$1,567,184	−10%	$1,410,466	$50,000	$1,360,466
13	$1,360,466	−10%	$1,224,419	$50,000	$1,174,419
14	$1,174,419	−10%	$1,056,977	$50,000	$1,006,977
15	$1,006,977	−10%	$906,279	$50,000	$856,279
16	$856,279	−10%	$770,652	$50,000	$720,652
17	$720,652	−10%	$648,586	$50,000	$598,586
18	$598,586	−10%	$538,728	$50,000	$488,728
19	$488,728	−10%	$439,855	$50,000	$389,855
20	$389,855	−10%	$350,869	$50,000	$300,869

TABLE 1.2 The Unlucky Retiree Whose Funds Run Out Too Soon

Period	Beginning Amount	Unlucky Return	End of Period	Withdrawal	Remaining
1	$1,000,000	−10%	$900,000	$50,000	$850,000
2	$850,000	−10%	$765,000	$50,000	$715,000
3	$715,000	−10%	$643,500	$50,000	$593,500
4	$593,500	−10%	$534,150	$50,000	$484,150
5	$484,150	−10%	$435,735	$50,000	$385,735
6	$385,735	−10%	$347,162	$50,000	$297,162
7	$297,162	−10%	$267,445	$50,000	$217,445
8	$217,445	−10%	$195,701	$50,000	$145,701
9	$145,701	−10%	$131,131	$50,000	$81,131
10	$81,131	−10%	$73,018	$50,000	$23,018

strategy, it is not sufficient to look at the average case; the order of returns will matter, and it will matter a lot.

Another way of saying what I'm trying to get across is that modern portfolio theory creates good portfolios that work *on average*. For retirement income, however, the problem switches to ensuring that the income generating capacity of the portfolio works *regardless* of the path taken by the market but still has almost the same upside potential. There are both simple, passive methods for ensuring sufficient yearly income and methods that require more activity and thereby put more at risk that may or may not provide greater upside. The best approach for a particular person requires knowledge about that person; but we'll go through a variety of approaches that you and your client may want to use.

Making your client's money last does not mean putting everybody in bonds or annuities. It means managing their funds in a way that has them prepared for each year's needs. In many cases, it merely means taking advantage of the fact that bonds don't just dampen portfolio volatility, but they are generally scheduled to pay fixed amounts on set dates plus their face value on maturity.[2] Throughout the book, we explore both passive and active ways to take and maintain control of a portfolio throughout retirement. Advisers should come away with a firm grasp on how to help their clients, and frankly, *sell* the proposition. If you're not an adviser and not the type to do it yourself, you'll come away knowing how to interact more productively with your adviser, so that your adviser can act as an agent able to understand and meet your goals.

Here's the key concept: Once your client begins thinking of retirement, you want to help them to understand what they need as a lifestyle *floor* (the minimum amount of funding required for the client to keep their lifestyle viable) and begin to shift their portfolio's focus from pure accumulation, with its emphasis on maintaining balance, to a stance that protects their lifestyle while still offering the potential for upside. This floor isn't necessarily what they want to spend to maintain a lifestyle; it is what they need to spend to maintain their lifestyle. Protecting a lifestyle floor means changing the rebalancing rules that are used in accumulation to ensure that floor's protection.

Fixed Depletion Weights (Variable Spending) and Lifestyle Risk

There is an alternative that some of you may have already considered. It is possible to take a fixed proportion each year, while letting the amount vary depending on market conditions. If you think of someone starting out with 100 shares and they want to make the funds last for 20 years, then you could sell 5 shares per year. In such a case the fund will last, but they may end up with a few lean years and a few fat years along the way. For example, we consider our lucky, unlucky, and average retirees using this approach. With an average return of zero, our average retiree will take out $50,000 per year. But our lucky and unlucky retirees will end up with the consumption paths shown in Table 1.3.

A string of positive returns during the first 10 years of retirement means that except for the final year this individual supports a lifestyle greater than $50,000 per year.

Having the bull market at the beginning of retirement, "Lucky" was able to maintain a lifestyle that provided little in the way of income stability for planning but did provide a few fat years along the way. However as with drawdown plans, for the unlucky retiree of Table 1.4 who follows the same rule but gets hit by very different market dynamics, the scheme does not work nearly as well.

With the first 10 years of Table 1.4 sporting negative returns, this individual supports a lifestyle that can only be described as grim relative to sticking the money in a mattress.

TABLE 1.3 The Lucky Retiree Enjoys a Well-Funded Lifestyle

Period	Beginning Amount	Return	End of Period	Lucky's Withdrawal	Remaining
1	$1,000,000	10%	$1,100,000	$55,000	$1,045,000
2	$1,045,000	10%	$1,149,500	$60,500	$1,089,000
3	$1,089,000	10%	$1,197,900	$66,550	$1,131,350
4	$1,131,350	10%	$1,244,485	$73,205	$1,171,280
5	$1,171,280	10%	$1,288,408	$80,526	$1,207,883
6	$1,207,883	10%	$1,328,671	$88,578	$1,240,093
7	$1,240,093	10%	$1,364,102	$97,436	$1,266,666
8	$1,266,666	10%	$1,393,333	$107,179	$1,286,153
9	$1,286,153	10%	$1,414,769	$117,897	$1,296,871
10	$1,296,871	10%	$1,426,558	$129,687	$1,296,871
11	$1,296,871	−10%	$1,167,184	$116,718	$1,050,466
12	$1,050,466	−10%	$945,419	$105,047	$840,373
13	$840,373	−10%	$756,335	$94,542	$661,793
14	$661,793	−10%	$595,614	$85,088	$510,526
15	$510,526	−10%	$459,474	$76,579	$382,895
16	$382,895	−10%	$344,605	$68,921	$275,684
17	$275,684	−10%	$248,116	$62,029	$186,087
18	$186,087	−10%	$167,478	$55,826	$111,652
19	$111,652	−10%	$100,487	$50,243	$50,243
20	$50,243	−10%	$45,219	$45,219	$—

TABLE 1.4 The Unlucky Retiree Lives a Constrained Lifestyle

Period	Beginning Amount	Return	End of Period	Unlucky's Withdrawal	Remaining
1	$1,000,000	−10%	$900,000	$45,000	$855,000
2	$855,000	−10%	$769,500	$40,500	$729,000
3	$729,000	−10%	$656,100	$36,450	$619,650
4	$619,650	−10%	$557,685	$32,805	$524,880
5	$524,880	−10%	$472,392	$29,525	$442,868
6	$442,868	−10%	$398,581	$26,572	$372,009
7	$372,009	−10%	$334,808	$23,915	$310,893
8	$310,893	−10%	$279,804	$21,523	$258,280
9	$258,280	−10%	$232,452	$19,371	$213,081
10	$213,081	−10%	$191,773	$17,434	$174,339
11	$174,339	10%	$191,773	$19,177	$172,596
12	$172,596	10%	$189,855	$21,095	$168,760
13	$168,760	10%	$185,636	$23,205	$162,432
14	$162,432	10%	$178,675	$25,525	$153,150
15	$153,150	10%	$168,465	$28,078	$140,388
16	$140,388	10%	$154,426	$30,885	$123,541
17	$123,541	10%	$135,895	$33,974	$101,921
18	$101,921	10%	$112,113	$37,371	$74,742
19	$74,742	10%	$82,217	$41,108	$41,108
20	$41,108	0%	$41,108	$41,108	$—

Fixing the depletion weights and allowing the amount consumed to vary each year will always stretch the funds as far as needed, but is not always a satisfying approach. When returns are constant and without volatility, flexible withdrawals provide stable consumption. However, for portfolios having elements of risk, anyone who is even moderately risk averse will prefer a smoother, more predictable consumption path.

Falling for Murphy's Law of Timing Retirement

For most people, retirement isn't a spur of the moment act but part of a premeditated plan. Often the premeditation is colored by the current state of the economy as a whole and portfolio performance in particular. When markets are booming, people have a sense of financial well-being. That may lead some to underweight the probability or suddenness of a market downturn. This sense of well-being may make some more prone to choose early retirement after a long period of prosperity and near a market peak. This would be Murphy's Law of retirement: People tend to retire just before a market downturn and are thus more likely to be unlucky. We want to show you how to protect their gains in a way that allows for participation in opportunities for growth while managing against the risk of degradation in lifestyle. This further helps avoid the blame game and the potential for questions about suitability.

Drawdown Plans Are Sensitive to Longevity

All drawdown plans, whether fixing spending levels or fixing portfolio weights, are sensitive to longevity. The more that an adviser tries to optimize a drawdown plan to cover a retirement span, the greater the sensitivity of the plan's likelihood of success to living past the expected span's terminus.

For the fixed spending level plans, the longer the stream of income is expected to flow, the greater the probability that any depletion rate will fail. Few people want to constrain their lifestyle needlessly. That means that there is an incentive to seek the highest rate of drawdown that will be expected to work. But the rate that ought to work for a 10-year span is unlikely to be successful for a 30-year span. Advisers run the risk that the higher they try to manage or optimize a drawdown plan's cash flows, the greater the probability that the plan will run out of money if the client is blessed with longevity.

For the variable spending plans, there is also a danger in longevity. In a mathematical sense, the risk here can be somewhat mitigated by adjusting the drawdown rate to reflect conditional life expectancy at each point in time. However, what works mathematically is not necessarily sensible. The level of spending that falls mathematically out of a variable spending plan may not be high enough to sustain lifestyle. The likelihood that a variable spending plan will yield cash flows that are too low to sustain lifestyle is greater when the plan is adjusted for longevity.

RETIREMENT SAVING VERSUS RETIREMENT INCOME: AN ILLUSTRATION

Conceptually, the retirement saving problem is a problem of growing as big a pot as possible given a client's level of risk aversion. Once retired however, each client needs to maintain a lifestyle that works for him or her. Instead of thinking of the metaphor of the pot that keeps growing, what you want to do is begin to think of a problem where you create a floor amount of income for each year of retirement and your goal is to never let the client fall below the floor. As shown in Figure 1.1, accumulation eventually gives

Before the Retirement Planning Phase: Grow the Portfolio

Beginning with Retirement Planning: Protect the Lifestyle

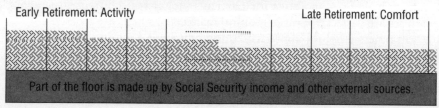

Consumption/Lifestyle Floor

FIGURE 1.1   Growing the Portfolio and then Protecting the Lifestyle

way to decumulation. It is useful to lay out assets and match desires against abilities, recognizing that some of their income may come from external sources and that the client may anticipate a slowing down of their lifestyle.

If your clients have been contributing to Social Security, or have other forms of social income such as veteran's benefits, then they will be eligible to receive benefits that can defray some of their lifestyle costs. In addition, although the participants of defined benefit retirement plans have become rare outside of governmental employment, some clients may get such income. Social Security and defined benefit plans aside, it's all up to remaining financial and human capital sources.

PRODUCTS VERSUS SOLUTIONS

Retirement income is a multifaceted problem. The objectives include securing a lifestyle, having the ability to meet contingencies, and being able to aspire to an improved lifestyle. The difficulties that people face include risks that the adviser can control and risks outside the adviser's control. The adviser can help mitigate market risks, credit risks, longevity risks, inflation risks, some of the risks associated with changing tax laws, and certain health risks. But he or she cannot control spending risks, public policy risks, and uninsurable catastrophic events. The focus of this book is on managing for and through the difficulties and finding solutions that help prevent difficulties.

Products are not solutions, but they help to effect solutions. With different segments for lifestyles relative to wealth, risk aversion, health, and longevity, there will be different solutions. Quite often products are touted as solutions. In a few cases, products exist that meet the needs of a particular slice of a segment. This book, however, does not endorse individual products. There are no products that offer solutions for all segments. Products have pros and cons for particular segments. For some segments, annuities are perfect, for others capital markets products are a better choice, for still others a hybrid approach combining capital market products with insurance-related products can be appealing.

This book weighs product types for their ability to help effect solutions for individuals. We show how to build portfolios and, where necessary, manage the risk within the portfolios. In most cases, the right solution is static or, with occasional rebalancing, nearly static. There are solutions where the risk needs to be actively managed.

SUMMARY

This chapter showed that traditional portfolios, built for accumulation of wealth, frequently fail during withdrawal in retirement. In a nutshell, the problem is that traditional portfolios are designed around the principle of finding what is, on average, the best alternative—and finding the best portfolio for an individual client out of those that will not fail. These first few examples are designed to reinforce the notions that drawdown plans suffer from major weaknesses.

- When making withdrawals the order of returns matters
- The timing of retirement can have a significant impact on the likelihood of success or failure
- Unexpected shocks, even one-time shocks, can destroy a plan
- Outliving ones assets becomes a more acute risk for an "optimized" withdrawal strategy

CHAPTER 2

The Top-Down View

A Short Primer on Economic Models of Retirement Income

Objectives

Understanding the framework for retirement portfolios
    Securing minimum needs
    Creating upside above the minimum

Understanding funding and the need to take risk
    Capital markets and capital markets risk
    Risk pooling: Monetizing your mortality and its risks

While many financial professionals are well schooled in the dynamic nature of asset markets and asset prices, most of the practical literature geared toward financial professionals gives short shrift to the basic point that clients are saving and investing for a reason. Even less guidance is provided to advisers on the dynamic nature of how the actions required for achieving the client's portfolio objective change through time. The standard framework in which most advisers operate treats the client portfolio as separable from desired future consumption. Separating out consumption and ignoring the reason that portfolios are created may make the material easy to teach, but reduces the material's relevance.

A half-century of literature exists that links investing to consumption. As you'll see in this chapter, a simple and subtle tweak to the standard framework provides substantial practical insight. We're not after an academic exercise, but in showing how recognizing a seemingly small change in framework provides enormous insight into how to build a business.

We start this chapter with a short primer on economic models of retirement income—pay special attention to the simplicity of the results and their business implications. We then reconcile accumulation portfolios with retirement income portfolios. Of practical interest is how the degree of client risk aversion evolves. When the client has an interest in lifestyle maintenance, the portfolio construction separates between lifestyle flooring and creating the potential for upside. We discuss client goals, the ability of clients to meet their goals, the role of taking market risk, and the role of insurance against risks by risk pooling.

AN OVERVIEW OF ECONOMIC MODELS OF RETIREMENT INCOME

Almost all structural models of lifetime consumption and portfolio selection yield strikingly similar results. It helps that the results are pretty intuitive. What is even more helpful is that we can take the important implications of the approach without being constrained by a particular parameter. To be technical for a moment, all members of the standard class of utility functions[1] yield optimal consumption plans implying optimal consumption in any period is given by an individually specified minimum consumption floor amount plus a fraction of wealth in excess of the present value (PV) of *all* future floor amounts (discretionary personal wealth). The salient differences between optimal plans for different preferences manifest themselves by differences in the drawdown fractions (x).

The English translation is this: Every model commonly used by economists takes you to the same place: An individual's optimal consumption is given by their specified minimum lifestyle plus some fraction of discretionary wealth.

Here is a mathematical representation:

$$\text{Optimal consumption} = \text{Consumption floor}$$
$$+ x\% \times [\text{Current wealth} - \text{PV(future floors)}]$$
$$= \text{Lifestyle floor} + x\% \times (\text{Discretionary wealth})$$

This allows us to characterize "optimal" portfolios as floor plus upside.

The primacy of securing a floor under lifestyle holds for all models. Some models leave the floor unchanged if wealth and consumption rise and others that are more elaborate allow the floor to rise when there is a bump up in lifestyle. All of the models emphasize the importance of some type of floor. The results of optimizing the remainder of the portfolio for alternative preferences are nuanced and subtle. Different preferences imply differences in portfolios and rates for drawing down from discretionary wealth:

1. Differences in risk tolerance will lead to discretionary wealth portfolios that have degrees of risk corresponding to where the individual sits along the aggressive–conservative risk-tolerance spectrum.
2. Those whose relative risk aversion is unchanged as wealth is drawn down will consume discretionary wealth in straight-line fashion while those whose risk aversion increases as they draw down total wealth will be more frugal with their resources and be less tolerant of risk as their wealth shrinks.

RECONCILING RETIREMENT INCOME PORTFOLIO CONSTRUCTION WITH ACCUMULATION

At first glance, the rationale and equation in the previous section may not look like the standard Markowitz (1952, 1959) model or the Modern Portfolio Theory (MPT) framework that we normally work with. In fact, the standard MPT framework is a special case of the more general life-cycle framework of Samuelson (1969) and Merton (1969, 1971) which we use here. Modern portfolio theory began with Markowitz, but it didn't end there. There are two main features that distinguish the life-cycle framework used here from the Markowitz special case. The first is that this framework is explicit in its acknowledgment that consumption has physical and psychological minimum requirements. By itself, this difference seems small but has a profound impact on portfolio construction. The second is that this framework takes into account the dynamic features of a lifetime portfolio problem rather than the single-period framework used by Markowitz.

The lifestyle floor recognizes that most people would seek to avoid outcomes if their basic lifestyle was in jeopardy. Security and fear are powerful emotions that drive behavior in virtually every financial model. The floor is a statement that there is an outcome where fear overwhelms the desire for potential gains. In brief, the floor is part of a total portfolio, but it is a subportfolio where safe, time-dated cash flows are desired.

The fraction of the portfolio that encompasses discretionary personal wealth—that is, wealth in excess of the amount needed to lock in a floor—is close in spirit to the standard framework. One important difference here is that the model is dynamic, linking the individual's desires and sense of well-being across time. This dynamic feature embeds a desire for smooth consumption that would not be captured in the standard model. That means that even in this Markowitz-like subportfolio, as wealth is drawn down, the risk aversion of the client will probably be changing and the optimal portfolio will change commensurately.

To give a little better feel for why the portfolio construction differs for retirement income and accumulation, we now go through the abstract setup for a two-period problem followed by a simple example of the way that the problem is changing.

Suppose that we are in a Markowitz world with two periods today and tomorrow. We'll make it even simpler by assuming that today's consumption has already been chosen so that the only decision is how to allocate the amount of unspent wealth among different assets. Formally, the investor/consumer's problem is to choose a portfolio to maximize the expected utility of next period's consumption subject to limited wealth and the characteristics of available assets. To put it in symbolic form the investor/consumer's problem is the following:

$$\max E[U(C_{t+1})]$$

subject to

$$C_{t+1} = W_{t+1} = (W_t - C_t)(1 + R_{t,t+1})$$

and

$$R_{t,t+1} = \sum_{i=1}^{N} w_i r_i$$

In this equation $E[]$ represents the expectation operator, C represents consumption subscripted by time period, W represents wealth similarly subscripted, $R_{t,t+1}$ represents the return on the portfolio of assets. The individual returns on the assets are given by r_i and the weights of the assets in the portfolio are given by w_i. As always, the weights sum to 1.

Since we've already chosen today's consumption the problem is equivalent to choosing the optimal set of portfolio weights w_i. If the utility function is quadratic, or if returns follow a normal distribution, then the preceding problem is a standard mean/variance optimization problem.

The retirement income problem can be seen as an almost identical problem, but with the addition of a constraint that next period's wealth must be above some floor level. The portfolio weights are still the choice variables in the problem, but the resulting portfolio will now reflect the imposition of the flooring constraint.

$$\max E[U(C_{t+1})]$$

subject to

$$C_{t+1} = W_{t+1} = (W_t - C_t)(1 + R_{t,t+1})$$

and

$$R_{t,t+1} = \sum_{i=1}^{N} w_i r_i$$

$$W_{t+1} \geq \text{Floor}$$

In this simple model a greater proportion of the portfolio will be dedicated to a risk-free asset to ensure that the floor is achieved.[2] The complications for modeling are trivial but the implications for portfolio construction are profound.

To see how profound the implications of the change, consider a very simple numerical example with two portfolios:

Portfolio 1

Probability	Outcome
0.5	22%
0.5	–6%

Portfolio 2

Probability	Outcome
0.08	90%
0.92	0%

We can calculate the expected return and volatility of the portfolios as follows:

$$\text{Mean} = \sum_{i=1}^{N} \text{Probability}_i \times \text{Outcome}_i$$

$$\text{Variance} = \sum_{i=1}^{N} \text{Probability}_i \times (\text{Outcome}_i - \text{Mean})^2$$

$$\text{Standard deviation} = \sqrt{\text{Variance}}$$

	Portfolio 1	Portfolio 2
Mean	8.0%	7.2%
Variance	0.0196	0.0596
Standard deviation	14%	24%

Portfolio 1 has both a higher mean and a lower variance than Portfolio 2. Portfolio 1 offers what some would call both first and second order stochastic dominance. A mean/variance investor will prefer Portfolio 1 as the higher return, lower risk portfolio. For an investor with an initial investment of \$100 and utility function is given by $U = \sqrt{\text{Final Wealth}}$, portfolio 1 will provide the higher expected utility.

For Portfolio 1:

$$U_{P1} = \sum_{i=1}^{n} \text{Probability} \times U(\text{Outcome}_i)$$
$$= 0.5 \times \sqrt{122} + 0.5 \times \sqrt{94} = 10.37$$

while for portfolio 2:

$$U_{P2} = \sum_{i=1}^{n} \text{Probability} \times U(\text{Outcome}_i)$$
$$= 0.08 \times \sqrt{190} + 0.92 \times \sqrt{100} = 10.30$$

In contrast, assume that the investor's initial investment is \$100 and the investor's utility function incorporates a consumption floor of 93, which is now given by $U = \sqrt{\text{Final Wealth} - 93}$. For Portfolio 1:

$$U_{P1} = \sum_{i=1}^{n} \text{Probability} \times U(\text{Outcome}_i)$$
$$= 0.5 \times \sqrt{122 - 93} + 0.5 \times \sqrt{94 - 93} = 3.19$$

While for Portfolio 2:

$$U_{P2} = \sum_{i=1}^{n} \text{Probability} \times U(\text{Outcome}_i)$$
$$= 0.08 \times \sqrt{190 - 93} + 0.92 \times \sqrt{100 - 93} = 3.22$$

With the incorporation of the consumption floor in the utility function, Portfolio 2 becomes the preferred portfolio.

As soon as a consumption floor is included, portfolios that violate the floor get ruled out and outcomes that exceed the floor become much more important for creating satisfaction. Even though Portfolio 1 has both lower variance and higher expected return than Portfolio 2, Portfolio 2 has less lifestyle risk and becomes preferred. This example was contrived to obtain the reversal of portfolio preference ordering but the point is that imposing a lifestyle floor creates a desire for asymmetric portfolio payoffs.

It is interesting to note that if the floor had been set above 94, then the investor would not even be willing to consider Portfolio 1. The adviser does not observe the client's utility function, but does observe what sells. Very few clients buy mean/variance optimal portfolios. Many clients simultaneously purchase annuities and speculative stocks. The import of the previous statements is that the adviser only observes behavior and not the underlying motivation; the client may seem to be acting suboptimally by refusing a portfolio that dominates in mean and variance. Some may even be tempted to call the behavior an anomaly or say that the client is irrational. In fact, the client isn't necessarily acting suboptimally or irrationally; a small change in the objective can lead to a large change in optimal solutions.[3]

In general, mean/variance optimization relies either on preferences defined only on the mean and variance of a portfolio or that the portfolio's returns follow a distribution that can be fully characterized by mean and variance. A minimum consumption level makes it a client's goal to seek assets and form portfolios with asymmetric payoff profiles that have less downside than if normally distributed.[4] Unless we keep the strict interpretation of preferences defined only on the mean and variance of a portfolio, we move to floor plus upside portfolios. The risk-return framework still applies, but risk means degradation of lifestyle not simply volatility.

Instead of limiting the analysis to the mean/variance notions of risk-return that often draw blank looks and may not be useful for our clients, we can use the more resonant framework of creating a consumption floor plus upside that is more broadly applicable.

Retirement requires outcomes, not just expectations. In a fuller and richer model, the portfolio dynamics will place greater emphasis on creating the floor the closer that the client is to the date when the floor begins to take effect. For retirement income, the process of beginning the switch from pure accumulation to a portfolio that evolves toward protection of the floor is known as the *transition*.

THE DYNAMICS OF RISK AVERSION

Most people exhibit behavior consistent with *decreasing relative risk aversion* (DRRA). When their wealth is rising, people are willing to take more and larger risks. After retirement, when wealth is decreasing, behavior and portfolio choices are more restrained. The restrained spending behavior stays in place until very late in life, when "saving for a rainy day" gives way to "you can't take it with you." Then you often see the anecdotal phenomenon of the very elderly reversing years of frugality by deciding to redecorate or splurge in some way. This phenomenon is neither simply a health-related issue nor a desire to avoid estate taxes; it appears to be common regardless of health or wealth; impatience overtakes frugality.

Figure 2.1 depicts the drawdown of wealth for an individual with *constant relative risk aversion* (CRRA). This individual remains tolerant of risk

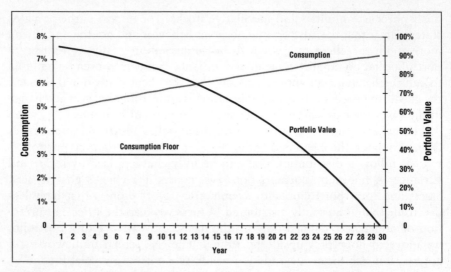

FIGURE 2.1 Wealth Drawdown and Consumption for Individual Exhibiting Constant Relative Risk Aversion

regardless of wealth. Consumption is planned to rise only because the individual wants to get as much incremental happiness from consuming tomorrow as today. Since the planning of consumption tomorrow is worth less than today (impatience), constant incremental happiness requires expecting more consumption tomorrow.

For an individual with CRRA preferences, consumption will be set at a fraction that depends primarily on the number of years remaining. The degree of impatience is what provides the upward tilt in the consumption path. Impatience values consumption now more than consumption later; the point of indifference is reached only when deferred consumption is high enough to compensate for foregoing higher consumption today. In the previous example, wealth is consumed and consumption rises at a constant rate reflecting the influence of impatience.

Figure 2.2 repeats the exercise shown in the CRRA graph for an individual exhibiting decreasing relative risk aversion. Here, the DRRA individual is less tolerant of risk as wealth declines. Consumption is deferred and the portfolio used sparingly as impatience gives way to fear—until very late in life. Near the end of life, as there is a shorter future to worry about, fear recedes, and impatience roars back.

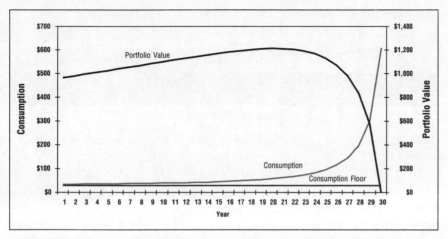

FIGURE 2.2   Wealth Drawdown and Consumption for Individual Exhibiting
Decreasing Relative Risk Aversion

In this case, since risk aversion is increasing as wealth is drawn down,
consumption plans reflect anxiety around the prospect of running short of
funds. Here we see a phenomenon that often surprises conventional wisdom:
Often those who retire hold fast to their assets until very late in life; impatience is held at bay by a decreasing desire for risk. Notice in Figure 2.2
that the dramatic rise in consumption and corresponding drop in wealth
has nothing to do with the state of health or pending estate taxes, it is
strictly a reflection of life-cycle planning among those with risk aversion
that rises as their horizon shrinks.

SEPARATION BETWEEN FLOORING AND UPSIDE

Rather than starting with a structural model for behavior and attempting
to design optimal solutions, we consider the simpler reduced form problem
of an individual who has specified a consumption floor and would, naturally, like to consume at or above the floor. Since the fundamentals remain
the same, we treat the simple two-part problem: How to build the flooring
and then what to do with the excess to build in the potential for upside.
By focusing on the flooring need first, we can better understand the self-
segmentation of individuals into groups who are more or less disposed to

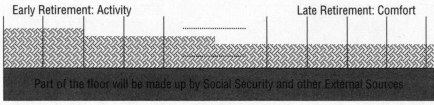

Consumption/Lifestyle Floor

FIGURE 2.3   Planning Covers the Level of Lifestyle and the Sources of Funding for the Lifestyle

capital-markets solutions versus insurance solutions. We will shortly discuss different types of flooring for different constituencies. After we complete the flooring, we address handling insufficient funds for flooring and alternatives for what to do with any leftover wealth.

We treat the floor shown in Figure 2.3 as comprised of the sum of both private (internal) and social (external) components such as Social Security income, defined benefit plans, etc., with the shape of the flooring completely dependent upon the individual's desires.

As before, in this example we have an individual whose retirement planning includes an active early retirement followed by decreasing activity.

With the guidance of the structural models showing the primacy of meeting the flooring needs, the reduced form approach becomes quite agnostic to flooring builds; engineering the portfolio to meet the flooring needs becomes a straightforward task.

FULLY FUNDED VERSUS UNDERFUNDED FLOORING

When today's wealth $W \geq$ PV(flooring needs),[5] we call the portfolio fully funded and there are myriad options available for building sustaining and sustainable portfolios. At a minimum one could build a floor using a ladder of bonds of different maturities or strips or zero-coupon components and place the excess in any arbitrary portfolio. In this example we express the portfolio as a sum of zero coupon bonds (ZCB) plus a standard portfolio for the funds that are in excess of what is earmarked for flooring:

$$ZCB_1 + ZCB_2 + ZCB_3 + \ldots + ZCB_N + \text{Portfolio of remaining funds}$$

Here we have a floor comprised of zero-coupon bonds from the first date of retirement up to a date at which we are fairly certain that the flooring will no longer be needed plus a portfolio which would depend on the individual's preferences.

When today's wealth $W < PV$(flooring needs), we call the portfolio underfunded. In this case, there are four options available: Work longer, reduce lifestyle, take market risk, or monetize mortality. Leaving the first two options of working longer or reducing lifestyle aside, we'll explore a little bit of the more interesting choice between taking market risk and monetizing mortality via a risk-pooling contract.

MONETIZING MORTALITY

Risk pooling is a way to monetize one's mortality. In one form or another, it places claims on assets at risk. At their heart, the insurance annuitant is willing to relinquish a claim on a percentage of assets (if dead) in exchange for a larger share (if alive)[6] of the assets of another person in the pool who has died. The question of whether the trade is worthwhile depends upon the following:

- *The price of mortality (how much/long does one expect to collect)*. That is, if the individual's subjective probability of survival is greater than the survival probability ascribed to the individual by the insurance company, then there will be a greater incentive for the individual to buy insurance.
- *Bequest desires (what does the client want to leave behind)*. An individual with a limited bequest motive would be more inclined to put assets at risk of mortality than an otherwise identical individual.
- *Reversibility (what if something happens or the probability of survival changes)*. Many annuities have charges for either outright surrender of the policy or changes in payout rates.

TAKING MARKET RISK

In conjunction with or in place of mortality risk, an individual who is underfunded may feel compelled to take market risk. In its simplest form, the addition of market risk could be in the form of corporate bonds or equity. In essence, credit ratings equal and credit risk aside, purchasing a corporate bond is equivalent to purchasing a fixed-term annuity that pays regardless of whether you're dead or alive. If taking, say, diversified equity risk, the individual becomes exposed to potential downside in exchange for higher expected outcomes. In the insurance context, the downside risk of too many people surviving too long is primarily borne by the unsecured creditors of the insurance company and only secondarily borne in the form of credit risk by policyholders.

By taking market risk, it is *possible* that the client may dig their way out of the hole in which they find themselves. However, there is a risk that they will dig themselves into a deeper hole. In fact, since for any maturity the price of vanilla put and call options are equal when struck at the (risk-free) forward price, capital markets offer no reason to expect that the odds of beating the risk-free rate are greater than 50/50. Later chapters will deal with the folly of raising the *expectations* that clients can dig their way out of a hole. As we discuss in Chapter 15 and show in the workbook, the cost of insuring that a portfolio's return exceeds the risk-free rate of interest does not decline for longer terms—as a former colleague used to say, "the long run is only longer than the short run, not safer."

RISK IS RISK, IS IT NOT?

In essence, taking mortality risk differs from market risk with respect to how those risks are priced and traded. At the retail level of the typical unaccredited[7] investor, capital market risks are traded with nomenclature that creates standardized products that trade in two-way auction markets: exchanges have standardized rules for market making, price discovery, delivery, settlement, and conflict resolution. In contrast, insurance markets are essentially monopolistically competitive, one-way contractual markets where the individual issuers offer differentiated products.

The other main difference between market risk versus mortality risk shows up if one looks at how insurance markets and capital markets price risk. In capital markets risk is priced by the cost of hedging out the risk via replication. In other words, the price is determined by the cost of getting someone else to bear the risk. In insurance markets, the risk is priced on an actuarial basis trying to charge the probabilistically right price for the risk. For example, a firm engaging in capital markets pricing will price an equity-linked, floored payout as if the issuing firm is short a bond and an equity call option. The cost of hedging out the short positions will be the basis for the pricing that the customer sees. In contrast, insurance contracts pool the risks and price based on expected payout and probabilities of capital sufficiency. Capital markets price based on what might happen rather than what is expected to happen; expectations play a far lesser role in capital markets pricing than in insurance pricing.

RISK, UNCERTAINTY, AND RISK AVERSION

Aside from the mechanical probability of ruin inherent in drawdown schemes—that is, the depletion of assets well before death—there remains the problem of inducing a risk-averse individual to be willing to accept a scheme which may fail. If we know that the after-the-fact results may not work, without a premium it would not appeal to risk-averse individuals before the fact. But for the risk averse, it goes a little deeper than the success versus failure outcome. For the risk averse, portfolios that offer smooth outcomes will be preferred—imagine if your consumption was highly variable. In retirement, portfolios offering both lifestyle security and the same expected return as accumulation portfolios will clearly be preferred. People may even be willing to pay to rid themselves of risk to lifestyle by purchasing solutions that are only desirable because of the absence of known alternatives. This may partially explain why annuities often appeal to those who have no need or desire to monetize their mortality.[8]

In accumulation portfolios, there is not only the risk associated with near-term market moves, but there is the uncertainty about the nature of future distributions of returns. Until 2008, no one would have expected that the S&P 500 would achieve a volatility more commonly associated with highly speculative single stocks, even for those who acknowledged the abstract possibility. Fortunately, there are some natural portfolio constructs that allow for reducing the uncertainty around lifestyle; lifestyle security is the major concern of most people planning for retirement. Ultimately, we will show portfolio constructs that look familiar, work in a way with which we are familiar, but allow for confident planning and have better outcomes for retirees.

SUMMARY

This chapter showed how the accumulation portfolios conventionally associated with Modern Portfolio Theory are really special cases of more general models. In general, garden variety accumulation portfolios ignore the importance of maintaining lifestyle. Retirement income portfolios seek to provide clients with flooring and upside in a way that balances ensuring adequate outcomes while maintaining the potential for upside.

The chapter also highlights the two main classes of flooring as tradable contracts, rather than individual contractual agreements:

- Decomposition of retirement income as floor + upside
- Risk aversion is likely to change with wealth
- Fully funded versus underfunded flooring
- Monetizing mortality through risk pooling
- Taking market risk is an oft considered alternative
- Capital markets contracts versus insurance contracts

CHAPTER 3

The Importance of Lifestyle Flooring

Objectives
Estimating the amount of flooring that is required
Anticipating the impact of inflation
Evaluating your choices in type of flooring

Setting explicit goals and planning to meet them is one approach that people can take for their retirement. The other approach is to save and structure retirement as intelligently as possible—but without knowing quite where it will all lead. This is planning implicitly but not explicitly. Both approaches are legitimate and the choice is a matter of preference. In this chapter, we focus on putting floors under lifestyles, laying out goals, and planning to meet them.

The concept of estimating and laying out retirement needs may end up sounding obvious to those predisposed to planning ahead. We call the lifestyle needs of clients their retirement floor—and understanding the floor is the start of the problem. How to construct and build up from the floor depends a lot on their individual preferences. If you're asking how much and what kind of flooring do they need, then this is the chapter for you. You should come away ready to segment your clients into one of three different flooring types: insurance, capital markets, or hybrid. In addition, you will be given pros and cons of having a nominal floor stepping up for expected price rises or flooring that automatically adjusts to inflation. Then you will be provoked to think about whether you are more comfortable as a nominal builder or an inflation-protected builder. The mechanics of laying down nominal or real flooring, however, will be covered in Chapters 6 and 7.

For those whose clients either do not want to reveal much or who are more of the freewheeling personality type, you may be tempted to skim until we discuss nominal versus real flooring in this chapter so you can move more rapidly to the chapters on building retirement income portfolios.

We will revisit flooring desires in Chapters 6 and 7 when we look closer at client assets and asset allocations. At that point, we will come back to flooring to try to figure out whether current assets (or likely future assets) can support client goals. If not, you can work with clients to choose whether to delay retirement, scale back their goals, monetize their mortality with insurance products, or put their late-stage retirement lifestyle at risk by swinging for the fences.

One very important point to make is that flooring is defined here as a guaranteed minimum payment, either nominal or real for some specified minimum amount of time.[1] We do not take the view that yield products constitute flooring unless the yield is based on a fixed minimum notional; in such a case the flooring value would be based on the minimum notional multiplied by the guaranteed yield. What we want to rule out are cases where the yield is a fixed percentage of a varying notional, such as some unprotected equity-linked funds.

As you go through this chapter, we start with a balance sheet view delineating the client's assets by category and placing the consumption needs within the balance sheet as liabilities. Retirement requires outcomes and not just expectations, as we discuss conditions for an asset or product type to qualify as flooring.

After this snapshot view of the balance sheet, we focus more deeply on an estimation of needed amounts, needed duration, and planning to meet the needs. We delve into the methodology and some definitional boundaries that are helpful in categorizing plans and assets. Since the concept of lifestyle is subjective and varies by client, we delineate between the bedrock floor and the aspirational floor to arrive at the finished floor.

We want to pay special attention to the potential impact of inflation. Inflation is sometimes considered a silent destroyer of lifestyle. While we'll try to avoid hyping the problem, we take it quite seriously—and note that a substantial number of the problems in the workbook focus on planning for the effects of inflation.

To conclude the chapter, we revisit the types of flooring; this time focusing on choosing a flooring type based on the client's capabilities, needs, and particular circumstances.

AMOUNT OF FLOORING: A BALANCE SHEET VIEW

Financial advisers generally focus on financial wealth. For life-cycle planning, it is important to remember that financial wealth is just one component of wealth. Most authors writing about this are likely to distinguish between financial wealth, human capital, and social capital.

This distinction separates the wealth that is based on past accumulation (financial wealth), wealth that will be monetized in the future via the direct efforts of the client (human capital), and wealth that is a claim on the efforts of others that is derived as part of the social compact and for which there is no direct quid pro quo (social capital).

Financial wealth is essentially comprised of claims that have accrued to the client through previous efforts. Some, but not all, of financial wealth is what financial services professionals are used to dealing with. With our definition, financial wealth includes the portfolio of traditional financial account holdings, home equity, art, collectibles, and liquidation values of the various knickknacks, bric-a-brac, and gewgaws that make up a household. This category also includes the present value of the flows that are expected to accrue based on equity ownership of businesses or other cash-producing entities.

Human capital is the present value of future earnings that will accrue to the client based on the individual efforts of the client. This category will include wages. For many clients this will also include the present value of expected patents, copyrights, and not yet achieved entrepreneurial activities. In short, this category includes the present value of all possible sources of income due to the effort of the client unit that are expected but not yet achieved.

Social capital is an interesting category that is often overlooked. To start with an example, the simplest element of social capital to understand is Social Security income. The Social Security system is a transfer program where the young, who are working transfer wealth to those who are no longer working but had previously contributed to the system. Whatever politicians may label things, the Social Security system simply acts as a pass-through service from the working to those no longer working. If the system were to be changed, the elderly would have no recourse. Similarly, there are other sources of wealth that are derived from society, charitable institutions, and family members.

Typically, advisers and wealth managers focus on the liquid portfolio subset of the financial wealth portion of the balance sheet and work on growing client wealth. For a client expected to live forever this is appropriate. However, retirement income clients need to match what they have, and be willing to part with on the left with what they need on the right. It may be helpful for you to ask your clients to get out a piece of paper and think of their lifestyle relative to their income and relative to their financial wealth.

Figure 3.1 highlights the analogy of a balance sheet for a hypothetical retiree. On the left side, we show assets and on the right side are liabilities (consumption, desired bequest) and any capital in excess of liabilities. In

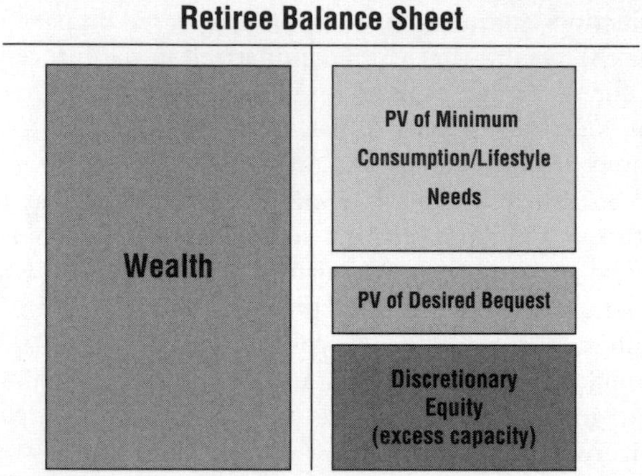

Retiree Balance Sheet

FIGURE 3.1 The Retirement Balance Sheet

concept, this is meant to be equivalent to a true economic balance sheet rather than a GAAP balance sheet—meaning intangibles like human capital are included. Please note that this illustration shows only the balance sheet and not the risks to the balance sheet (risky assets and unforeseen liabilities).

It is useful to think more deeply about the client's balance sheet and, depending on your business model, where your practice fits in with the following view of a client balance sheet as shown in Table 3.1.

RETIREMENT REQUIRES OUTCOMES, NOT JUST EXPECTATIONS

Markets are not merely collections of random variables that can be easily combined into stable portfolios. Markets are a reflection of the decisions of millions of participants who, at times, act autonomously and, at times, act as a mob. When the mob is out, markets can be discontinuous and temporarily unstable. We tend to be surprised more often—and by larger amounts—than our preconceived notions of risk lead us to expect. We often become lulled into a sense of complacency and a false sense of control by a market that remains stable for long periods of time. Depending on conditions, markets change course for longer and by a greater amount than we thought probable. We think that we have the ability to model the behavior of processes such as asset markets, but the market reminds us periodically

TABLE 3.1 Categories for a Client Balance Sheet

Assets	Liabilities
Human capital	PV of future consumption
Earnings	Preretirement
Patents	Postretirement
Entrepreneurial endeavors	
	PV of desired bequest
Financial capital	To offspring
Financial portfolio	To charity
Real assets to be monetized	
Accrued DB pensions	
Social capital	Discretionary wealth
Social Security	
Anticipated inheritance	
Expected assistance (family, community, etc.)	
Total	Total

that our models are imperfect representations of outcomes that are themselves representations of collective individual behaviors.

Much investment planning related to accumulation focuses on managing total return and risk exposure. An exclusive focus on risk-return ignores why we create portfolios: to make the most of our deferred consumption. Exclusive risk-return focus ignores differences in the reasons that the portfolios are being created or the timing of "planned harvest." An exclusive focus on risk-return implies consumption foregone rather than consumption deferred. Figure 3.2 shows the range of possible outcomes—simulated accumulation paths—for a portfolio: risk is no guarantor of return We can see that most but not all paths achieve our consumption floor. What works on average may not work for your clients. With a floor, one can avert disaster rather than planning in the face of it. Planning is more definitive when outcomes are bounded. Unbounded outcomes make planning more difficult.

Retirement-income planning needs to place an emphasis on creating a floor under the client's lifestyle. Financial planning for retirement is about creating outcomes while recognizing the importance of aspirations. With downside outcomes eliminated, the client can handle the planning around how to spend his or her retirement; after all, it is harder to make concrete plans in the face of greater uncertainty. This very change in focus, from

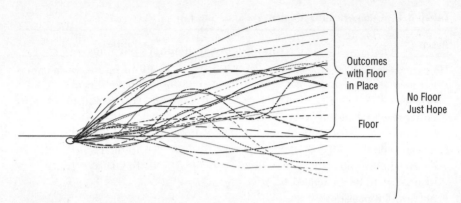

FIGURE 3.2 Simulating Paths for Accumulation

expected outcomes that have a wide variance creating outcomes and a limited downside, helps us deal with some of the difficulty of planning.

Investment in a pure accumulation framework focuses on the risk-return tradeoff and the client's risk tolerance. In this setting, the client may win some and lose some, but he or she can always try again. In retirement there are risks for both the financial plans and for the retirement plans. The adviser who leaves the client at such risks faces unhappy clients, CRD complaints, arbitration cases, and lawsuits. With alternatives that are available, practical, and able to avoid the previously described problems, failure to act appropriately is unwise.

CONSUMPTION NEEDS

It may be true that on average retirees spend about 70 percent of their preretirement income, but that is a useless factoid where almost any specific case is concerned. It's not what they earn, but what they spend that's important. Figuring out how much is needed in today's dollars to maintain clients living in the style to which they are accustomed is the first part of the problem; paying for it is another problem to solve; managing the funds securely is yet another. So let's go through top-down and bottom-up ways to narrow the client's spending needs. As individuals, they should be encouraged to do this before starting to plan with you. Any conscientious adviser will ask clients to go through this exercise before prescribing a course of action. The thing you want to do is have clients estimate their consumption expenditures as they are now and adjust for anticipated changes.

An important, but often overlooked point is that consumption needs represent a risk-free liability. A person has to eat; money for food needs to be there when the client gets hungry. An individual's earnings or portfolio returns may be risky, wants being discretionary may be discounted at a risky rate but the needs are "must have" amounts. How those needs are met and matched with assets is covered in Chapters 4 through 6; whether the liabilities are matched with assets of the same level of risk and how that gap in risk can be managed are important issues to think about.

The risk-free nature of needs makes them look expensive. This is both a daunting problem when dealing with clients but also an opportunity. One of the positive ways to use the risk-free discounting of needs versus wants is that the higher present value of needs can be used to get clients to rethink needs versus wants and get them to think about the aspects of their lifestyle that are most important.

First, we undertake the simplest possible yes/no exercise to help give an idea of where clients could end up if their current contributions are maintained but directed, metaphorically, into an inflation-adjusted mattress. After this section, we move to a more concrete planning process for determining needs.

YES/NO PLANNING

The idea behind yes/no planning is to allow an individual to see if they're comfortable with the road that they're currently traveling down; illuminating one feasible destination for the trip. The question is whether the destination that is laid out, with its implied lifestyle, is acceptable. This is similar to the way that many of today's planning tools work, but we want to strip out as many assumptions about portfolio performance as possible. No one comes away happy from this exercise and the answer to the yes/no question is almost always a no. But the exercise helps to set a baseline for getting people to think about their lifestyle needs.

The method is very simple and requires only a little arithmetic. The individual simply multiplies his or her current annual contributions to retirement savings by the number of years left until retirement and then adds his or her current retirement savings. Don't even adjust for the risk-free rate of growth. Since most money market funds earn a rate of interest imperceptibly different than the rate of inflation, the net effect of a cash account is that they go nowhere in real (inflation-adjusted) terms. Don't create the illusion of growth by looking at nominal funds without acknowledging inflation. Once you have the result of first calculation, divide by the number of years of retirement that are expected.

For example, suppose that your clients are a couple who are both 45 years old and have savings for retirement valued at $400,000, which includes not just their qualified plans but all savings earmarked for retirement. Suppose further, that they're saving $30,000 per year in various accounts meant for retirement. With 20 years to go before retirement, then the cash account mattress should hold $1,000,000 in today's dollars. If this couple thinks that one or both might live for 40 years after retiring, then the implied floor becomes $25,000 that their portfolio can provide plus any Social Security or external payments.

The couple may do better or worse by taking market risk. But the question here is whether the simplest and safest handling of current and planned savings could be used as the basis for an acceptable lifestyle.

We now switch to a more formal planning process conducted in two steps. First, we engage in constructing what we call the client's bedrock floor and second, add in what we'll call the aspirational floor. The bedrock floor is a measure of the cost of his or her current lifestyle without work-related costs.[2] The aspirational floor is not meant to be a wish list, but the realistic plan that the client has for living what they consider a full life during retirement.

THE WINDOW FOR MAINTAINING LIFESTYLE

Another simple test gauges a lifestyle against a wealth level to see how long it takes for the money to run out. To start this game, we construct an estimate of a portfolio on one year before retirement begins. We'll play the game by assuming the purchase of an ordinary annuity one year before retirement begins, with a payment equal to the stated lifestyle desire. The question that we try to answer is the length of the annuity that can be purchased.[3]

Table 3.2 shows the maximum number of periods that an ordinary annuity could be constructed to provide level payments. The payout percentage is given on the left side and the discount rates are given along the top. For example, for $100 up front, an annuity that pays $9 per period would last 22 periods at a 7 percent discount rate.

Table 3.2 can be seen as either ignoring inflation or pretending it away. Along the left we have the lifestyle choices as a percentage of wealth. For example, an individual with a $1,000,000 portfolio and lifestyle needs of $150,000 per year would, depending on the discount rate for the annuity, find themselves somewhere along the bottom row of the table. The columns of the table are the discount rates used for present value calculations. The values in the table are the maximum number of periods that a full annuity

TABLE 3.2 Thinking About Level-Payment Annuities

Maximum Annuity Length by Draw Rate and Discount Rate

		Discount Rate							
		3%	4%	5%	6%	7%	8%	9%	10%
Lifestyle as a Percentage of Wealth	3%	∞	∞	∞	∞	∞	∞	∞	∞
	4%	46	∞	∞	∞	∞	∞	∞	∞
	5%	30	41	∞	∞	∞	∞	∞	∞
	6%	23	28	36	∞	∞	∞	∞	∞
	7%	18	21	25	33	∞	∞	∞	∞
	8%	15	17	20	23	30	∞	∞	∞
	9%	13	14	16	18	22	28	426	∞
	10%	12	13	14	15	17	20	26	∞
	11%	10	11	12	13	14	16	19	25
	12%	9	10	11	11	12	14	16	18
	13%	8	9	9	10	11	12	13	15
	14%	8	8	9	9	10	11	11	13
	15%	7	7	8	8	9	9	10	11

payment can be made. For example, someone with lifestyle needs of 10 percent of wealth in an environment of 4 percent discount rates would be able to annuitize his or her lifestyle for 13 periods. Note that as long as the lifestyle does not exceed the discount rate for the annuity, the portfolio is able to perpetuate the lifestyle. The next table shows the impact of even moderate inflation on the length of survivability.

Table 3.3 shows the maximum number of periods that an ordinary annuity could be made to last with payments rising for anticipated inflation of 3 percent. The payout percentage is given on the left side and the discount rates are given along the top. In comparison with our previous example for $100 up front, an annuity that pays $9 the first period but rising at 3 percent per period to keep pace with expected inflation would only last 14 periods at a 7 percent discount rate.

In Table 3.3, we adjust the lifestyle payments to take anticipated inflation into account. In this case, with inflation expectations of as little as 3 percent, a 10 percent lifestyle can only be maintained for 10 periods when the discount rate is 4 percent. Notice that the largest changes are for low lifestyle percentages. For example, a 4 percent lifestyle's survivability in a 3 percent discount rate environment drops from 46 to 25 periods; longevity becomes a risk.

TABLE 3.3 Thinking About Level-Payment (real) Annuities with 3 Percent Expected Inflation

		Maximum Annuity Length by Draw Rate and Discount Rate							
					Discount Rate				
		3%	4%	5%	6%	7%	8%	9%	10%
	3%	33	40	54	123	∞	∞	∞	∞
	4%	25	28	34	45	92	∞	∞	∞
	5%	20	22	25	30	39	74	∞	∞
Lifestyle as a Percentage of Wealth	6%	16	18	20	23	27	34	62	∞
	7%	14	15	16	18	21	24	31	53
	8%	12	13	14	15	17	19	23	28
	9%	11	11	12	13	14	16	18	21
	10%	10	10	11	11	12	14	15	17
	11%	9	9	10	10	11	12	13	14
	12%	8	8	9	9	10	10	11	12
	13%	7	8	8	8	9	9	10	11
	14%	7	7	7	8	8	8	9	10
	15%	6	6	7	7	7	8	8	9

THE BEDROCK FLOOR

In budgeting problems, there are two main strategies for estimating the amounts of funding needed. One approach, the top down approach, starts with current budgets and attempts to drill in to adjust values for future budgets. For new projects with no history or where the budgets are seen as layered with extras, there may be a desire to start over from scratch and build up the budget anew from the bottom up.

Top-Down Estimates

Top-down estimates are often called ballpark estimates, but they can be quite good[4] if the user thinks through his or her big-picture finances. First, that person needs to think of income similarly to the way the IRS does as income from *all sources*. In a nutshell, either you or your clients should add up their income from all regular sources for the last couple of years. That means to add all of the things like wages, interest, dividends, and other regular sources of income that they count on year in and year out. Leave off things like lottery winnings and other one-time income. There are many variations on this theme; pick the easiest way, but try to be honest and complete. Second, look at their financial statements and see how much has been socked away each year over the last couple of years. Using the relationship that Consumption = Income − Saving, you can calculate their current consumption by subtracting annual savings from annual income.

Take what you have just calculated and adjust for *necessary* consumption expenditures that they anticipate will either crop up during retirement or go away before they retire. Tell the client to be realistic—their kids will still cost them money after they move out; commuting and other work-related expenses will go away. Will the mortgage be paid off? Don't worry about emergency contingencies at this point, we account for them later.

Bottom-Up Estimates

Here you try to estimate your client's consumption needs directly by either using his or her current budgeting methods or by having the client go to his or her checkbook and add up every check written or withdrawal made. The goal is to try to build up the estimate of flooring by building up the expenses that this client is expected to incur during retirement. Try to get the client to leave off expenses that he or she knows will not be incurred after retirement. Similarly, add in expenses that the client knows he or she will regularly incur during retirement. To get a better picture of the steady-state requirements, you'll want to understand potential one-off expenses such as weddings and their timing.

The bottom-up approach really requires a much fuller accounting of sources and uses of funds than generalist financial advisers will be willing to undertake. However, for those advisers who seek to be retirement specialists, knowledge of the client's balance sheet and pro forma income statements are an important part of the process.

THE ASPIRATIONAL FLOOR

On top of the bedrock floor is the layer of flooring for the things that clients truly intend to do in retirement, things they would do now but don't have the time. We call these *retirement aspirations*. Here is the place to add their reasonable desires for what clients consider a full life during retirement. Perhaps they plan on traveling, taking courses at a university, or engaging in a costly hobby. The important question that you need to get clients to answer for themselves, before adding these in, is whether these are expenditures for the floor or pure wishes. There is no bright-line test that you or

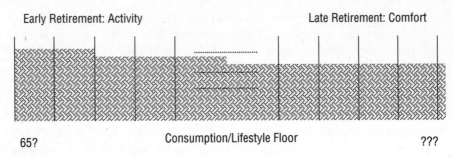

Early Retirement: Activity   Late Retirement: Comfort

65?   Consumption/Lifestyle Floor   ???

FIGURE 3.3 What Lifestyle Does the Client Desire?

your clients can apply, but use the best judgment. If they are niceties or pure wishes, then leave them off and perhaps they can be funded out of the discretionary wealth or upside from their portfolio. If the expenditures are reasonable for your clients' aspirations and within their grasp, then include them here. The main thing that we are trying to do here is to find the lifestyle that defines who they are, while they are still standing firmly in the real world of what they can afford.

THE FINISHED FLOOR

Now that you have your estimates of their bedrock and aspirational floors, it is time to put them together. Laying out the floor visually may be extremely helpful for you and the client as shown in Figure 3.3. Here one can see, again, that for flooring we plan for lifestyle desires and maintenance even in the face of longevity. For the client, it is especially helpful as this illustration forces him or her to think about the length of the active phase and potential longevity.

NOMINAL VERSUS REAL FLOORING

Inflation is the silent enemy of retirement plans. People are often awed and dismayed by the impact that inflation can have on their lifestyle. If their flooring is not made up entirely of Social Security income, which is automatically adjusted upward for inflation, both you and the client need to face it head on. Neither of you need to panic, you don't necessarily have to do anything differently, but you do have to be aware.

   The two main paths that people can choose to mitigate inflationary impacts are to build a nominal floor that takes expected inflation into

TABLE 3.4 Nominal Flooring versus Real Flooring Needs with Inflation Running at 4% Per Year

Years From Today	0	1	2	3	4	5	...	15
Nominal Floor	$50,000	$50,000	$50,000	$50,000	$50,000	$50,000	...	$50,000
Anticipated Inflation-Adjusted Floor	$50,000	$52,000	$54,080	$56,243	$58,493	$60,833	...	$90,047

account or to buy real flooring that will adjust at some specified and observed rate of inflation. Adjusting nominal flooring is a simple task. If you're starting today and want to build a floor of $50,000, you can adjust for 4 percent inflation as in Table 3.4, $52 = 50(1.04)$, $54.08 = 52(1.04)$, $56.243 = 54.08(1.04)$, and so on.[5]

If not purchasing inflation-protected flooring outright, then plan for maintaining lifestyle with the effects of anticipated inflation.

To get an idea of when inflation is an important consideration, consider Table 3.5. It shows the number of years that it takes for prices to double for different inflation rates given in the left-hand column.

TABLE 3.5 The Half-Life of Nominal Funds

Inflation Rate	Time (in years) It Takes for Prices to Double
1%	70
2%	35
3%	23
4%	18
5%	14
6%	12
7%	10
8%	09
9%	08
10%	07

TABLE 3.6 Common Inflation-Protected Securities

Security Types	Caveats
TIPS	If outside of IRA, 401(k), etc.; taxes at Federal level including "phantom" income
Foreign TIPS equivalents: UDIs	Currency risk, U.S./Foreign inflation will differ; taxable
Inflation-linked structured products	Not widely known, complex, credit risk of issuer; taxable
Equities	Not guaranteed; capital gains and dividends are taxable

Nonsecurity Types	Caveats
I-bonds	Creates ordinary income each period; taxes at Federal level
Real assets	Not guaranteed; taxable; not universally eligible for inclusion in IRAs
Inflation-linked annuities	Credit risk of issuer; taxes depend on wrapper

With the cheeriness of Table 3.5, you can see how quickly inflation becomes important and how even a couple of years of high inflation can hurt your client.

The alternative to adjusting for inflation up front is to buy flooring that will automatically ratchet up at some specified rate of inflation. At this juncture, it would be a little premature to get into too much detail about specific products. However, let's think about inflation-protected products by categorizing them and thinking about where they belong in a portfolio construct.

Treasury Inflation-Protected Securities (TIPS) are the most commonly referenced source of guaranteed inflation protection. In a sense, they are the standard against which all other inflation-protected securities can be judged. Table 3.6 shows a partial list of security types usually associated with inflation protection.

Both TIPS and I-bonds are issued by the Treasury but they work a little differently and have different tax consequences. TIPS work in the following way: Suppose a TIPS is issued with par = $1,000 and a 3 percent coupon. If inflation runs at say 5 percent, then the notional amount of the TIPS will step up to $1,050 and 3 percent coupon will be based off of the new notional.[6] The tax rub is that the IRS treats the $50 increase in notional as income for this year, even though it is only a notional increase that the holder will have to wait until maturity to actually realize. This is what is generally referred to as "phantom income." The important point to take away is that TIPS work best in tax-deferred accounts where there are no tax consequences until withdrawal. I-bonds were created for smaller savers and not issued as trading securities. In contrast to TIPS, where TIPS adjust the notional, but leave the coupon rate fixed, I-bonds adjust the coupon rate for inflation.[7] I-bonds have no phantom-income consequences.

Some foreign governments issue their own version of inflation-protected securities. Probably the most popular are the Latin American UDIs (pronounced oo-dees). These are also valuable for inflation protection, but putting these in a portfolio puts the holder at risk for currency fluctuations, sovereign risk, and the differential between different country's inflation measures.

Some of the leading thinkers about retirement have argued that the risk of inflation means that all flooring should be real flooring.[8] I am less dogmatic for two related reasons. First, there is a more subtle interpretation of the pricing differential between inflation-protected and nominal yield assets, not as a difference driven by expected inflation, but as earned premium for writing an option on inflation. Second, given the dominant volume of nominal rate securities being placed versus inflation-protected, even when inflation-protected securities are available suggests that there are many who understand the concept and magnitude of risk, but are seemingly comfortable writing the inflation call option.

With both nominal rate and inflation-protected securities trading, it is more fruitful to think of the difference as the value of an option on inflation. The buyer of a nominal rate bond receives a fixed payment for each coupon period and the principal of the bond does not adjust. If inflation rises, the nominal rate buyer loses; if inflation is low or negative, the nominal rate buyer wins. In essence, the buyer of nominal rate debt is short an option on inflation to the issuer of the bond. In that light, the difference between coupon rates on TIPS and coupon rates for nominal rate securities can be thought of as option premium received by the buyer of the bond in exchange for being the payer on the inflation option. When anxiety about future inflation is high, the spread between real and nominal rates will rise; the option premium received by the nominal rate holders will rise.

In that light, buying nominal rate securities when there is high anxiety about the potential for future inflation may be an attractive proposition for those who do not share the anxiety. This may manifest itself either by relatively high coupon rates for nominal rate debt or very low yields for inflation-protected securities. The difference is the inflation premium. Those who can either hedge the effects of being wrong, or those implicitly comfortable that the wider spread sufficiently compensates for the risk of being wrong, may prefer to buy securities that are not inflation protected. The time to buy TIPS and inflation protection is when no one else is worried about inflation.

Both equities and real assets are also often used for inflation protection. The caveat there is that neither is guaranteed to keep pace with inflation. It is true that equities have, in their broadest measures, kept pace with inflation on average. However, equity prices do not adjust in lockstep with each other or inflation. It should also be remembered that the past does not always presage the future. Without a contractual arrangement, there is no guarantee. It may be a reasonable long-term bet, but it is still a bet.

Similarly, real assets are not guaranteed to keep pace with inflation. Real assets also have two other considerations to keep in mind. First, real assets are often traded in forms other than as financial securities such as gold coins, rare stamps, art, commodities, and so on. They may be highly sensitive to specific features such as location (real estate), condition (coins, stamps), or other features (art, oil, agricultural products), and having periods of low liquidity or wide bid/offer spreads. Second, and more importantly, many real assets are not simply investment assets but they offer consumption benefits. This brings up a subtle but important point: For any asset, total return can be decomposed as the sum of consumption return plus financial return.[9] Purely financial assets have no consumption value. Some assets, such as rare stamps, coins, and art are primarily held for consumption and only secondarily for investment purposes; with some notable temporary exceptions, housing usually falls into this category. For some real assets, such as gold and a subset of agricultural products, the demand is primarily for consumption but the price volatility may be driven by investment movement. In equilibrium, the greater the consumption return, the lower the financial return. Also, keep in mind that consumption demand is, for most real assets, procyclical; demand for particular real assets may rise or fall as tastes change. In short, like equities, real assets may be helpful in hedging inflation, but they are not without their own substantial risks.

TYPES OF FLOORING

Now that we have an idea of the amount of flooring that is needed, we turn to the choice of type of flooring. This is not the final word on flooring choice. Just as we have to revisit and double check the amount of flooring, we also check back on the type. Here we get the ball rolling for thinking about the best flooring types for different consumption segments. Our approach is to compare flooring desires with wealth. The more that the client's consumption desires eat up available and prospective assets, the more important it is to secure the floor.

The first step is to ask the question: "How much do you need to retire?" I love when this question is asked because there is a way to provide an answer. If the client is sure about the floor, then the answer is just the cost of locking in the floor. So if we calculate the PV of the lifestyle floor amounts,[10] we are able to say something like "if you want a government secured floor it will cost you x dollars." This is a powerful and useful piece of information.

Revisiting the Balance Sheet

Comparing the PV of their flooring needs to their current financial assets gives us an idea of where clients stand in terms of meeting their goals for retirement. Ignoring insurance for a moment, our goal is to compare your client goals to their wherewithal. In Figure 3.4, we use comfortable and stressed as shorthand ways of describing people whose needs are low relative to their wealth versus stressed where there is little, if any, slack. Here wealth isn't the sole determinant of lifestyle or even what would be called

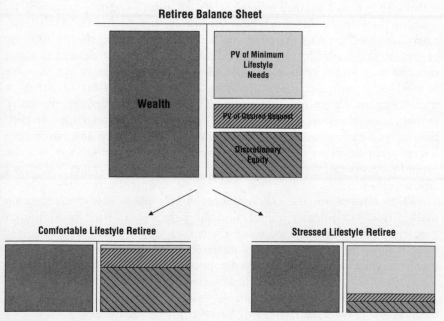

FIGURE 3.4 Balance Sheet and Lifestyle Revisited

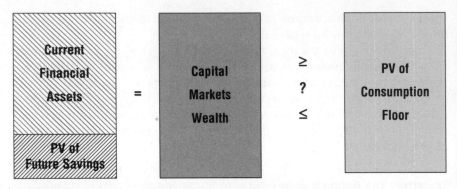

FIGURE 3.5 Assets, Wealth, and Capital Markets Capability

a comfortable lifestyle. Similarly, the risk of the sustainability of a lifestyle is determined by spending relative to wealth.

If not constructing a full balance sheet, it may be useful to calculate an alternative measure of financial wealth restricting attention to traditional financial products. To go from financial assets to our alternative and restricted view of financial wealth[11] as shown in Figure 3.5, as one of the steps you may want to add the PV of future contributions to the client portfolio. Call this your clients' *capital markets wealth*. Be aware that if constructing a full balance sheet, the PV of future contributions will be accounted for in the difference between human capital and the PV of consumption over the client's remaining working life. Using the measure of capital markets wealth, find the maximum percentage of desired flooring that can be afforded with wealth. An obvious question to ask at this point is whether a sufficient lifestyle can be built without resorting either to monetizing mortality or taking market risk. As a very rough mortality monetization measure, find the PV of the maximum percentage of client flooring you can source using all of their capital markets wealth purchasing a fixed-term mortality-monetizing annuity to the same date as used for the capital markets calculation.[12,13,14] Call this the client's *mortality-monetized consumption.*

Place bounds on the cost of your client's plans before considering market risk. For a lower bound, find the percentage of the consumption floor that can be constructed using the treasury yield curve. For an upper bound, find the client's mortality-monetized consumption by seeing how much flooring can be purchased by putting all of the client's financial assets into an annuity. If the client's expected lifespan is so short that mortality-monetized consumption is lower[15] than the client's capital markets floor, then the client will have no *purely* financial reason to buy an annuity.

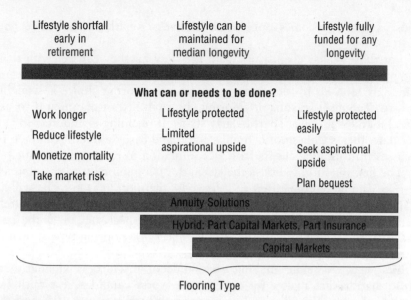

FIGURE 3.6   Segmenting Flooring Types

CHOOSING A FLOORING TYPE

In this section, we discuss the flooring types and the "gravitation" that individuals may feel toward a flooring type. As Figure 3.6 illustrates, there is no purely prescriptive answer as to what a particular client should do—it is his or her choice. However, there are some factors that you can use to help guide the client make a decision.

For those whose lifestyles are a substantial fraction of wealth, planning to monetize mortality may be the only way to maintain lifestyle. As lifestyle relative to wealth decreases, then it becomes possible to build capital markets flooring, putting less at mortality risk. (In Chapter 7, we discuss feasibility of approaches and specific allocation needs by age.) This shows that options are few for those whose wealth is less than the PV of their consumption needs. The simpler the lifestyle the easier it is to craft more varied portfolios. Again it's not wealth that matters, it is the lifestyle relative to wealth that is important.

Naturally, advisers have a preference for the distribution of particular types of products, but this view may be helpful in trying to establish a motivation for an approach effective for different client types. It is intuitively clear that a simpler lifestyle allows more options for meeting client needs; as lifestyle becomes more lavish relative to wealth the choices become constrained.

For those whose clients just want see how far they can get with their current rate of saving and have no intention, at present, of trying to measure their lifestyle needs to set a specific target, the flooring choice is straightforward. The most reasonable flooring choice in lieu of planning is to use capital markets products, particularly strips. If planning is undertaken at a later date, then such a floor is highly liquid and easily altered. (Chapter 10 discusses transitioning clients from accumulation to retirement income.)

The first question to ask is the strength of commitment to the planned lifestyle. The more committed to a lifestyle, the more reason to be willing to "lock it in." The second question is what does an objective, but purely financial analysis based on the personal balance sheet suggest as the best way forward. Take a look at the balance sheet and flooring type shown in Figure 3.7. It should provide guidance toward understanding how at risk the lifestyle is and help in making a sound decision. Third, is whether there is information that makes for a better or worse candidate for outliving assets. If the expectation is to live into extreme old age, say 105, and the capital markets wealth is unlikely to last past 90, then a pure annuity or hybrid approach, including longevity insurance, will be more appealing. Fourth, is to consider whether there are dependents or other reasons to

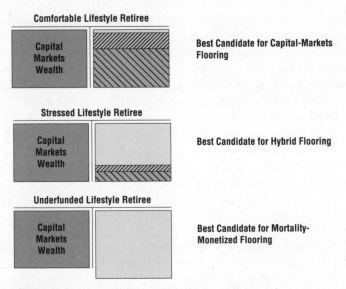

FIGURE 3.7   Balance Sheet and Flooring Type

demur from monetizing mortality rather than risk assets for those who may rely on an estate. Fifth is a matter of being honest about impulsiveness. Figure 3.7 helps to illustrate the classification of client lifestyle types. It provides another way to view segments purely based on feasibility. In the top of the figure, all flooring types are feasible as wealth does not appear to constrain lifestyle. In the middle section, lifestyle can be maintained for some period of time without resorting, by necessity, to monetizing mortality; longevity insurance on top of a long capital markets floor may work best. In the lower portion of the figure, pure capital markets flooring would be insufficient to maintain lifestyle needs—the individual's lifestyle is underfunded. In the bottom case only, and only possibly, will mortality credits be sufficient to support lifestyle needs. For those who don't need steady-as-a-rock dynamic flexibility, a simple annuity could be the best option. On the other hand, for those who are impulsive and prone to act on whims, sticking to capital markets solutions will offer lower-cost reversibility than a typical annuity.

For those falling into the category of a comfortable lifestyle retiree, consumption needs are low relative to wealth and worrying about flooring becomes less important. In percentage terms if annual consumption/wealth is below about 3.5 percent per year, then the portfolio can probably be set up to throw off yield sufficient to meet lifestyle needs for an indefinite

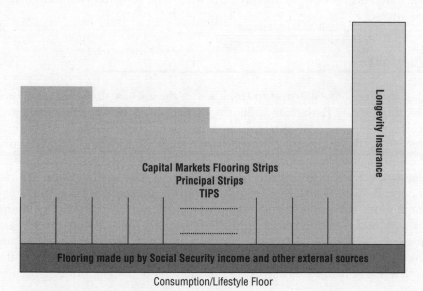

Capital Markets Flooring Strips
Principal Strips
TIPS

Longevity Insurance

Flooring made up by Social Security income and other external sources

Consumption/Lifestyle Floor

FIGURE 3.8 Hybrid Retirement Flooring

future. Unless there is a preference there is no need-based reason in this case for the client to feel compelled to monetize mortality.

At the other extreme, for those who fall into the underfunded lifestyle retiree category, then monetizing mortality may be the only hope to maintain an adequate lifestyle. In percentage terms, if annual consumption needs exceed about 7 percent of total wealth, a safe plan is unlikely to last longer than 15 years;[16] there is a need to either be aggressive about taking market risk or there needs to be a willingness to monetize mortality.[17] Depending on the depth of the hole, there may be potential for upside on top of the lifestyle floor with either an insurance wrapper on an annuity/mutual fund combination or by annuity plus capital markets products.

Even in the stressed lifestyle category, as long as consumption is fully funded there are many options available from period certain annuities to full capital markets approaches back to partial annuitization, and on to capital markets for a fixed window topped up with longevity insurance. In the hybrid flooring model shown in Figure 3.8, consider a case where capital markets products, particularly government securities, are used to make up the bulk of the flooring out to a specified date at which longevity insurance kicks in. The essence of hybrid flooring is that it combines capital markets products with longevity insurance. Capital markets products create flooring for the majority of the postretirement planning horizon and the longevity insurance (mortality monetization) kicks in if the holder survives. The value of mortality is the greatest where the probability of survival is the lowest.

SUMMARY

This chapter showed a way to think about the client's ability to fund consumption during retirement using the familiar tools of a balance sheet and pro forma income statements. It is shown how the economics of meeting lifestyle needs sets a floor under consumption and changes the advisory framework from one of expectations to both outcomes and expectations. Outcomes are the important facet of flooring and expectations are the important facet of upside. Methods useful for gauging flooring needs that range from the ad hoc and unsophisticated tools like yes/no planning through both top-down and bottom-up methods for estimating needs are covered. Finally, the chapter circles back to the balance sheet to discuss how the client's lifestyle relative to available wealth helps to inform the adviser about the proper choice and positioning of flooring for a particular client.

CHAPTER 4

Monetizing Mortality

Annuities and Longevity Insurance

Objectives

Understanding risk pooling
    The trade-off between lifestyle and estate

Classes of retirement insurance
    Pure longevity
    Annuities
    Annuities coupled with capital markets products

Credit risk and annuities

A s mentioned earlier in the book, risk pooling is a way to monetize mortality.[1] People put assets into a pool with other mortals. The amount received in return each period depends on whether you survive or perish. With retirement income–oriented insurance, your clients get less if they're dead in exchange for more if they're alive.

In this chapter, we have a few goals centered around intuition rather than detail. First we'll go through the basics of risk pooling. We'll then move into the straightforward area of pure longevity insurance. Pure longevity insurance is one of the few areas of insurance related to retirement that is intuitive and lends itself to easy quantification. Once through longevity insurance, we can then move through the traditional areas of annuities. We cover vanilla annuities and complex annuities, including annuities with death benefits, and variable annuity types. Particularly in light of the recent credit crisis and the bailout of AIG, we would be remiss if we did not spend some time on the issues of credit risk in insurance contracts.

TABLE 4.1 In the Absence of Risk Pooling

Outcome	Probability	Needs	Assets	Result
Survive	0.5	$100	$50	Starve
Die	0.5	$0	$50	No worries

RISK POOLING

As a starter, let's go through a trivial example. Suppose that your client (A) and a neighbor (B) each need $100 next year to avoid starvation. Each of them has an independent 50/50 chance of surviving until next year. Neither has the needed $100, but your client has $50 and their neighbor has at least $50 to put into a risk pool managed by XYZ Insurance.

As you can see from Tables 4.1 and 4.2, without risk pooling, the future looks bleak regardless of the outcome. With risk pooling the probability of being free and clear with no worries rises. If neither A or B survive, then XYZ gets to keep the money contributed by the two parties.[2] If only one of the two people survive then all that XYZ needs to do is make sure that there is $100 to pay out. The only hitch is that if both survive, then the result depends on the ability of XYZ to make good on both A's and B's claims. I will refer back to this result when we talk about insurance and credit risk. For the sake of a little foreshadowing, there is credit risk in each of the cases where XYZ must make a payment, but the credit risk is greater when XYZ must pay both parties.

PURE LONGEVITY INSURANCE

Suppose that you have clients who are 65 years old and fairly comfortable with the plan you've made for their retirement funds that will maintain

TABLE 4.2 In the Presence of Actuarially Fair Risk Pooling Through XYZ Insurance Co.

Outcome	Probability	Needs	Assets	Result
A&B dead	0.25	$0	$100	No worries
A survives, B Dead	0.25	$100	$100	No worries
A dies, B survives	0.25	$100	$100	No worries
A&B survive	0.25	$200	$100	XYZ on the hook

their lifestyle and last at least until they reach age 90—25 years into the future. However you and they are concerned that if they live past 90, they might outlive their money. One alternative would be to buy a bullet bond[3] that matures in 25 years. If the current rate of interest is 5 percent for government securities, then the rough cost of the bullet can be computed as follows:

Bullet bond cost = $1/(1.05)^{25} = 0.2953 \approx 30$ cents per dollar of notional

The easiest bullets to find are principal strips of government securities. They are regularly offered for sale by broker/dealers and the prices are observable, meaning that you don't need to calculate the cost; you can see what it is going for in the market.[4] All you'd need is the ability to look up bonds using the "bond look-up" tool provided by your broker/dealer. For now, let's suppose that we found a government principal strip trading at our aforementioned price.

In this case, if they want to top their portfolio up with a million dollars at age 90, then they can spend just under $300,000 today to buy a bullet bond that will pay no coupon interest but will pay the notional amount of $1 million in 25 years. However, $300,000 may be too much money for them to tie up for that long.

Suppose that the probability of living another 25 years until age 90 is 20 percent.[5,6] A no-fee, no-overhead, actuarially fair, risk-free insurance company would be willing to pool individuals and offer million-dollar policies of pure longevity insurance for $0.20 \times \$300,000 = \$60,000$. In other words, for our example, the odds that they die before receiving payment means longevity insurance costs 6 cents on the dollar.

For every year the need for longevity insurance can be deferred, the cheaper it becomes. With higher rates of survival, a 25-year policy should be more expensive for someone who is 50 as opposed to someone who is 65. Conversely, a policy that pays at age 90 should be cheaper for the 50 year old than a 65 year old because the odds of surviving to 90 are higher for someone who has already survived to 65. For someone buying longevity insurance for age 95, the lower likelihood of survival cuts the fair-game cost of longevity insurance to a couple of cents on the dollar.

The mechanics of an insurance company's operations are thematically similar to the simple example of risk pooling that started this section. The insurance company will pool the funds that they receive from contract holders to buy bonds that will, in turn, provide payments to the survivors. If the insurance company "hits the odds" of survival right, they will pay off the surviving policyholders and reap a profit for their shareholders.

ANNUITIES

Since we've already gone through longevity insurance, basic annuities are difficult to price but easily grasped. Under the right circumstances, they can be thought of as a stream of longevity payments, conditional on continued survival since the previous payment. For someone buying a $10,000 annuity, the cost will roughly be given by calculating an infinite sum of the probability weighted present value of annual payments of $10,000; the complicated part of annuity pricing lies in the probability weighting. For each payment in the annuity stream, the present value of the payment needs to be adjusted by the probability of surviving until the next payment is due while having survived through the previous payment. Somewhat formally, for each payment this can be represented as the probability of continued survival conditional on surviving through the previous payment multiplied by the probability of surviving through the previous payment.

$$\Pr(\text{continued\_survival}|\text{survival\_thus\_far})\Pr(\text{survival\_thus\_far})$$

As an example, suppose that the mortality rate is a constant 40 percent per year and the prices in the market conform to interest rates of 5 percent at every maturity. That is, for our example we're assuming that 40 percent of people die off each year[7] and that survival one year does not improve one's chances of survival for the next year.[8] Then the probabilities of survival will follow column B in Table 4.3.

In Table 4.3, a $10,000 single payment will be worth what is given in column E. To obtain the cost of each payment, multiply column B × C × D, the result is shown in column E. You can see how quickly, with a mortality rate of 40 percent per year, the cost of a year's insurance drops off: by age 90 it's virtually free. Adding the values in column E to construct a makeshift annuity gives a cost $13,333.32 Our main inputs here are the survival probabilities and the cost of the bonds we need to buy. If interest rates change or survival probabilities change then the costs will change.

For those purchasing an annuity, the big winner will be someone with a Methuselah gene who lives long enough to beat the odds. The losers in the annuity game will be those who have the misfortune of an early death. If insurance companies were allowed to discriminate by price in annuity sales, then for those described as heavy drinkers, smokers, or obese, annuities would be cheaper. One reason that is often given for popular resistance to annuities is that those who view themselves as likely to die before the annuity "pays for itself" will simply not want to subsidize those more likely to survive.

TABLE 4.3 Hypothetical Longevity Payment Costs by Client's Age

A Age	B Survival Probability	C Payment	D Per $ Cost of Bullet	E Longevity Cost
66	0.6000	$10,000	$0.95	$5,714.29
67	0.3600	$10,000	$0.91	$3,265.31
68	0.2160	$10,000	$0.86	$1,865.89
69	0.1296	$10,000	$0.82	$1,066.22
70	0.0778	$10,000	$0.78	$609.27
71	0.0467	$10,000	$0.75	$348.15
72	0.0280	$10,000	$0.71	$198.95
73	0.0168	$10,000	$0.68	$113.68
74	0.0101	$10,000	$0.64	$64.96
75	0.0060	$10,000	$0.61	$37.12
76	0.0036	$10,000	$0.58	$21.21
77	0.0022	$10,000	$0.56	$12.12
78	0.0013	$10,000	$0.53	$6.93
79	0.0008	$10,000	$0.51	$3.96
80	0.0005	$10,000	$0.48	$2.26
81	0.0003	$10,000	$0.46	$1.29
82	0.0002	$10,000	$0.44	$0.74
83	0.0001	$10,000	$0.42	$0.42
84	0.0001	$10,000	$0.40	$0.24
85	0.0000	$10,000	$0.38	$0.14
86	0.0000	$10,000	$0.36	$0.08
87	0.0000	$10,000	$0.34	$0.04
88	0.0000	$10,000	$0.33	$0.03
89	0.0000	$10,000	$0.31	$0.01
90	0.0000	$10,000	$0.30	$0.01

What about buying now versus later? For the general population, the main difference in pricing annuities for someone who buys an annuity at age 45 versus someone who buys an annuity at age 55, and where both begin paying at age 65, comes from stretching out the payment period and the changing of conditional probabilities of survival as an individual ages. If an individual buys an annuity at age 45, the conditional probabilities of survival until receiving payments are lower than for someone age 55. At age 45, individuals may be able to stretch out the payments over 20 years instead of paying for the annuity over 10 years. The big kicker for monetizing mortality is past middle age, when the survival probabilities start to decrease rapidly. For actuarially fair insurance, as a pure matter of present value, absent material differences in mortality, there is no reason to prefer buying sooner rather than later. With life expectancy conditional on age, there is an incentive for those who expect to live the longest to buy annuities early, before their longevity becomes apparent. Surrender charges, difficulty in reversing nontradable contracts, and fear of early demise all work against early annuitization.

COMPLEX ANNUITIES

Insurance is a very flexible platform for creating variations on a theme. Since insurance is a business based on individual contracts rather standardized products as in exchange markets, it is much easier for companies to differentiate their products and try to earn higher profits than would exist in a perfectly competitive market.

Death Benefits

For a simple example of complexity, death benefits[9] or annuities with surviving spouse benefits are easy modifications of the standard problem. These are all modifications that stay within the core competency of insurance actuaries—understanding mortality risk. Death benefits are easy to understand and pretty popular, but they are not free.

Let's go back and revisit our longevity insurance example. The PV factor 25 years out implied that the cost of a zero-coupon bond was 30 cents on the dollar. Remember that for our 65-year-olds, the odds of cheating death by age 90 were only 20 percent. That meant they were able to buy their longevity insurance for 6 cents on the dollar ($0.3 \times 0.2 = 0.06$). Now just suppose that they wanted to add a death benefit. Clearly, the insurance company would be best off if they expired the day before they were able to collect on the longevity insurance. But the odds of having already experienced death are, by then, 80 percent. So if they died anytime before the longevity insurance paid off—even if it was written into the contract that their heirs would not receive the death benefit until the same date that the longevity insurance had been paid—the death benefit would cost four times as much as the longevity insurance ($0.3 \times 0.8 = 0.24$). Death benefits are usually paid shortly after death, the sooner someone is expected to die, the higher the PV of the death benefit for their heirs. Since the question is not whether they will die but when, it is those who die early who are the big winners for the death benefit component of a policy.

Variable Annuities

For the past several years, insurance companies have been moving towards products that combine mortality risks with market risk components. The thinking is that while fixed annuities are desirable for some people, an annuity that provides potential upside might be even more desirable.

Conceptually, it is straightforward to take a simple annuity, such as the type discussed previously, charge a little extra, and attach an arbitrary mutual fund. In the parlance of the financial products business, what you have is a mutual fund in an insurance wrapper or a wrapped product. One advantage that an insurance-wrapped mutual fund would have over an ordinary mutual fund is that the insurance wrapper creates a tax-deferred income stream. The tax rules get complicated quickly, but you need to be careful about two things. First, buying insurance in a 401(k) or IRA is a waste of the tax-deferral features that are already part of retirement accounts. From a tax perspective, buying insurance products outside of the umbrella of retirement accounts makes more sense. Second, if the income stream created by the insurance payments is ordinary income then, depending on holding period and intermediate cash flows from the fund, your client may be worse off than if they paid capital gains rates on any increase in value of the mutual fund.

Guaranteed minimum accumulation, income, or withdrawal benefits (*GMAB, GMIB* and *GMWB*) plans are types of variable annuities that do more than simply tack mutual funds to annuities. On top of the annuity payments, they provide guarantees on the performance of the embedded mutual funds. In essence, this is a combination of an insurance contract with a capital markets–style[10,11] financial product. For the most part, these products can be thought of as the sum of an annuity plus a mutual fund plus a long put position.[12] For these products, it is important to understand how the risk of the put option is being hedged. Two ways that the insurance company may be hedging the risk of the embedded put are via direct hedging or engaging in a trade with a financial intermediary that will itself hedge the put. A third possibility for an insurance company would be to forego hedging and take the actuarial bet that the long run performance of the fund will provide sufficient resources to pay the policyholders the contractual minima.

CREDIT RISK AND INSURANCE

If you want to sell insurance, your client will certainly expect to pay production costs, overhead and a reasonable profit margin. However, clients seem aware that private insurance without a government guarantee contains an element of credit risk; the recent bailout of AIG has reinforced the fear that an annuity provider has the potential to fail. When a client buys insurance they are executing a contract with a private company that will probably, but may not, be around when it's their turn to pay. Alternatively, if your client buys a government bond there will be no credit risk: The U.S. Treasury can always pay—they run the printing presses.

The credit risk of an insurance contract by the purchaser needs to be evaluated with an eye to both the assets and the liabilities of the insurance company. On the asset side, many insurance companies have, as part of their required capital, government and AAA-rated securities. Typically, the higher the quality of the assets that are on the insurance company's balance sheet the stronger the insurance company. However, ratings alone are not a sufficient metric of quality. Remember that the insurance companies were often eager purchasers of the AAA tranches of CDOs because of the enhanced yield that they offered relative to ordinary AAA bonds.

On the liability side, there is generally very little concern with insurance companies that stick to ordinary markets of property, casualty, and life insurance. Hurricane Andrew in 1992 made it clear to property insurers that geographic concentration can spell disaster for liability management.[13] Insurance companies have had a tougher time pricing extreme tail events with other types of insurance such as catastrophe insurance. Unhedged market protections also have the potential to pose problems for insurance companies. An insurance company that writes GMAB, GMWB, GMIB, and other assorted *GMxx*'s (i.e., GM-type plans) without an active in-house trading desk to hedge the market risk, or standard contracts with an entity that can hedge, would be a greater credit risk than otherwise.

What all of this means is that insurance contracts for retirees are little more than corporate debt with a mortality pooling component; the correct rate to discount payments that an insurance contract will pay would be the rate that the insurance company would pay to issue debt at that maturity— because that is what the pool of purchasers is really buying. That is not to say that an insurance company with a solid credit rating (AAA) can't fail or that a company with AA, A, or lower should be avoided. It does mean however, that the principles of diversification apply to credit risk. Fortunately, the diversification of credit risk is more straightforward and transparent than the diversification of market risk.

In principle, the credit risk disincentive to purchase annuities can be overcome. With standardization, annuity contracts can be bundled in a similar, but not identical fashion[14] as mutual funds. Some individual plan sponsors offer diversified annuity packs, but at the retail level many financial advisers face the hurdle of working in a closed architecture firm meaning that credit risk diversification of insurance products, on behalf of the client, runs counter to the adviser's compensation scheme.

SUMMARY

This chapter provided a light introduction to the mechanics of risk pooling and its application to the market for mortality-based payouts. The traditional range of products associated with retirement, longevity insurance, annuities, and complex annuities are covered. Most of the pros and cons of using insurance products to provide basic flooring or the more elaborate products offering flooring plus upside relate to the client's circumstances, needs, and preferences. For advisers dealing with clients about insurance, it can be difficult to distinguish a client's underlying preferences from their private information about longevity.

This chapter also touched upon the credit risk associated with insurance claims. Inducing clients to place their financial assets in a debt obligation of a single entity is something about which advisers should be very cautious; it is as true of insurance as it is of corporate bonds.

CHAPTER 5

Flooring with Capital Markets Products

Objectives

Understanding how to create a floor with bonds
    Strips, zeroes, and OID bonds
    Ladders
Government vs. corporate vs. municipal bonds
    Avoid callable bonds in flooring

I start this chapter with a story about a make-believe couple with a traditional portfolio who contribute to both a joint IRA and their employer-sponsored 401(k) plans. Their 401(k) plans offer the typical menu of mutual funds. Since they feel the 401(k)s offer limited flexibility for customizing their retirement, our intrepid couple invests in an array of domestic and foreign equity funds within their 401(k) plans. Within the IRA, they've done something far more interesting, they're working with their adviser and using their IRA to build a floor. Until they turned 40, they used the IRA to moderate the volatility in their overall portfolio by buying shares in a high-grade bond fund. As soon as the older of the two turned 40, they began instructing their adviser to allocate 50 percent of their incremental contributions in zero-coupon bonds with a maturity 25 years in the future, when the oldest would turn 65. Each subsequent year the bonds would always be purchased for 25 years in the future, paying at 65, 66, 67, and so on. Although the cost of flooring has fluctuated, the cost has averaged roughly 30 percent of the notional amount—that is, $3,000 would, on average, buy $10,000 of flooring 25 years out. Until the younger spouse turned 40 they still put 50 percent in the old bond fund. Now that both are over 40, each year they place what they can in their IRA contributions buying zeroes always for 25 years in the future. When they're done, their flooring will last until the younger one turns 90. At some point, they will take rollover distributions from their 401(k) plans and reallocate the wealth that currently sits in those plans.[1] For now, they're comforted by the thought that the systematic plan that they have followed has allowed them to build a floor for retirement several thousand dollars per year above that which will be provided by Social Security income.

In this chapter, we mainly focus on using government securities to create flooring. For our purposes, government securities have the advantages of ready availability, familiarity, and standardized features. Treasury strips are included in what we term government securities—even though they are not technically issued as zero-coupon bonds by the government— because of their ubiquitous nature, CUSIP designations as individual securities, and ease of use for creating capital markets flooring.

There is nothing wrong with, and many positive aspects for using corporate bonds or municipals to create flooring, and we will discuss their use. It would be possible to create flooring with corporate or municipal liabilities at any desired level of credit risk. Some would argue that, with proper selection and/or diversification, it would be preferable to buy flooring cheaper using corporate and municipal securities than government securities and get more flooring for the dollar.

Many advisers will probably prefer to use government and corporate bonds to create flooring[2] for their mass-affluent[3] clients and municipal flooring for their high-net-worth clients. Indeed, as a liability of a corporation, an insurance annuity falls into the category of debt containing credit risk. The reason for the focus on Treasury markets is one of ready availability in the market given the way it currently trades and the ease with which one can find Treasury strips. There are many bond funds and individual bonds that could be created to really target the retail retirement income market but, for the most part, that development lies in the future.

GOVERNMENT-ISSUED SECURITIES

The U.S. government and its many agencies often issue bonds to finance their operations. These bonds differ from corporate bonds and, indeed, even the bonds of government-sponsored entities (GSEs) by the fact that the government has the capacity to print money to pay off its debts. There may be a question about how much a dollar will buy when the debt is paid off, but there is no question that the government can find the money: either through tax revenues, rolling over the debt to borrow from a new lender, or printing the money needed to pay the debts. Technically, it is possible for a sovereign government to repudiate its debts, particularly foreign-held debt, but absent extreme social upheaval, it is rare. Since neither corporations nor GSEs have recourse to the taxpayer or the printing press, they contain an element of credit risk. Credit risk is the risk that the borrower will not be able to make some or all of the payments that it has promised.

Trading in government securities is highly liquid and transparent. For the most part, government securities have standardized features and their conventions are well known. As mentioned before, government securities do not have credit risk. Within such a highly liquid market, some specialized products have been created within the aftermarket. Strips are the most commonly created aftermarket product.

One other benefit of most government securities is that government issuance is generally noncallable. This means that even if interest rates fall, the debt cannot be called back by the issuer and reissued at the new, lower rate. Many corporate and municipal issues are callable, and you need to be very wary about including them in the flooring part of retirement portfolios. Callable securities and their stripped components are not good choices for flooring. When flooring is purchased, the purchaser needs to know that it will not be called.

CREATING A FLOOR OF STRIPS

Whether using the principal or coupon, strips are ideally suited to create capital markets flooring. However, taxes on accretive bonds can substantially reduce their allure: keep strips in client IRAs or other tax-deferred accounts. Except for zero-coupon tax-exempt securities, bonds that sell at a discount create taxable phantom income as the discount diminishes and the value of the bond rises to par at maturity. Even tax-exempt securities can create phantom income if the discount is due to interest-rate fluctuations. In an account where taxes can be deferred until funds are withdrawn, there is no taxation of phantom income.

Principal strips offer no coupon payments and only pay the par value of the bond at maturity. They are, therefore, ideal for creating a known cash flow at the date of maturity. By creating a ladder of strips, one at each year of retirement, it is easy to lay down a floor that fixes the payment and the times that cash flows will be received. Table 5.1 illustrates the cost of providing $10,000 worth of flooring using bullet payments. The numbers are hypothetical assuming a yield curve that is a flat 5 percent.

The values in Table 5.1 are calculated using the relationship that the results in column B for a present value N periods into the future are $1/(1.05)^N$. The value in column C is simply the value in column B multiplied by $10,000.

TABLE 5.1   The Cost of Flooring Year by Year

Years in the Future	PV @ 5%	Cost of $10,000 Floor
1	0.9524	$9,523.81
2	0.9070	$9,070.29
3	0.8638	$8,638.38
4	0.8227	$8,227.02
5	0.7835	$7,835.26
6	0.7462	$7,462.15
7	0.7107	$7,106.81
8	0.6768	$6,768.39
9	0.6446	$6,446.09
10	0.6139	$6,139.13
11	0.5847	$5,846.79
12	0.5568	$5,568.37
13	0.5303	$5,303.21
14	0.5051	$5,050.68
15	0.4810	$4,810.17
16	0.4581	$4,581.12
17	0.4363	$4,362.97
18	0.4155	$4,155.21
19	0.3957	$3,957.34
20	0.3769	$3,768.89
21	0.3589	$3,589.42
22	0.3418	$3,418.50
23	0.3256	$3,255.71
24	0.3101	$3,100.68
25	0.2953	$2,953.03

You can see in Table 5.1 that the further out in the future they purchase a year's worth of flooring the lower the per dollar cost. Here, someone with sufficient funds, who began placing money into flooring within their IRA at age 40, for $3,000 per year could purchase more than $10,000 of flooring per year to begin paying out at age 65. In this example, to buy the whole floor in one shot would cost a little under $141,000. Since the person in this example waited to buy the flooring until just before retirement, roughly the same flooring could have been constructed, at a similar cost, using an appropriate number of coupon strips (IO) from the 25-year bond.[4]

Naturally, in the real world, the prices of the strips will vary every day. For some this will be an annoyance, for others an opportunity to exercise discretion: When rates are abnormally low, say, during a recession, some may choose to hold off on the purchase. By deferring purchases, they are having the client take the bet that rates will go higher and the flooring thus cheaper. Conversely, during the tail end of a business boom, some may choose to suggest accelerating flooring purchases, taking the bet that rates will fall and flooring will become more expensive. For those dollar-cost averaging, purchase prices can vary, thus allowing the purchase of more when rates are high and less when rates are low. Table 5.2 is a partial listing of principal strips by maturity. Prices implied by yield curves derived from Government securities during the second week of October 2008, when rates were extremely low—if ever there was a time of panic this was it.

Values in Table 5.2 approximate prices for strips on October 9, 2008. The first column represents the maturity date. The second column shows the CUSIP (the security identifier established by the Committee on Uniform Security Identification Procedures) for the principal strip. The third column shows the approximated prices per $100 of notional. The yields were provided with the prices.

Figure 5.1 provides a visual comparison between the cost of flooring on October 9, 2008. The curves from bottom to top represent the calculated cost assuming a flat 5 percent yield curve. The hypothetical prices shown assume a constant 5 percent discount rate and constant notional amount for each year to be paid by the February 15th series of strips in the payment year. As always, the higher the discount rate for a particular maturity, the lower the cost of flooring.

Coupon strips are a good way to lay a bed of level flooring over an interval of time, particularly when there will be a need to receive cash flows in the near term. Principal strips, on the other hand, are well suited to either legging in to flooring on a set schedule or providing some refined shaping for a level floor. Both coupon strips and principal strips are valuable tools for creating flooring in a retirement income portfolio.

TIPS

TIPS—Treasury inflation-protected securities—are an excellent way to build a government guaranteed floor in real (inflation-protected) dollars. TIPS provide a coupon rate that is fixed at inception, but the principal off of which the coupon is calculated changes. TIPS work by having the principal adjust monthly with changes in the CPI (urban, not seasonally adjusted, three-month lag). The principal amount will be adjusted upward whenever the CPI is positive. The principal will only adjust downward for negative CPI values when the principal is above $1,000. For example, a TIPS with

TABLE 5.2 Approximated Cost of Treasury Strips during Panic of 2008

Maturity	CUSIP[a]	Price	Yield
2/15/09	912820JW8	$99.80	0.35%
2/15/10	912820EM5	$98.38	1.10%
2/15/11	912020GC5	$96.56	1.41%
2/15/12	912820GV3	$92.91	2.11%
2/15/13	912820HR1	$89.51	2.47%
2/15/14	912820JX6	$86.67	2.60%
2/15/15	912803AA1	$80.49	3.36%
2/15/16	912803AF0	$76.66	3.57%
2/15/17	912820PE1	$73.54	3.64%
2/15/18	912820QN0	$69.53	3.96%
2/15/19	912803AQ6	$64.09	4.28%
2/15/20	912803AS2	$60.76	4.38%
2/15/21	912803AV5	$57.72	4.44%
2/15/22	912833LG3	$54.88	4.50%
2/15/23	912803BB8	$52.59	4.49%
2/15/24	912833LQ1	$50.53	4.46%
2/15/25	912803BE2	$49.03	4.38%
2/15/26	912803BG7	$46.25	4.47%
2/15/27	912803BK8	$44.73	4.41%
2/15/28	912833RY8	$43.17	4.37%
2/15/29	912803BW2	$41.86	4.31%
2/15/30	912833XX3	$40.12	4.31%
2/15/31	912803CK7	$39.12	4.18%
2/15/32	9128334T4	$37.96	4.18%
2/15/33	9128334V9	$36.65	4.15%
2/15/34	9128334X5	$35.35	4.13%
2/15/35	9128334Z0	$34.12	4.11%
2/15/36	912803CX9	$33.74	4.00%
2/15/37	912803CZ4	$33.05	3.93%
2/15/38	912803DC4	$32.40	3.87%

[a]The 9th column of a CUSIP (for Committee on Uniform Security Identification Procedures) is a checksum digit that is algorithmically derived from the first eight characters; CUSIPs are often shown in eight-character truncated form.

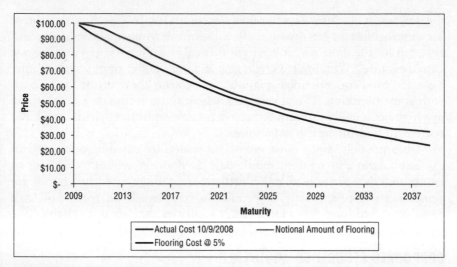

FIGURE 5.1 Cost of Flooring Using Principal Strips by Maturity (10/9/2008)

a 6 percent coupon rate will adjust to 5 percent inflation by having the new notional of $1,050, and a semiannual coupon payment based on 6% × 1050/2 = $31.50. Even ordinary TIPS can be problematic for taxable accounts since the changes in principal are treated as phantom income. When using principal strips from various TIPS to build an inflation-protected floor, it is once again most beneficial to use a tax-deferred account where taxes are only applicable upon withdrawal.

As with nominal bonds, TIPS can be stripped. Using TIPS strips one can construct an inflation-protected floor under lifestyle. Some authors, including William Sharpe, have argued that TIPS strips are the ideal flooring for retirement income.[5] I've already argued elsewhere that this may not be the optimal approach for everybody. However, this is a very sensible approach that can be implemented with more or less a "set it and forget it" program. TIPS can also be used within the insurance context for companies to use TIPS as the backbone for real longevity protection either via pure longevity insurance or annuities.

MUNICIPAL SECURITIES

Municipals securities ("municipals") can satisfy the requirements for tax exemption. These securities are tax exempt at the federal level, and often tax exempt at the state level, and they can provide a great way to augment the tax-favored status of retirement accounts with a pseudo-retirement account that has no penalty for early withdrawal. Municipals do have credit risk, but for the most part it is a hypothetical risk as municipal defaults are extremely rare.[6] With limited credit risk and their tax-exempt status, municipals are good for retirement planning at present; they can be made great with some tweaking. This is one area where those fortunate enough to be in a high tax bracket can earn attractive taxable-equivalent yields[7] and build retirement flooring at the same time.

Unfortunately, since most municipal issues are callable, one needs to exercise caution in treating municipals as flooring without checking to ensure that they are noncallable. Furthermore, though municipal bonds are sometimes stripped, mostly they trade in complete bond form. Still it is possible to find long-dated tax-exempt securities that are not callable.[8]

CORPORATE SECURITIES AND OTHER FINANCIAL PRODUCTS

In general, flooring can be created out of any time-dated product that has a fixed minimum payment and is noncallable. Many corporate bonds can be laddered or are issued as OID bonds or can be stripped to fit the generic description of flooring. However, with corporates, and to lesser extent municipals, credit risk calls for diversification. There are better ways to seek yield enhancement for a portfolio than having concentrated credit risk in the part of the portfolio that is designed to provide lifestyle security during a person's retirement years.

In principle, corporate securities could include certain types of structured products that are often created by their originators. For transaction-based advisers, it is easy to conceive of products that would have appealing usability for retirement income. Of course, there are certain restrictions on advisers placing these in fiduciary accounts. In addition, there are whole classes of structured products that are not floored, but sold as enhanced-yield products where the enhanced yield is created by having the client take enhanced risk. However, firms often issue principal-protected notes that, for some, may be a useful way to plug gaps in, or add shape to, flooring.

Another possibility for capital markets creating flooring is the use of options and other derivative contracts to create a secured income stream. In principle, it is possible to lock in a minimum value on a portfolio or some of the individual elements therein. A client with substantial share ownership in a firm may have reasons to want to hold onto shares, while simultaneously desiring to nullify the risk of the shares. In such a case, a staggered ladder of put options or similar derivative contracts could be used to create a floor out of the shares. As a practical matter, this approach is made difficult by the general unavailability of listed and even over-the-counter (OTC) equity options. An additional hurdle for using this approach is that a hedge that neutralizes risk is typically treated as equivalent to a sale, and thus constitutes a taxable event. Since neither impediment, short duration and taxation, are likely to be reduced in the foreseeable future, the practicality of this approach will remain limited.

SUMMARY

Capital markets provide an array of products that can be used to create lifestyle flooring. The capital markets products that are the building blocks of flooring include both governmental and corporate securities. Two of the most readily available products for creating capital markets–based flooring are Treasury strips and Treasury inflation-protected securities (TIPS). Both have the advantages of high liquidity and being free of credit risk. Coupon-bearing bonds, both corporate and governmental, can be used for flooring, as can structured products and derivatives. The adviser needs to be wary of using callable bonds to create a client's retirement flooring.

PART TWO

Adapting Portfolios for Retirement Income

CHAPTER 6

Building Retirement Income Portfolios

Objectives

Create floor and upside portfolios

Building over time

By definition change is disruptive. Too often the planning for retirement income really begins in earnest on the date of retirement or at the time of the 401(k) rollover distribution. As a general rule, proposing large changes always faces more resistance than proposing small changes. Annuitization, which is essentially a transformation of a large part of most portfolios, is a big change. In retirement, the portfolio change is also linked to a profoundly personal acceptance of mortality. This helps to explain those who ultimately annuitize only after experiencing some period of retirement and becoming comfortable with the idea. Any steps taken prior to that point will be helpful. Structuring retirement income portfolios to look and feel like accumulation portfolios minimizes disruption and maximizes flexibility.

We always want to keep in mind the cognitive dissonance associated with change. Questions like "Why now?" and "Was the old way wrong?" are questions that can be avoided by letting the client know what changes are to be expected as accumulation gives way to retirement income planning.

The trick, the subtlety, and the art lies in making the change both expected and seamless—both for the client and the adviser. Portfolio proposal tools can easily be enhanced to facilitate both accumulation and retirement portfolios; the approach and sleeving of products should be enhanced so that it is backward compatible with traditional portfolio construction.

Along with the theme of retirement income, there need to be concrete methods or approaches for both setting and meeting goals. To that end, we offer three generic templates that can be used to motivate anything from an informal to a pitch-book approach. Three generic templates for creating retirement income accumulation plans are described. Here they are labeled as "Brick Layer," "Track Layer," and "Surge Maker." Their dual purpose is to provide the client with a plan of action and you with a backstory for marketing.

Within this chapter, we also cover some of the advantageous ways to build accounts from a tax perspective as well as some of the taxation pitfalls associated with retirement portfolios. Our objective is to use the tax shields most advantageously for creating a retirement portfolio. Taxes act as a friction in the machinery of retirement. Tax laws have a habit of changing over time, so our focus is on the nature of the rules rather than the specific rates.

What is true of the client is also true of the financial professional. Extensions or tweaks to a business model, which offer incremental upside with no downside, are more likely to gain acceptance than major shifts that create risks along with the opportunities. Much of what we show in this chapter is that a major gain to retirement practice works out to being analogous to a slight change in the sleeving of products. Until the market catches up with more dedicated fund offerings for retirement income, the retirement income sleeve will be filled with more individual securities, but to the professional it should feel as before. For managing multiple clients, it is as simple as starting the Smiths' retirement income in 2018 and Joneses' in 2021.

Traditional intuition about the trade-off between risk and return works quite well in this framework. To motivate a visual interpretation we can think of the familiar construct of the *capital market line* (CML) shown in Figure 6.1. The CML links a risk-free asset and the efficient frontier[1] of risky assets by showing the best ways to combine the risk-free asset with portfolios on the efficient frontier. The efficient frontier gets its name from the idea that if we take all risky assets and consider all possible combinations of those assets, the efficient frontier will represent the portfolios of risky assets with lowest possible risk for a particular expected return (or conversely the highest expected return for a given level of risk).

PORTFOLIO SLEEVES FOR RETIREMENT INCOME

In Chapter 2, we saw that the top-down view of the retirement problem allowed us to write the consumption solution as the following:

$$\text{Optimal consumption} = \text{Consumption floor} +$$
$$x\% \cdot [\text{Current wealth} - \text{PV}(\text{Future floors})]$$
$$= \text{Lifestyle floor} + x\% \cdot (\text{Discretionary wealth})$$

This framing provides us with a natural way to create product sleeves that take the optimal from the hypothetical to the practical. *Sleeving* is a common way to build a portfolio composed of modules that allow the adviser to stay within a disciplined framework while offering clients a customized portfolio.[2] For advisers, whether on a single-fee or transaction-based model, the commonality between the sleeving presented here and the sleeving that sits in their proposal-generating tool will help create a natural bridge to cross from pure accumulation to accumulation for retirement income. The basic construct for retirement income, shown in Figure 6.2, involves two sets of sleeves—one for flooring and the other for the excess portfolio, which shows one of the main distinctions of retirement income portfolios: assets committed to lifestyle security and assets that represent discretionary wealth or funds intended for but not yet committed to flooring. The roles change a little, but, in spirit, this should feel no different than a sleeving of fixed-income and equity. The excess portfolio sleeving will, at first glance, be entirely familiar. The difference here is that the excess portfolio is only part of the total retirement income portfolio, so the familiar can be interpreted as a subset of a broader view.

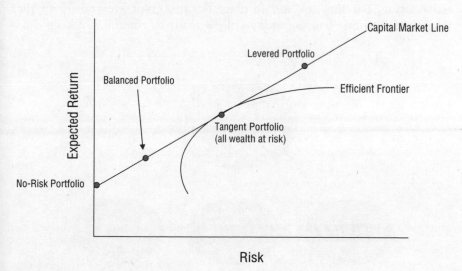

FIGURE 6.1 Allocation along the Capital Markets Line (CML)

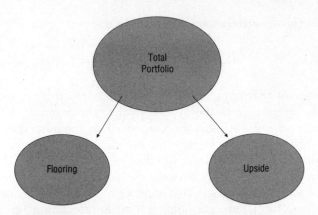

FIGURE 6.2 Creating Initial Allocations

The mechanical view of how the sleeving works is best illustrated by thinking of a two-track process. Along the first track we move to flooring. We will break this down further at a later point, but for now flooring includes longevity protection—lifetime flooring. The second track takes us to the sleeves for the management of discretionary wealth shown in Figure 6.3. Later on this will also be broken down to be more inclusive of liquidity balances. You'll notice that the bottom right of Figure 6.3 has a placeholder for discretionary wealth. If the funds are in risky assets, they may be potential flooring, but they are not in-place flooring. Not everyone with the wherewithal to buy flooring today will be ready to commit; we keep it as

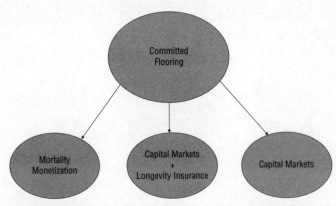

FIGURE 6.3 Flooring Sleeves

a placeholder for now.[3] We treat this segment in great detail in Part Three, where we discuss techniques for managing portfolios in the presence of flooring risk.

Moving down a level first to the committed flooring node, we see in Figure 6.3 that there are three groupings of sleeves for products: annuities, hybrid, and capital markets. Of the roughly 20,000 financial advisers at Bank of America/Merrill Lynch, a significant majority are registered to be able to sell both capital markets and insurance products. For retirement income products, having both registrations is desirable. Note that the different nodes are the natural flooring solutions for different levels of relative wealth (Wealth/PV/Lifestyle needs).

Annuities sit within the first grouping in Figure 6.3, sleeves for mortality monetization; this includes variable annuities.[4] As its name implies, the sleeves should contain all products for which there is a sizeable component of mortality monetization: fixed annuities and variable annuities. Folks choosing flooring via mortality monetization fall into two camps: (1) those who choose it as a way to provide a tax-advantaged floor outside of the constraints of their retirement accounts; and (2) those who feel that monetizing mortality is the best way to maintain lifestyle. These are two very different constituencies.

Not all products that are placed in an insurance wrapper constitute flooring. Many financial products are placed in an insurance wrapper to confer tax deferral, even though the insurance component is essentially secondary; such products would best be described and sleeved as discretionary wealth products; not all insurance products monetize mortality; not all insurance products constitute flooring.

The capital markets node in Figure 6.3 would encompass all fixed income instruments that can be used to create flooring. To reiterate an important point from Chapter 2, "flooring is defined herein as a guaranteed minimum payment, either nominal or real." Yield-based products without a fixed minimum notional do not constitute flooring. We rule out cases where the yield is fixed or floored, but the notional varies, such as certain equity funds. Sleeves would contain options for government securities and funds—nominal, government securities, real, corporates, and municipals.[5] In contrast to the mortality monetization node, those desiring capital markets flooring generally are not only unwilling to monetize their mortality, nor do they feel compelled to do so. For those with sufficient wealth to meet their lifestyle needs, mortality monetization is an option, not a necessity. This means that there is a greater opportunity for both high-end and low-end flooring products to be created and sleeved within this node. A simple but powerful start on this sleeve can be made by listing available strips by maturity.

The central node in Figure 6.3, capital markets plus longevity insurance, would not simply copy and add to the capital markets sleeving. It is important to remember that the typical hybrid flooring purchaser is motivated by a desire to maintain lifestyle in the face of longevity risk. Without longevity insurance, they only have enough to maintain lifestyle for a finite period of time. Flooring choices located off of this node should be of the more basic and most secure types; kept straightforward, secure, and affordable. For those in this category, separating flooring and discretionary wealth, securing the flooring, and concentrating efforts on the discretionary wealth provides the best opportunity for incrementing lifestyle at a later date.

The sleeve contents for discretionary wealth are the same as those for ordinary accumulation portfolios. The difference here lies not in the content, but in the construction. If we have taken care to set up a floor for the client, then they have more freedom to take risk in the discretionary wealth subportfolio to move the portfolio as a whole to a desired risk-return structure. I am not advocating using the discretionary wealth subportfolio to gamble, but pointing out that the flooring subportfolio has the volatility dampening characteristics of the fixed-income portion of an accumulation portfolio. In a simple sense then, the discretionary wealth subportfolio would be expected to have a higher weight in equity than the equity sleeves of an accumulation portfolio.

PORTFOLIO INTUITION

Once again we refer to the concept of the capital market line. In Figure 6.4, we show the retirement income analog to the ordinary accumulation view of the CML. We use the notion of the CML to illustrate retirement income allocations between lifestyle security (flooring) and risky assets (the discretionary wealth portfolio). We want our discretionary wealth to be in an efficient portfolio and we wouldn't knowingly construct our portfolio to be inefficient. Professionals may differ in the construction of portfolios, but they all aim for maximum reward per unit of risk.

One main difference in Figure 6.4 is that we now have the concept of lifestyle risk replacing the concept of risk merely for return distributions as in the accumulation CML. Here the risk-free end of the spectrum refers to allocations that correspond to a 100 percent fixed lifestyle (insurance or capital markets). For this case, there is no allocation to discretionary wealth whether bundled into a variable annuity or in an unbundled fashion comprised of risky capital markets products. For practical purposes, the other

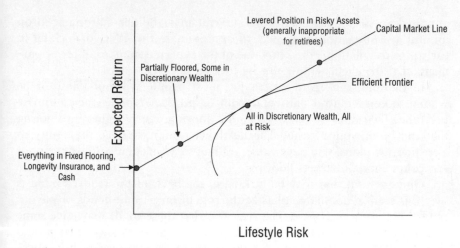

FIGURE 6.4 CML Analog for Retirement Income

end of the spectrum that we consider would be a portfolio with no allocation to lifestyle security and 100 percent in at-risk assets. Except for the very young, or those actively engaged in risk managing portfolios, this would not be recommended. In between those two endpoints would be all shades of balanced approaches that are more or less appropriate depending on age and degree of activity allowed for risk management.

BASIC PORTFOLIO CONSTRUCTS

There are many ways to structure portfolios during the transition period from pure accumulation to preretirement, covering the 25 years leading up to the act of retirement. There is no single best way. There is one fork in the road that if chosen is hard to reverse—the question of monetizing mortality. But if it is the right path for your client, then the earlier they head down that path the better. If your client *knows* that annuities are for them, then the earlier that you secure them flooring with an annuity, the more their mortality is worth. By monetizing their mortality preretirement, they are increasing the odds of dying before ever receiving a check; that means that a vanilla annuity that begins payment at 65 is cheaper for a 45-year-old than a 65-year-old. Unlike life insurance (death benefits), annuities are cheaper when people are expected to die sooner;[6] mortality monetization pays off more when survival is less likely. Choosing the right time for an annuity can be influenced by the survival probabilities starting to drop around age 60. One simple way to approximate the effect of locking in early is to calculate the present value of the expected number of fewer payments that the client will receive by locking in early.

In the long run-up to retirement, most people will not know or be willing to commit to a particular path or product type as their ultimate portfolio. That does not mean to ignore flooring, but it argues for flooring that can be unwound easily. The flexibility option, that is, the ability to alter flooring plans, will have value, leading to an accumulation-stage preference for capital markets flooring.

One question that may be lurking in the back of the reader's mind is why this section doesn't emphasize the role of target date funds or payout funds in retirement income. The reason is that these funds may have some appeal to investors, but they do not secure flooring. As such, they would therefore be more appropriate for discretionary wealth sleeves. In particular, payout funds, lacking in guarantees, are best thought of as distribution plans for discretionary wealth. What target date funds do is reduce the two-sided volatility of a portfolio over time. For example a target date fund may begin with a 90 percent exposure to equity and 10 percent exposure to fixed income (90:10). As it moves toward its target date, it will reduce the equity exposure moving from 90 percent to, say, 60 percent (90:10 to 60:40). However, current target date funds do not secure flooring. By reducing the portfolio volatility, reducing upside as well as downside, and without securing a floor, your client may just as likely drown, but in a shallower pool.

We move on to illustrate three simple accumulation plans for creating retirement income portfolios. These three plans are designed to be reversible, but they are also designed to give a head start to the retirement income portfolio that will be managed during retirement. These are all presented as plans that are compatible with current portfolio management processes. This compatibility should help the adviser adjust focus in a seamless fashion. These plans should also help to avoid the cognitive dissonance associated with sudden and major shifts in portfolio emphasis. All of the basic portfolio constructs here are designed to illustrate that the effective changes here are not in the portfolio risk characteristics, but in the focus on lifestyle maintenance and the addition of the concept of notional flooring laid down for retirement.

Brick Layer

The brick layer accumulation plan follows the notion that some clients desire to fix a window of time for which they need to build a floor. During accumulation, knowledge of whether the fixed window will be (1) kept as a standalone, (2) augmented with longevity insurance, or (3) ultimately sold off and replaced by a mortality-monetizing annuity is not essential. A simple portfolio construct that would completely dovetail with current accumulation plans would simply swap out a traditional accumulation plan's fixed-income component for a fixed-income component that will be allowed to mature. The simplest thing to put in for flooring in this case is a coupon strip.

As an example, suppose that a 50-year-old client wants you begin a bricklaying program for them. Suppose also that they have been comfortable with their portfolio weights set at 70 percent equity and 30 percent fixed income. Now your client decides that they want to put in a floor to cover ages 60 (when they plan to retire) to 75. The easiest way to begin laying down a floor here, while maintaining portfolio style, is to begin to purchase coupon strips on a coupon-bearing noncallable bond maturing in 25 years. Similarly, next year you can purchase a coupon strip on a coupon-bearing noncallable bond maturing in 24 years. In essence, this individual will be dollar-cost averaging into a fixed window. You will always know and be able to let this client know his or her flooring by the dollar amount of the coupon payments to be received. If purchasing government securities, then there is no credit risk to worry about; however, if purchasing securities with credit risk, diversifying by using bonds from different corporations and even different industries is recommended.

This accumulation plan is quite flexible. The "old" fixed-income component of a portfolio can be kept in its current form, typically bond funds, or converted to additional flooring. It allows for the size of the bricklaying window to be widened in later years. It can be augmented for shape by overlaying zero-coupon bonds on top for years where higher flooring is required. Finally, it can all be easily reversed and converted into a mortality-monetizing plan if that becomes desirable.

Track Layer

The track layer is our second portfolio building construct. It is in some senses easier for individual clients to intuit and grasp than brick layer. This can be started anytime during middle age, but for our example we consider starting at age 40. The main difference between the track layer and brick layer is that instead of fixing a wide window and then trying to fill as much as possible as the brick layer does, the track layer relies on principal strips and other zero-coupon bonds to create a small section of track with a new bit of track, created a little bit further out each year.

The example that we use here is very similar to the story that was used to introduce Chapter 5. Suppose that your client has several years to go until retirement but wants to lay down a year's flooring with each passing year. This will be best accomplished by purchasing bullet payments for each year. Unlike the brick layer, diversification to avoid credit risk must be conducted each year. As a practical matter, given the credit-risk possibilities, and the current lack of fund choices, government-backed zero-coupon securities are ideally suited to track layer.

As with the brick layer, it is possible to do this while maintaining the same portfolio weights as a pure accumulation portfolio. However, by focusing on a single year of retirement at a time, this approach really seems to hammer home the link between the amounts saved today and the lifestyle secured during retirement; it is likely that the client's desired portfolio weights may shift to a greater emphasis on flooring.

Surge Maker

The surge maker is a construct that is best suited to those for whom it is unclear whether they will need to fully monetize mortality or whether there are sufficient resources for a hybrid floor. In its mechanics, the surge maker builds up a relatively narrow window to a desired level of flooring before moving out to build an adjacent window. For those starting more than 10 years before the act of retirement, or if the window being filled is more than 10 years away, bonds can also be used. However, it would be useful to have a plan for layering the coupon payments that are to be received. When the window being filled is close at hand, then using bonds or their coupon strips to the window's edge will work just as well.

For example, suppose that at age 50, Pat begins a surge maker program. Not having thought much in the past about retirement, but being caught in the pincers of panic over maintaining lifestyle after retirement and needing equity exposure for upside, Pat has you put 60 percent into flooring and is willing to take greater than normal risk with the remaining 40 percent. The flooring component can be built up with a variety of (noncallable) corporate bonds. The coupons that are received will be directed to discretionary wealth where the portfolio that Pat has chosen is weighted toward small and midcap stocks. Pat's target for flooring, excluding Social Security income, is $30,000. If Pat can surge to $30,000 out to age 80 with the flooring portfolio, then Pat will reallocate some of the excess portfolio to longevity insurance, holding most of the rest in equity to use as a bequest for a couple of grandchildren; if not Pat will convert all current flooring and most of the excess to an annuity; expectations for the grandchildren will be lowered.

GENERAL ACCUMULATION PLANS
FOR RETIREMENT INCOME

Regardless of the portfolio construction theme, the first question to answer has to do with the percentage of the current total that needs to be locked down and committed to flooring. The principal that we stringently adhere to is that once flooring is laid down for a client, you stick with it except under predetermined conditions.[7] Many, but not all, rational individuals will want to lock in flooring as soon as the wherewithal to buy the flooring is available. However, some, equally rational but of higher risk tolerance, will keep their flooring funds at risk as long as the at-risk fund total exceeds the cost of locking in the needed flooring. A large part of Part Three of this book is devoted to active management of retirement income portfolio allocations to ensure safety while still allowing for taking market risk.

For those least tolerant of risk, there is no question of when to buy flooring. The answer is to keep locking in flooring first until the required amount of flooring is secure—only then are there excess funds for investing in risky assets.

For those with greater risk tolerance, there may be a desire for either passive or active strategies. Some may want to create an initial balance of components for the portfolio that ensures the flooring considered necessary will be met eventually. Others may be interested in a minimal initial floor, keeping open the possibility of their flooring desires ratcheting upward in future years. For some others an accumulation plan that targets all flooring securely in place by retirement will be the most appealing.

For the most risk-tolerant investors, which funds are reasonable candidates for remaining uncommitted? The most important factor in the answer depends on the ratio of wealth to the present value of flooring needs. While there are rules of thumb for specific year's floors, the main rule is concerned with the total needed for creating flooring versus the funds available. The risk is that the value of the available funds drops below the present value of the cost of locking in flooring. Once contributions have ceased, a shortfall in value means the individual faces the prospect of taking on market risk, mortality risk, or accepting a reduction in circumstances. Part Three will cover the active management of this type of risk.

TAXES AND RETIREMENT INCOME PORTFOLIOS

When it comes to retirement income portfolios, how you navigate the tax landscape can have a dramatic impact on how well the portfolio performs. There are two categories of accounts to think about:

1. *Fully taxable*. After-tax earnings on accumulation, taxable income created
2. *One-sided taxable*
   - Tax-deferred. Pretax in, taxable out (pretax income throughout the accumulation phase is taxable as ordinary income during distribution)
   - Taxed prior to accumulation. After-tax in, tax-exempt out (after-tax income treated as tax-exempt accumulation with no tax liability on distribution [Roth IRA])

There are a few considerations to keep in mind that provide both generic rules and special cases that help the decision of which type of account is the best location for different types of products. To that end, we work backward and start with the Roth IRA–type accounts.

- *Roth IRA accounts*. Roth IRA accounts take in after-tax funds, however, all gains and income created within the account are tax-exempt on distribution. This makes the Roth IRA an ideal location for income-producing assets; particularly assets that produce phantom income. Phantom income that is taxed at ordinary rates is perhaps the most onerous problem for retirement income that is alleviated by the Roth IRA.

   In the absence of constraints on annual contributions, there would be no question but to put all retirement assets into tax-favored accounts. However, with the limitations on contributions that affect all of the favorably taxed retirement accounts, there is a question on how best to use the accounts in the event that the total retirement savings exceed the capacity of the favored accounts. When retirement funds exceed the capacity limits of the Roth IRA, it is not the best location for assets that qualify for favorable dividend or capital gains treatments. Similarly, the Roth IRA is not the right place for assets that have a significant possibility of incurring capital losses.

   Roth IRA accounts are the right place to locate assets that produce ordinary income, phantom or otherwise. A secondary question with respect to Roth IRA accounts is whether it is worthwhile to rollover assets from a 401(k) or ordinary IRA into a Roth IRA. Such rollovers create a taxable event at the time of conversion. It is sensible to convert if tax rates are expected to be significantly higher in the future and the Roth IRA will be used for locating the highly taxed assets discussed previously. To give an example that will clarify the issues, consider a client who is currently in a 35 percent marginal tax bracket. Suppose the client expects tax rates to double in the near future. If the client still expects to be well in the top bracket after retirement and is using the Roth IRA for "ordinary income," then the conversion will make sense. A Roth conversion may also be a good way to take advantage of a temporary bout of unemployment or income diminution, particularly if the conversion can be effected at a low tax rate. Keep in mind that the conversion will not make sense if tax rates are expected to fall or if the client expects to be in a lower marginal bracket during distribution.

- *Tax-deferred accounts.* Tax-deferred accounts encompass the bulk of assets held for retirement. The most popular versions are the traditional IRA, 401(k), and 403(b). These accounts allow annual contributions of pretax income, subject to limitations, that grow tax-deferred until withdrawal where the distributions are taxed as ordinary income. The tax deferral feature is essentially a way to lever the deferred tax liability. In essence, the account holder accrues a tax liability that they can reinvest until the year of withdrawal, at which time tax is paid on both the original tax-deferred deposit plus the gains as ordinary income.

  As with the Roth case, things become a little more nuanced when retirement savings exceed the capacity of tax-favored accounts. The tax deferral is valuable in all cases, but it is less valuable for assets that generate preferential treatment such as capital gains and dividend income. That is because all withdrawals from the accounts are treated as ordinary income, with no preferential rates applying.

- *Fully Taxable accounts.* Fully Taxable accounts are places where asset choice is most important. There are products that can be placed in fully taxable accounts that are tax exempt, some that are taxed preferentially, and others that are tax deferred. Municipal securities are among those that are tax exempt at the Federal level.[8]

  Aside from the exempt securities, there are instruments such as insurance products that can be placed in fully taxable accounts that create a tax deferral. Both simple and complex annuities[9] have an important tax-deferral feature that is often overlooked. Annuities work well in fully taxable accounts because they can free up capacity in the accounts that have restrictions on deposits and withdrawals. Buying an annuity in a tax-deferred account is a waste of a tax shield and should only be done when other options are unavailable.

Tax-favored accounts are the first-best place for instruments that produce ordinary income. With capacity constrained in the tax-favored accounts, instruments that obtain capital-gains treatment or have dividend yield are preferred instruments for fully taxable accounts.

It is a well-known and sad fact that most people do not take full advantage of their ability to shield income from the taxman. The reasons given for underutilizing tax shields range from a lack of awareness to unwillingness to fill out a form. Whatever the reason, the important question is whether the shields that are being used are being used properly. So let me mention a few simple rules.

Some Tax Dos and Don'ts

- Don't waste tax shields. Municipal bonds and insurance policies are best kept outside of your client's retirement accounts. (Even if you want to violate this rule, deferred annuities are problematic in IRAs.)
- Tax treatment of discount bonds creates phantom income that can create current-year liabilities before the bond matures. Taxes on phantom income can be avoided if discount bonds are kept in retirement accounts. Your client still pays taxes upon withdrawal when they realize the gains, but not before.
- For assets of equal expected return, the value of the tax deferral in retirement funds is greatest for assets that would otherwise be producing yearly, ordinary income as opposed to capital gains or dividend income.
- For assets of differential expected return, the higher the expected return, the greater the value of the income deferral tax shield at maturity.
- If your client's 401(k) does not have a sufficiently varied menu to allow building flooring, then a rollover IRA provides the opportunity to move all or part of their 401(k) to a self-directed plan offering more flooring flexibility. Rollovers from a 401(k) to an IRA have no tax consequences. This should not be treated as a way to prove stock-picking acumen; this is the place primarily for flooring, not off-track betting with discretionary wealth.
- For pretax funds in an IRA, the higher the return on assets, the greater the long-run value of the tax shield.
- For after-tax funds, a Roth IRA is an all around better deal than putting after-tax funds into a traditional IRA.
- For after-tax funds in a traditional IRA, the value of the tax deferral is greatest for assets that would be continuously creating ordinary income. Don't unintentionally waste the tax shield on assets that would have deferred taxation by their nature such as the capital gains on equity.
- Don't waste after-tax funds in a traditional IRA by converting what could be deferred capital gains into deferred ordinary income. When using after-tax income, any nondistributing capital-gains asset will get lower tax treatment outside the traditional IRA. Assets that produce ordinary income, especially phantom income, are natural candidates for any after-tax funds in a traditional IRA.
- A Roth IRA (after-tax on the way in, tax-exempt on the way out) is a great place for all assets, but the relative advantage is greatest for those that generate ordinary income.

- Although retirement accounts do remove the tax disadvantages of short-term trading, once retired it becomes much harder for clients to come back from a bad gamble, so unless they expect to die soon or are enamored of cardboard housing, don't gamble away their retirement lifestyle.

SUMMARY

This chapter served as a foundation chapter for turning the concepts of Part One into usable, recognizable, and scalable portfolios. As we cover the basics of constructing portfolios of floor plus upside, we keep the familiar context of portfolio sleeving. By using the familiar sleeving, it becomes clearer how a small change in practice can lead to portfolios that have profoundly better outcomes for clients who become retirees. To help illustrate the process, basic portfolio constructs that we call brick layer, track layer, and surge maker were used to help simplify how to bring retirement income into a standard adviser's practice. We ended the chapter with some tips for locating retirement assets within different accounts subject to differing tax rules.

If one of the goals is to revamp a practice that was dealt a hard blow in the recent crisis, then it is important to think about how to explain your enhanced practice to clients without a hint of regret for the practices that have been in place. It is as important to make retirement income a seamless addition to your practice as it is to make the transition from pure accumulation to retirement income seamless for your clients.

Creating Allocations for Constructing Practical Portfolios by Age and Lifestyle Needs

Objectives

Providing usable allocations and allocation methodology for creating actual portfolios

Adjusting allocations for lifestyle, age, anticipated inflation, and life expectancy

When it comes to building portfolios, the engineer will look into a toolkit and say, "Here's what I can do for you." The economist will look into the models and say, "Here's what you ought to do, assuming you are of this type." The marketing manager will look around and say, "Here's what everyone else does, let's call it new and improved." This chapter focuses on the actual allocations that fall out of analyzing what can be done with available wealth.

In traditional accumulation portfolios, an allocation centered around 60 percent equity, 30 percent bonds, and 10 percent cash is a well-worn standard. For retirement income, the economic models are too crude and the retirement income industry is too new to have an industry standard for providing default allocations. Therefore, what follows is an engineering approach meant to place emphasis on the possibilities for creating portfolios. We benchmark the engineering implications of what can be done with client portfolios to achieve particular objectives; we derive allocations to flooring, longevity risks, precautionary balances, and risky assets to achieve these intuitive objectives.

First, we look at how age, inflation, and expected horizon affect the required minimum flooring allocations for a static and secured flooring plan. Said another way, we find allocations for flooring that could be purchased and, once purchased, would require no further action. I stress this point here because in Chapter 9 when we discuss active risk management, we cover methods where the allocation to risky assets changes. Under active risk management, the amount of in-place flooring changes as the portfolio value changes relative to the targeted flooring amounts; then there may be a difference between the target flooring level and the actual amount that we have secured. For now, we want to focus on allocations that fix the floor as a percentage of current wealth, but allow the dollar value of the floor to rise if wealth rises.

Second, we turn our attention to the issue of longevity risk. Even if flooring is in place until extreme old age, the possibility remains that the individual may still be vigorous in spirit and possibly vigorous in body. If it were certain that extreme longevity meant dementia then the incentive to guard against running out of money before running out of time might be lower for some individuals.[1] Being fearful of a diminished lifestyle is the risk that is discussed in this chapter.[2] There are profound societal issues associated with the reality of providing care for the elderly, but the fears of frailty, dementia, and poverty are universal yet always personal.

Third, we look briefly at precautionary allocations. During accumulation, precautionary balances are suggested not only as portfolio stabilizers but also as a ready source of funds in the event of employment interruptions or other unplanned needs. In retirement, there is also a precautionary motive for holding cash balances. The circumstances and surprises are different, but the needs are no less real.

Finally, we look at allocations to risky assets and how having flooring in place and secured provides greater incentive for risk taking in discretionary wealth. It turns out that with flooring securely in place, the payoff in any period becomes equivalent to having a call option. Once the downside risk is mitigated by flooring, there is a greater risk tolerance for discretionary wealth. This result is in stark contrast to optimal allocations for drawdown plans without flooring in place.

If you are impatient and want to jump ahead to allocations that can be used in a plug-and-play context, then you can skip to the table on the last page of this chapter. You can always double back later to read the contents of the chapter to create your own allocation schedules. There are also several problems that you can tackle in the companion workbook, designed to help you construct allocation tables that can be dynamically tailored to the needs of your clients.

FLOORING ALLOCATIONS

To start, we look at the simplified case of finding flooring allocations for someone who expects to need to fund their retirement for 20 years until

TABLE 7.1 Flooring Allocations to Allow for Consuming at a Steady 5 Percent Beginning at Age 65

Age	Anticipated Inflation		
	0%	2%	3%
30	12%	28%	43%
35	15%	32%	47%
40	19%	37%	52%
45	25%	43%	57%
50	31%	50%	63%
55	40%	58%	69%
60	51%	67%	76%
65	65%	77%	84%
70[a]	73%	82%	88%
75[b]	81%	88%	92%

[a]In this case, someone at age 70 expects to fund to age 85, implying a baseline flooring of 6.7 percent per year.
[b]In this case someone at age 75 expects to fund to age 85, implying a baseline flooring of 10 percent per year.

age 85, receiving payouts beginning at age 65. If flooring is purchased prior to retirement, we target 5 percent of initial wealth to be secured as flooring. In other words, until retirement a $1,000,000 portfolio would be floored to provide a minimum of $50,000 per year for each of 20 years. If locked in prior to retirement, each period's retirement income will total $50,000 plus the fraction of discretionary wealth that the individual chooses to monetize.[3] For a client who arrives on our doorstep after retirement commences, the flooring would be designed to cover the years remaining until age 85. Table 7.1 shows the allocation to flooring for a client creating a 5 percent floor covering ages 65 to 85, while Table 7.2 shows allocations to flooring at 4 percent of current wealth covering the range from age 65 to 90. Don't worry too much about the percent of wealth used in the tables since the results scale directly.

Previously, and in what follows, we show two tables (Table 7.1 and Table 7.2) illustrating allocations for individuals who build flooring to ages 85 and 90 respectively. As you read through these, keep in mind that the differences between allocations can be interpreted as largely due to the difference in lifestyle needs of the two individuals. For retirement saving, "start

TABLE 7.2 Flooring Allocations to Allow for
Consuming at a Steady 4 Percent Beginning at Age 65

Age	Anticipated Inflation		
	0%	2%	3%
30	11%	26%	41%
35	14%	30%	45%
40	17%	35%	50%
45	22%	40%	55%
50	28%	47%	60%
55	36%	54%	66%
60	46%	62%	73%
65	59%	72%	80%
70[a]	65%	77%	84%
75[b]	73%	82%	88%

[a]In this case someone at age 70 expects to fund to age
90, implying a baseline flooring of 5.0 percent per year.
[b]In this case someone at age 75 expects to fund to age
90, implying a baseline flooring of 6.7 percent per year.

early and save until it hurts" is a well-worn cliché. The point to make here
is that for retirement income, along with an early start and a high saving
rate, a lower floor with simpler lifestyle "needs" can make for a much more
flexible portfolio.

In Tables 7.1 and 7.2, the horizontal rows show the allocations to
flooring for individuals purchasing the flooring at different ages. The verti-
cal columns show the allocations to flooring if that flooring were to be
adjusted, beginning at date of purchase, for anticipated rates of inflation of
0 percent, 2 percent, and 3 percent. The column corresponding to 0 percent
anticipated inflation can also be interpreted as pure nominal flooring. It is
purely coincidental, but interesting nonetheless to see that the nominal
allocations to flooring in this example are not totally dissimilar to the standard allocations in pure accumulation.

One implication for professionals is that the allocations currently utilized for clients as accumulation portfolios may be naturally transformed
into retirement income portfolios by transitioning the fixed income component of the accumulation portfolio into the proper securities for the flooring

component of a retirement income portfolio. The major difference between these flooring allocations presented here and the fixed income allocation used in accumulation portfolios is that having the flooring in place eliminates the probability of ruin inherent in drawing down accumulation portfolios; this is designed to work, whereas drawdown is based on hope.[4]

Each element of Table 7.1 represents a prospective allocation to lifestyle protection (flooring) for an individual whose age is given by the row, with an expectation of lifestyle needs rising at the rate of inflation given by the columns. For simplicity, underlying Table 7.1 is an assumption that retirement commences at age 65. The flooring funds would pay until age 85 after which longevity protection would be needed. (Longevity allocation is discussed in the next section.)

Table 7.1 provides allocations for an (Income)/(Initial wealth) ratio of 5 percent per year. It is interesting to note that the nominal allocations by age here are quite similar to the rule-of-thumb allocations that are used for pure accumulation portfolios. In pure nominal terms, a 50-year-old individual in the baseline case above would have a 30 percent allocation to flooring. Similarly, the nominal allocation to flooring by someone 40 years old would be 20 percent. It is quite important to notice that the allocations for inflation-adjusted flooring increase more than proportionately for younger individuals. Upon reflection, this should make sense. At 3 percent inflation, the flooring for someone who is 30 will be 2.8 times the nominal amount—such as someone needing $10,000 worth of flooring at the price level existing when 30 years old will equate to needing $28,138 at age 65 if inflation runs 3 percent.

For someone using TIPS or real annuities to build flooring, there is no need to adjust notional amounts for inflation. However, Table 7.1 will still provide indicative information about portfolio allocations. TIPS for example, are more expensive than nominal securities. It will require a greater allocation of today's funds to protect against inflation than given by the 0 percent inflation column. Somewhere in between the 2 percent and 3 percent columns is, in recent circumstances, probably not far off the mark.

For individuals with higher (Lifestyle)/(Initial wealth) requirements, the ratio would be proportionately higher; for individuals with lower (Lifestyle)/(Initial wealth) requirements, the ratio would be proportionately lower. For example, if instead of 5 percent, the individual needed the portfolio to provide 10 percent flooring, then the allocations in Table 7.1 would all double. For anyone with a lifestyle requirement implying an allocation to flooring of more than 100 percent, it is necessary to consider monetizing mortality, working longer, reducing lifestyle needs, or taking significant market risk; only the first three options are reasonable recommendations; the fourth risks turning what may be a minor shortfall into a major shortfall.

For our second case, Table 7.2, we consider someone who desires to fund retirement flooring beginning at age 65. As before, we allocate baseline funding percentages to the retirement horizon. With the five-year longer horizon, we lower the baseline flooring level to 4 percent per year, if purchased at or before retirement. In similar fashion to the previous case, a $1,000,000 portfolio would be floored to provide a minimum of $40,000 per year for each of the 25 years. Funding preretirement, total income in any period will be $40,000 plus whatever fraction of discretionary wealth that the individual chooses to monetize. As before, the horizontal rows show the allocations to flooring by age; vertical columns show the allocations to flooring by anticipated rate of inflation.

The results shown in Table 7.2 are quite similar to the baseline flooring allocations shown in Table 7.1. Adjusting for both the longer desired window for lifestyle security and lower rate for drawing on the flooring portfolio yields allocations that are once again quite similar to the rule-of-thumb allocations in accumulation portfolio construction.

Each element of Table 7.2 represents a prospective allocation to lifestyle protection (flooring) for an individual whose age is given by the row, with an expectation of lifestyle needs rising at the rate of inflation given by the columns. For simplicity, the table assumes that retirement commences at 65. The flooring funds would pay until age 90, after which longevity protection would be needed. (Longevity allocation is discussed in the next section.)

In practice, one would be able to directly observe the prices of instruments useful for flooring. For the time being, our purposes are better served by focusing on the centering point allocations rather than focusing on the pinpoint precise allocations implied by today's prices.

The general rule for finding flooring allocations by age, length of window, and expected inflation can be found by valuing an annuity that begins in M periods, and lasts for N periods. Assuming a constant with a payout ratio of $(L/W)\%$, constant rates r, and constant expected inflation i^e, the allocation to flooring can be found by using the following formula:

$$A\% = \left(\frac{L}{W} \right)\left(\frac{1+r}{r-i^e} \right)\left[1 - \left(\frac{1+i^e}{1+r} \right)^N \right]\left(\frac{1+i^e}{1+r} \right)^{-M}$$

where $A\%$ is the flooring allocation, L = lifestyle expenses, W = wealth, r = interest rates, i^e = expected inflation, M = periods from now that the payout is to begin, and N = number of periods that the payments are meant to cover once they begin.

One useful adjunct of the previous formula is that it can be used to help provide a lifestyle feasibility test. If we write the formula in shorthand as $A\% = (L/W)K$, with L/W being the client's relative lifestyle and K being the present value factor for our client's base lifestyle. K encompasses everything to the right of L/W in the previous formula and can be calculated either by formula or by direct observation of market values. Whenever wealth is insufficient for an allocation, $W < KL/A$ and the lifestyle is infeasible. If the entire portfolio is to be used for a floor then the maximum flooring constraint is $W = KL$. When conducting this exercise, it is important to remember that K is a function of the variables $\{M, N, r, i^e\}$.

LONGEVITY ALLOCATIONS

With flooring in place, we now turn to the problem of longevity. Even if you plan for client funds to last until age 90 or 95, it may come as a pleasant surprise to your client to still be alive and healthy at that age; it is a happy circumstance, but one that will require continuation of income. To prepare for longevity, there are three options. From the most expensive to the least, these options include locking in a floor, hedging for lengthening lifespan, and buying longevity insurance. First, one can create fixed capital markets flooring out past the longest reasonably feasible life span. Second, one may choose to delta hedge for longevity by trading small increments of future lifestyle or future aspirations to protect a lengthening view. The third option is to buy longevity insurance, which enables a client to take advantage of mortality credits that increase the longer the client can defer the starting pay date.

Placing a small amount of assets into pure longevity insurance can provide a contingent claim where the cost is low due to the low probability of surviving until able to collect on the claim. Purchased outside of retirement accounts, both pure longevity insurance and deferred annuities are assets that protect against the risk of longevity. In accumulation, we hold precautionary balances against the risk of near-term disruptions in income; in retirement income longevity, risk is a far-term diminution in income. The precautionary motive for holding cash in a retirement income portfolio differs only to the extent that once retirement commences, unemployment is not a temporary phenomenon but the reason for the floor.

At birth, life expectancy is just under 80 years for a female. However, life expectancy increases the longer one survives. The median life expectancy for someone still alive at age 65 is around 85 years. This means that half of all people alive at 65 will still be alive at 85. Unless there is private information about family medical histories or known chronic health problems, longevity is a possibility that should not be quickly dismissed.

The question for the individual is whether flooring past a fixed window is important. If once past the window where flooring is laid down, there is a desire to plan for the option of a continuation of lifestyle. In other words, is there a desire to protect a move toward higher-end assisted living if frail, and a desire to continue a normal lifestyle if not impaired?

Before turning directly to longevity insurance, we note health-related contingencies about which individuals should become more aware. This book isn't the place to do justice to the topic of long-term health care insurance for the elderly. However, nursing home insurance is more beneficial to those with above-average wealth and above-average lifestyle desires. Furthermore, the benefit may be higher for those who are healthy near retirement and thus have longer expected life spans and may face a slow but long diminishment in ability to remain independent.

Longevity insurance can be a valuable precautionary component for a portfolio structured to last through retirement. The concept of longevity insurance was discussed in Chapter 4. Our task here is to discuss how to estimate the client's baseline coverage needs based on relative lifestyle and age when needed.

With the exception of a frightening uptick in the late teenage/early driving years deaths, mortality rates do not rise dramatically until after middle age. This means that even with the possibility of deferring annuity income until age 65, there's not much value in trying to monetize mortality until past middle age. The longer that self-funding of lifestyle is possible, the lower the amount that one needs to put at risk buying longevity insurance. For people over 65, a simple rule of thumb[5] for estimating remaining lifespan is (100 − age)/2. For example, if find yourself alive at age 90, then you can roughly expect to live about another five years. This provides a way to gauge whether a deferred annuity or pure longevity insurance is a better fit. A portfolio only structured to last until age 85 is a better candidate for a deferred annuity, whereas a portfolio structured to last beyond age 90 is a better candidate for single-payment longevity insurance.

Each element in Table 7.3 represents a prospective allocation to longevity protection for an individual whose age is given by the row, with an expectation of lifestyle needs rising at the rate of inflation given by the column. For simplicity, the table assumes that retirement commences at 65. The longevity protection would commence at age 85 and pay as an annuity for the remaining lifetime.

In Table 7.3, we approximate the cost of building lifestyle-maintaining longevity insurance with columns representing both nominal and inflation-adjusted values. The table's values correspond to constructing a sequence

TABLE 7.3 Longevity Insurance for Continuing a 5 Percent Draw Rate as an Annuity Beginning at Age 85

Age	Anticipated Inflation		
	0%	2%	3%
30	1%	3%	6%
35	1%	4%	7%
40	2%	4%	7%
45	2%	5%	8%
50	3%	6%	9%
55	3%	7%	10%
60	4%	8%	11%
65	5%	9%	12%
70[a]	7%	11%	13%
75[a]	9%	12%	14%

[a]With 3 percent inflation, the allocations for flooring until age 85 plus longevity insurance exceed 100 percent. Waiting until after age 65 to put in flooring and longevity insurance in an inflationary environment may be infeasible. Full annuitization may be required and not just a choice.

of pure longevity payments commensurate with the earlier lifestyle beginning at age 85 and lasting until age 101. As before, the yield curve is assumed to be a flat 5 percent. Not surprisingly at age 30, the 55 years until first payout and the low probability of surviving until being able to collect makes for a low allocation to longevity insurance. For someone 60 years old, who assumes long-run inflation at 2 percent, longevity insurance requires only an 8 percent portfolio allocation.

Any individual whose combined allocation to flooring and longevity insurance approaches or exceeds 100 percent is more properly a candidate for annuitization. We see in the example above that (using Tables 7.1 and 7.3) for the lifestyle we presume, building the flooring only to age 85 consumes such a large fraction of the portfolio that there is little left for longevity insurance and virtually no discretionary wealth. In such a case, it would be wise to weigh a full monetization of mortality against a reduction in lifestyle. Having the ability to build flooring out to age 90 widens our options substantially.

TABLE 7.4   Longevity Insurance for Continuing a 4 Percent Draw Rate as an Annuity Beginning at Age 90

Age	Anticipated Inflation		
	0%	2%	3%
30	0%	1%	3%
35	0%	2%	3%
40	1%	2%	3%
45	1%	2%	3%
50	1%	2%	4%
55	1%	3%	4%
60	2%	3%	4%
65	2%	4%	5%
70	3%	4%	5%
75	3%	5%	6%

Table 7.4 illustrates allocations for an individual capable of laying flooring out until age 90. For preretirement allocations, laying flooring per year at 4 percent of wealth to age 90 helps to keep longevity insurance a much lower allocation than in our previous case. Obviously, a simpler lifestyle can be maintained for a much longer period of time without causing stress to a portfolio. By laying flooring down for a longer period, longevity insurance naturally becomes less important and less of a drain on resources.

Each element in Table 7.4 represents a prospective allocation to longevity protection for an individual whose age is given by the row, with an expectation of lifestyle needs rising at the rate of inflation given by the columns. For simplicity, the table assumes that retirement commences at 65. The longevity protection would commence at age 90 and pay as an annuity for the remaining lifetime.

PRECAUTIONARY ALLOCATIONS

During retirement, unanticipated expenses differ in nature from preretirement contingencies but are no less probable. Preretirement cash balances are often held as self-insurance against job loss or other unanticipated expenses. Postretirement job loss isn't a problem; it's the reason for laying down the floor. Spur of the moment expenses may be more or less likely depending on the individual. However, unanticipated medical expenses, whether out-of-pocket or just a bridge until reimbursed, are a greater risk in retirement.

If capital markets flooring is locked in and longevity insurance has been secure, then there is little motive for holding any significant cash reserve beyond a desire to control timing the disposition of, or better tax-manage, risky assets held in the discretionary wealth segment of the portfolio. One of the benefits of capital-markets products is that they are liquid. If a spouse dies, or if there is an adverse change in life expectancy, then capital markets products, including flooring, can be easily reconfigured for the new circumstances; reconfiguration of capital markets products is always possible in whole or in part.

However, if the flooring is constructed of annuities, then deviations from the contractual withdrawal/payment rate of the annuity can have significant adverse consequences. The possibility of surrendering and reformulating an annuity is contract-specific. Often annuities have surrender charges that make it costly to adjust for contingencies.[6] Even annuities with flexible withdrawal riders may be subject to guardrails. A complete reset of the annuity is triggered by withdrawing beyond a yearly limit, which is part of the contract for some plans. This is not meant as an argument against annuities. It is meant as recognition that the need for precautionary balances is greater when flooring is insurance based.

While it is difficult to derive specific allocations for a precautionary motive during retirement, the previous discussion should indicate that the less flexible the portfolio construction is for dealing with contingencies, the greater the need for precautionary balances. Retaining cash and its inherent flexibility is more important for those who annuitize. Even for someone without comprehensive health or nursing-home insurance, having a portfolio of capital markets assets may provide sufficient flexibility for most contingencies. Prior to retirement, precautionary allocations are best left for their traditional purposes. For our summary of allocations, I use 10 percent cash as a placeholder for those who are in preretirement. Once in retirement, I use 10 percent for those who annuitize but only 5 percent for those who are retired but have fully fungible assets.

DISCRETIONARY EQUITY ALLOCATIONS: ASSETS WITH RISK

Discretionary wealth is not an end in itself, but a means to an end. It serves two primary motives:

1. As a subportfolio, it is a means to aspire to a more affluent lifestyle.
2. As a source of funds, it is a means to consume in excess of lifestyle minimums.

Our focus here is on using the subportfolio of discretionary equity as a means to raise standard of living. By doing so, we are consciously understating the important motive of having discretionary equity: so that it may be spent.

As we saw in Chapter 2, the planned drawdown will only be linear for individuals with risk aversion that stays relatively constant as across changes in wealth. For those with *decreasing relative risk a version* (*DRRA*), the drawdown will start slowly before accelerating dramatically near the end of life. Most people fit into the DRRA category. Portfolio planning should take into account the likely consumption needs of individuals based on their "type" and not merely their current consumption.

Most often in accumulation portfolios, by virtue of their higher expected return, risky assets form the backbone of the portfolio. For retirement income portfolios, the emphasis turns to creating an asymmetric payoff, with lifestyle security, while retaining the opportunity for upside. Before going too far, it is important to note that the risky portfolio here does not just refer to the equity allocation as in an accumulation portfolio. Risky assets in this context could include any asset, even government bonds not held to maturity, where there is the possibility of market fluctuation; in this context all bond funds are risky. By segregating the flooring portfolio, the constraints that we place on the discretionary equity portfolio are to ensure that the downside for discretionary equity is limited to 100 percent so that losses cannot eat into the client's lifestyle floor.

The allocation of the portfolio to risky assets is at first blush simply dependent upon what's left over after we create security of lifestyle flooring for which we have planned. However, it is a little more nuanced than the simple view suggests. We can break this down into two areas of impact that come out of this. First is the swapping out of generic fixed income for targeted flooring. Second is the nature of a call payoff having an impact on incentives and behavior toward risk.

It is reasonable on first pass to treat the retirement income portfolio problem as an analog to accumulation. In this interpretation, flooring is analogous to the fixed-income portion of an accumulation portfolio; while the security choices may differ, the essential construction remains unaltered. As we have seen already, for brokers, advisers, and planners, the first task of moving clients from an accumulation posture to creating a lifestyle defense is straightforward to customize and implement. The flooring stage requires relatively little in terms of understanding a particular individual's risk tolerances and how those risk tolerances change. Completing the task of providing lifestyle protection is important but it is probably not the end of the ultimate changes.

The second stage involves the change in risk-tolerance brought about by the creation of a "call-option" payoff. It is well known that when downside is removed, volatility ceases to be a threat and becomes an ally. Many know, all too well, those traders who essentially held a call option granted by their employers have occasionally destroyed their employers[7] by taking risks offering upside but limited downside.

The impact of creating an option-like payoff may not manifest itself immediately, but the effects should not be surprising. The total effect will also depend upon individual preferences. Those who are most risk averse will be impacted relatively the most but practically the least. However, even someone acting in a fiduciary capacity may find it reasonable to tilt the risky part of the portfolio toward corporate debt from government debt, toward midcap stocks from large-cap stocks, or from midcap to small-cap.[8] A question that we address in Part Three is how to rebalance the portfolio as the original allocation drifts due to market moves.

SUMMARY OF ALLOCATIONS

Before moving to the risk management part of the book, we pause to summarize the thinking behind allocations of portfolios for retirement income. We want to try to crystallize the impacts that lifestyle, age, anticipated inflation, and flooring horizon will have on allocations. We do this by combining the example allocations provided in the previous paragraphs and showing the examples as complete portfolio constructions. Our allocations are an example and not set in stone; they illuminate the factors above but they also help to illustrate how the ratio of lifestyle/wealth can have an impact on the decision to monetize mortality fully with an annuity, partially with a hybrid structure, or not at all.

Once again we use the capital market line to provide a graphical representation, shown in Figure 7.1, of how the allocations to flooring products and discretionary wealth differ by age. Remember, the allocation differences show the effects of the lessening of time until retirement, driving up the cost of flooring for a given lifestyle/wealth consumption ratio. In this figure, we see how the allocations of the portfolio change as the individual ages. For anyone less than 30, there is hardly a lifestyle to floor. However, as the individual settles into middle age the lifestyle becomes more habitual and a floor is created. The present value of a given lifestyle, even a simple

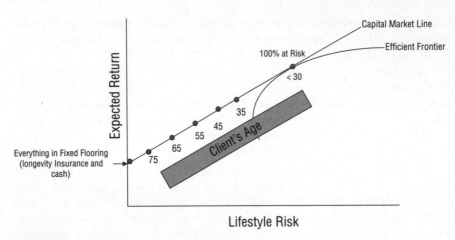

FIGURE 7.1 CML Allocations by Age

lifestyle, will increase thereafter, taking up a greater percentage of the allocation as the individual ages.

The results are all displayed in Table 7.5. The entries shown in italics depict those portfolios where the wealth is insufficient for maintaining lifestyle without a fuller monetization of mortality; that is, lifestyle needs take the lion's share of the funds leaving less than 10 percent of the portfolio in discretionary wealth. There are those who choose to insure, and those who need to insure, these are the latter. We use as our measure of sufficiency whether the discretionary equity (the At Risk column) is greater than 10 percent. If there is less than 10 percent of the portfolio available to put at risk, then there is little upside to be expected without taking outsized risks. For entries where the at-risk allocation is negative, resources are insufficient to maintain lifestyle without monetizing mortality.

This is a good place to think back to Chapter 1 and contrast these portfolios with trying to use a drawdown approach on an accumulation portfolio. Most of the retirement income portfolios that we've discussed look and feel quite similar to traditional accumulation portfolios. The differences are that all along the accumulation and decumulation path these retirement income portfolios allow for smoother consumption plans and always perform. Regardless of the degree of risk aversion, at equal cost, all risk-averse clients will prefer secure consumption paths.

There are six tables nested within Table 7.5. The rows of each table sum to 100 percent. Each column provides a prospective allocation to four areas: flooring, longevity protection, cash, and risky assets. Any row where the lifestyle needs leave less than 10 percent for risky assets, should consider

TABLE 7.5 Tables of Portfolio Allocations for Different Lifestyles, Ages, and Anticipations of Inflation (percentages)

Allocations for Flooring to 85 Nominal Values, 0% Anticipated Inflation					Allocations for Flooring to 90 Nominal Values, 0% Anticipated Inflation				
Age	Flooring	Longevity	Cash	At Risk	Age	Flooring	Longevity	Cash	At Risk
30	12%	1%	10%	77%	30	11%	0%	10%	79%
35	15%	1%	10%	74%	35	14%	0%	10%	76%
40	19%	2%	10%	69%	40	17%	1%	10%	72%
45	25%	2%	10%	63%	45	22%	1%	10%	67%
50	31%	3%	10%	56%	50	28%	1%	10%	61%
55	40%	3%	10%	47%	55	36%	1%	10%	53%
60	51%	4%	10%	35%	60	46%	2%	10%	42%
65	65%	5%	5%	25%	65	59%	2%	5%	34%
70	73%	7%	5%	15%	70	65%	3%	5%	27%
75	81%	9%	10%	0%	75	73%	3%	5%	19%

2% Anticipated Inflation					2% Anticipated Inflation				
Age	Flooring	Longevity	Cash	At Risk	Age	Flooring	Longevity	Cash	At Risk
30	28%	3%	10%	59%	30	26%	1%	10%	63%
35	32%	4%	10%	54%	35	30%	2%	10%	58%
40	37%	4%	10%	49%	40	35%	2%	10%	53%
45	43%	5%	10%	42%	45	40%	2%	10%	48%
50	50%	6%	10%	34%	50	47%	2%	10%	41%
55	58%	7%	10%	25%	55	54%	3%	10%	33%
60	67%	8%	10%	15%	60	62%	3%	10%	25%
65	77%	9%	10%	4%	65	72%	4%	5%	19%
70	82%	11%	10%	−3%	70	77%	4%	5%	14%
75	88%	12%	10%	−10%	75	82%	5%	10%	3%

3% Anticipated Inflation					3% Anticipated Inflation				
Age	Flooring	Longevity	Cash	At Risk	Age	Flooring	Longevity	Cash	At Risk
30	43%	6%	10%	41%	30	41%	3%	10%	46%
35	47%	7%	10%	36%	35	45%	3%	10%	42%
40	52%	7%	10%	31%	40	50%	3%	10%	37%
45	57%	8%	10%	25%	45	55%	3%	10%	32%
50	63%	9%	10%	18%	50	60%	4%	10%	26%
55	69%	10%	10%	11%	55	66%	4%	10%	20%
60	76%	11%	10%	3%	60	73%	4%	10%	13%
65	84%	12%	10%	−6%	65	80%	5%	10%	5%
70	88%	13%	10%	−11%	70	84%	5%	10%	1%
75	92%	14%	10%	−16%	75	88%	6%	10%	−4%

an annuity for all or part of the flooring needs. When the percentage allocated for upside (At Risk) is negative, creating a retirement portfolio using only capital markets products is infeasible. For simplicity, the table assumes that retirement commences at 65.

The importance of the allocations in Table 7.5 go far beyond the numbers contained within and may get to the heart of transforming business models. Suppose a 45-year-old client with a $1 million portfolio comes to you. In the current accumulation framework, you'd probably gravitate toward a portfolio with something near the 60/30/10 standard (equity/bond/cash). With such a portfolio, the client could expect to have $4 million at 65. But you really have no idea where the portfolio will end up and there is a significant possibility that the client could get whipsawed at any point. On the other hand, by carefully putting down flooring as part of the portfolio construction you are able to offer the same expected outcome of $4 million at age 65, but you are now also able to say that "I've built in plenty of upside potential for you and I've also put in a failsafe so that in the worst-case retirement you still will be able to count on $40,000 per year for life."

Table 7.5 helps guide what to sell, to whom, and when. Stepping back away from them for a moment, you will notice that within each table we have different allocations for different individuals at different ages. Age provides the "when" dimension. We also have different tables for different lengths of flooring, with flooring for 20 years and 25 years illustrated in the table. More broadly, these different-length-of-flooring windows can be seen as providing schedules of different flooring for different lifestyles. Equivalent allocation tables are shown for differing views about expected inflation. Different flooring for different lifestyles and inflation views tells us the "to whom" part of the problem.

The "what" is then simple—the tables provide the cost of a particular level of flooring at any point in the client's life. Instead of offering a 45-year-old client a long-term bond fund, flooring can be as simple as having bonds that begin to mature in 20 years. Depending on your business model and your client's lifestyle, the flooring options you offer may be individual insurance products or individual capital markets products or bundled units. The at-risk components may be anything from a simple index exchange-traded fund (ETF) to a balanced portfolio construct to a full-blown unified managed subaccount.

The allure of the flooring providing an explicit notional that can be grasped by any client is not to be overlooked. The client is able to see the floor, know what the current floor looks like, and effect creation of a higher floor by higher rates of saving. People tend to be task oriented and prefer tasks that create immediate positive feedback. Every dollar that is added to a retirement income portfolio is able to show a higher floor. In an accumulation portfolio, a deposit of additional funds brings more hope and more fear. With the minor tweak that turns a portfolio into a retirement income portfolio, there is the same additional hope, but any additional fear is countered by locking in a higher floor. At the risk of sounding like a campaigning politician, what was an outcome of Opportunity + Fear is transformed into an outcome of Opportunity + Progress.

SUMMARY

This is one of the keystone chapters of the book. First, we break the portfolio down into four components: lifestyle flooring, longevity, precautionary, and discretionary. By using the simple construct of finding the present values of future estimated cash flows, we can create usable allocations for building retirement income portfolios that have a solid floor, protect against longevity, take precaution against the uninsurable, and provide upside opportunities. The two key parameters for driving the allocations are years until retirement and desired lifestyle. Other parameters that are influential are the estimates of inflation, potential for longevity, and willingness to take precaution with a portion of the funds.

Managing Portfolios for Retirement Income

Rebalancing Retirement Income Portfolios

Objectives

The importance of rebalancing rules and how they differ for the retirement income problem

Ratcheting floors and habit formation

I n traditional accumulation portfolios, rebalancing is a two-sided affair centering on the target portfolio allocation. This means that as equity values rise relative to bonds the portfolio rebalances toward bonds, and as bonds rise relative to equity the portfolio rebalances toward equity. Fundamentally, the idea of moving assets toward the weak performer reflects an optimistic belief in some form of reversion to past performance. In traditional accumulation, this type of rebalancing requires faith that the deviation is due to a cyclical rather than structural phenomenon. Time to reversion doesn't matter as the horizon is effectively infinite.

In retirement, the horizon is not infinite, meaning that even if the optimism is warranted and reversion occurs, it may not happen quickly enough to help. An old saying among risk managers, and once again traceable back to Keynes, is that the market can stay irrational a lot longer than you can stay solvent. In 1981, when that latest bull market began, the S&P 500 was at nearly the same level as it was in 1964. Rebalancing toward equity may have worked fine for someone retiring in 1981, but it would have been a disaster for someone retiring in 1973. Retired or not, anyone in Japan rebalancing toward target allocations since 1989 is still waiting for the uplift.[1]

In retirement income, the allocations are selected for specific functional reasons rather than simply by asset class in order to create a theme. Risk management of the portfolio also has a functional dimension—the goal of protecting the lifestyle floor. With a goal of protecting the lifestyle floor rather than simply protecting a target profile, the rebalancing rules need to be adapted. Fortunately, the adaptation is simple for static portfolios. For static portfolios the adapted rule for the flooring function is to permit only one-sided rebalancing: Rebalance to add flooring when feasible, but never rebalance in a way that removes or endangers lifestyle security. In the next chapter, on active risk management, the rule will be given some nuances. But it should be understood now that active risk management requires active vigilance and a readiness for disciplined action.

Let's suppose that we have secured a lifestyle floor, longevity risk has been mitigated, and a stash of cash is readily available. There are two kinds of portfolio balancing to consider. The first is the traditional notion of rebalancing that applies to accumulation portfolios; for retirement income that notion still applies to the discretionary wealth subportfolio. There is nothing new here except that this rebalancing only applies to a part of the portfolio and not the entire portfolio. The second rebalancing is geared toward a functional rebalancing, moving funds from discretionary wealth to flooring, longevity, and/or cash. This functional rebalancing is critical to building a rising floor.

Over the course of this chapter, we start with an overview of portfolio rebalancing in a retirement income context. We move next to the more familiar area of rebalancing the discretionary wealth subportfolio. Then we work through rebalancing the functional components and finally how rebalancing helps to ratchet up the floor.

REBALANCING THE DISCRETIONARY WEALTH SUBPORTFOLIO

Within the discretionary wealth subportfolio, the target allocations can be thought of as fixed points, but it reduces transaction costs to relax the targets and to think of them as windows. It is usually best to think of the windows as having a predetermined size rather than sizing them on the fly. The problem with unspecified windows is that the portfolio may keep drifting away from the target risk or return without the rebalancing ever being triggered until a disaster occurs.

With a presized window, movement outside the window triggers rebalancing. The next issue is whether to realign the portfolio to the precise target allocation or simply whack it back inside the window. Here the answer is a definitive "it depends." However, absent tax consequences and transactions costs, the answer is unambiguous.

With transaction costs, the right rule for rebalancing depends on how the transaction costs behave in proportion to the effort. If the transaction costs are falling in proportion as the amount rebalanced increases, then it is optimal to rebalance to the precise target. For example, if transaction fees are independent of the size of the transaction, then they are a declining proportion. In this circumstance, rebalance to target; by completely reverting to the target allocation, you lower the frequency and long-run cost of rebalancing. On the other hand, if transaction costs rise in proportion to the effort, the major rebalancing is more costly—that is, trying to lower the frequency of rebalancing trades off against the higher cost of rebalancing to the center. For traditional portfolios consisting of listed and liquid securities, transaction costs are typically declining in proportion to the amount of the trade; absent taxes, rebalancing to the center is desirable. For portfolios comprised of alternative assets such as hedge fund shares, private equity, or real assets, good luck.[2] With atypical assets, rebalancing is harder and costlier. In such cases, the best that can usually be done is a reentry inside the target window.

Taxes are another factor that can complicate rebalancing. The generic advice is to recognize losses or at worst offset gains with losses. While that sounds simple, usually rebalancing is toward the area of loss and away from the area of gains. This isn't just a problem related to the wash sale rule,[3] the problem is that the flow from stronger to weaker performing areas means that you are most likely trying to monetize the area where you have gains and pour funds into the area with losses. Usually you have some wiggle room to the extent that not all of the losses are on the side toward which you rebalance. It does mean that a pecking order for disposition during rebalancing needs to be created. If you are rebalancing to target return, then the final amount to rebalance in the presence of taxes requires comparing the after-tax-expected return from rebalancing to the expected return from not rebalancing. If you are rebalancing to target risk, in a mean-variance framework, comparing pre- and post-rebalancing dollar volatility is required.[4]

REBALANCING THE FUNCTIONAL COMPONENTS

In robust market environments, the problems are the related issues of when to take some chips off of the table and where to put them. This is a nice problem to have, so let's cover this case last—that way, we can end this section on a positive note. Most retirement income portfolios, particularly for annuitants, are built to be more or less static constructs. The goal is to lay down flooring without touching it until the scheduled cash-flow date. For anyone unable to actively manage the risks, or unwilling to incur the transaction costs of active management, the only safe course to take is through one-sided rebalancing.

The reason that flooring is put in place is to ensure lifestyle. With one-sided rebalancing, if the discretionary wealth subportfolio contracts and you're thinking of rebalancing from flooring to discretionary wealth—don't. With one-sided rebalancing, if the discretionary wealth portfolio contracts and you're thinking of rebalancing from longevity protection to discretionary wealth—don't. With one-sided rebalancing, if the discretionary wealth portfolio contracts and you're thinking of rebalancing from cash to discretionary wealth—it's up to you and your client. The motives and needs for holding cash vary over time so it is feasible to rebalance between cash and the at-risk assets comprising discretionary wealth. However, the point of securing the floor is for the client to avoid reduced circumstances if asset prices fall.

Within functional components, there may be legitimate tactical reasons to switch one type of flooring for another, such as reduction of credit risk. Certainly the upside portfolio of discretionary assets may be more actively managed for expected performance. Chapter 9 delves into active management of strategic allocations, but tactical allocations within the components are usually the province of traditional investment analysis and beyond the scope of this book.

In a static portfolio construction, never rebalance away from the floor or away from longevity protection unless facing a shorter horizon. Your client only gets one portfolio to live off of and you get one chance to make the portfolio last. Chasing returns with what ought to happen may be acceptable in accumulation, but in decumulation it puts the entire remaining path of consumption at unnecessary risk. Without active risk management, one can raise the expected return of the portfolio by taking more risk in the discretionary wealth portion of the account rather than by placing the consumption floor at risk.

Consumption of discretionary wealth should be expected. With flooring and longevity protection firmly in place, the funds in the discretionary wealth subportfolio that are at risk are a combination of discretionary and precautionary. There will always be a legitimate desire to treat discretionary wealth as a piggybank for travel or discretionary expenditures. Even with some drawdown, in robust markets the at-risk assets may grow beyond their original allocation window. With lifestyle security in place, it may seem that there is no compelling need to rebalance. There is. In the next section of this chapter, we discuss reasons for setting an allocation window for discretionary wealth. For now, we'll take it at face value and consider rebalancing from discretionary wealth to flooring.

If taxes are a consideration, then rebalancing by first selling assets where there are losses is always preferred. However, tax strategies are not always feasible. Occasionally, if rebalancing away from discretionary

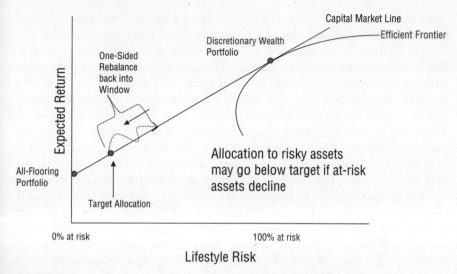

FIGURE 8.1 Target Allocation with Periodic One-Sided Rebalance (adding to flooring)

wealth toward flooring is anticipated early in the portfolio construction process, there are some feasible financial products that can be created to ease the transition. Tax-advantaged financial products could easily be engineered for rebalancing discretionary wealth type assets[5] that would qualify for capital-gains treatment. Creative monetization can also be easily accomplished in structured note form. The product segment financial services industry has yet to sense the profit potential of meeting the retirement needs of the mass affluent.[6]

RAISING THE FLOOR

In general, rebalancing from discretionary wealth to the floor involves raising the whole floor. Many individuals will want to build the floor through time. Still others, comfortable with current lifestyle, will want to upgrade their lifestyles if there is a substantial change in wealth. In the first case, the floor rises slowly and, in the second, the floor undergoes periodic jumps. The motives are different and the methods for accommodation also differ. Figure 8.1 illustrates the approach within the context of the capital market line. As shown with one-sided rebalancing, we allow our discretionary wealth allocation to drift upward under favorable market conditions until the allocation grows beyond the limits of the window and triggers a rebalance. In this illustration, we never rebalance away from flooring.

In Chapter 7, we saw pro forma allocations for individuals by age. From the same tables, we can see how the allocations change through time. Most of the change in allocation is not from raising the notional value of the floor; but it is driven by amortization of the discount in the zero-coupon bonds that we used to make up the lifestyle floor. It's not that building the floor doesn't appeal to the young or that retirement is not yet a tangible concept for them. For someone far from retirement, flooring is cheap. It captures only a small part of a portfolio's allocation. For the young, saving may be a problem, but the lack of allocation to flooring is not a problem. For the earliest starting group, it may be sufficient and desirable to simply divert the portfolio's own natural yield to build flooring. As the individual ages it is easier to dedicate a higher percentage of contributions to flooring. However, keeping the notion of yield flowing from the at-risk assets into flooring, especially preretirement, keeps the floor rising, putting a natural rebalancing mechanism in place. Of course, flooring can be discussed both in terms of yield to maturity and notional. Nonprofessionals tend to think in terms of notional amounts rather than yields, and with flooring for retirement income it is doubly useful.

Understanding the client is crucial to understanding the desirability of a wider or narrower rebalancing window. Almost all of us have some degree of habit formation. As our wealth increases our lifestyles increase. For some it is a smooth transitional process and for others it is an equilibrium punctuated by jumps. For those with smooth habit formation, the rebalancing window will be narrower and the desire to take money off the table will be more constant.

In contrast to the evolving floor described here, many people will have no desire to capture small changes in wealth by making small changes in flooring. For the most part, these people are subject to sticky habit formation: They get used to a lifestyle and do not change unless there is a step-change in lifestyle. For these people, the rebalancing window on the discretionary wealth portfolio will be quite wide. To them, small rebalancing changes will have little value.[7] It is not necessarily the case that they will have riskier assets, but they will be comfortable having assets at-risk beyond where others would want to take some money off of the table.

SUMMARY

The essential feature of rebalancing for retirement income is to treat the floor as sacred. One can rebalance to add flooring, but one of the main tenets of retirement income is that the floor is not placed at risk. The net effect of the importance of the floor is to imply that rebalancing rules become one sided. One-sided rebalancing rules stand in contrast to the two-sided rebalancing rules of accumulation portfolios that tilt funds toward the underperforming components of the portfolio. Two-sided rebalancing can cause a cascade of declines to persist into making withdrawals. Here the effects become catastrophic.

CHAPTER 9

Active Risk Management for Retirement Income Portfolios

Objectives

Actively managing the risk of retirement income portfolios

How to manage for both safety and growth

Active management conjures many images and is sometimes used to describe either strategic or tactical portfolio adjustments. This chapter is concerned with the implications of actively managing a portfolio with the twin goals of maximizing the opportunities for portfolio upside while ensuring that retirement lifestyle can be maintained.

It is one thing to choose to take risks, it is something else to ignore them. Risk management is not about avoiding all risk, it is about choosing the risks that one is comfortable taking; that and having a backup plan. The questions to be asked are "If I'm right, then what?" and "If I'm wrong, then what?" Many portfolios look to be shining brightly and only after the crash and burn is the original "shine" seen for what it was—a gamble with little forethought for how to get out while the gettin' was good, and no predetermined exit strategy for when markets turned. To paraphrase Thomas Edison, good risk management is 1 percent quantification and 99 percent beating the cocksure over the head with a stick.[1]

Risk management conjures a lot of images. Often risk management is confused with risk measurement. Measurement is important for gauging how similar positions have fared in the past or might fare in the future; however, much of risk management deals with uncertainties of the future that cannot be measured precisely. The system is always evolving, and so too are the probability distributions of asset prices. Just as often risk management is confused with active management. Risk management is quite necessary for active management but also useful for passive management.

For our purposes, we define active management to mean constructing a portfolio with a view to outperformance based on superior selection ability; active risk management is defined to mean predetermining the amount of movement in the portfolio that we are willing to tolerate before adjusting in a predetermined direction. It can mean rules for both limiting losses and protecting gains.

Risk management is quite useful for both active and passive management styles. In passively managed portfolios, occasional rebalancing to within the target allocation windows to prevent style and profile drift is a common risk management technique. Without rebalancing, the risk of a portfolio can drift as the uneven nature of gains and losses upends the portfolio's risk profile.

For actively managed portfolios, risk management is a way to enforce disciplined actions around being either right or wrong about the views expressed by the portfolio. Active management without risk management can lead to disaster—see Lehman Brothers, Bear Stearns, or any of a number of Wall Street firms that deemphasized independent risk management prior to 2008.[2] Risk management techniques can range from simple to the highly complex; fortunately simple usually works pretty well. With the goal of protecting a lifestyle, any portfolio that does not have the needed flooring fully locked in must undertake some form of risk management.

Even though I come from a background of considerable interaction with brokers, advisers, and planners, I generally manage my own financial planning at least in the larger sense of deciding on asset types and goals. However, when it comes to risk management, I want my adviser to act when the triggers that we have discussed and agreed on are reached. The hardest part of risk management is in taking necessary action without hesitation. Often individuals, me included, will suffer from inertia and inaction while a position blows through limit after limit. The truest value of a financial professional for a do-it-yourselfer may not be in stock selection, manager selection, or even asset allocation; the value may lie in the professional doing what needs to be done when it needs to be done. In sympathy with the medical or legal professions, never try to risk-manage yourself or you will have a poor client.

As we start this section, we need to define a few terms that will make for a much simpler exposition:

- *Locked-in flooring.* Any allocation where the appropriate flooring is purchased outright is referred to as locked in. If the allocations schedule of Chapter 7 is followed, then the flooring is locked in.
- *Notional flooring.* The payout amounts for the target level of flooring or lifestyle needs.

- *Flooring cost.* The current cost of locking in the required amount of notional flooring.
- *At-risk flooring.* Having funds available to purchase flooring without actually executing the transactions will be termed at-risk flooring.

For a moment, let's ignore longevity risk and cash needs. Suppose all of our client's assets are either in flooring or in the discretionary wealth portfolio. Just to make the example concrete, let's suppose that financial assets are $100 and our client's flooring allocation is 30 percent. For a static allocation, we'd put $70 at risk and $30 into flooring. However, suppose our client wants to take more risk than the static allocation permits. They may be willing to keep the full $100 at risk in hopes of achieving higher returns. But we're not going to have them rely on hope alone. Our plan is to keep close tabs on the portfolio. If the value of the risky portfolio falls we'll move to lock in the flooring before the portfolio falls below $30. We'd like to keep as much as we can comfortably keep at risk unless we begin to fall toward the amount needed to lock in flooring. If we get close to falling below the amount needed for flooring, we take them out of risky assets.

What I've described above is an example of rudimentary risk management. As I've laid it out, it isn't the cleanest of plans, but it gets the idea across: As long as the portfolio is worth more than the cost to buy flooring, we can take more risk in the client portfolio and seek higher returns. If we adopt this approach, we need to be vigilant and ready to act if the value of the (risky) portfolio falls. The important point is to ensure that action is taken before the portfolio can crash through the present value of the floor.

In Chapter 8, we discussed flooring and included the following lines:

The reason that flooring is put in place is to ensure a lifestyle. With one-sided rebalancing, if the discretionary wealth subportfolio contracts and you're thinking of rebalancing from flooring to discretionary wealth—don't. With one-sided rebalancing, if the discretionary wealth portfolio contracts and you're thinking of rebalancing from longevity protection to discretionary wealth—don't.

We slightly modify the rule in this chapter. That is, if you're actively managing the risk of the portfolio and the portfolio expands, then it may be okay to rebalance from flooring to risky assets to achieve higher expected returns. The salient differences are that there is some slack or cushion above the amount needed for flooring and that must be ready to move back to protect lifestyle if things don't go the way you'd like. The point is to try to create slack and use the slack advantageously, but be ready to take in the slack if necessary.

One mischaracterization of active risk management is that its methods generally boil down to "buy in a rising market and sell into a falling market." If the goal is to protect a lifestyle floor, then it is very true that exposure to risk will be reduced as the portfolio falls toward the floor. As noted before: your client only gets one portfolio to live off of and one chance to make the portfolio last. On the upside, when the portfolio is growing rapidly, it may be fun to watch, but it is more useful to have a plan in place to hold on to the gains. Looking backward on the U.S. experience, buy and hold may have historically been the best long-run strategy and, after the fact, it may work out as the best strategy, on average, in the future. But we won't know what would have worked best until we get there. As has been said before, although in retirement each portfolio, not just the average portfolio, needs to be protected; each client only gets one shot at it.

With most of the long introduction for this chapter behind us, I'll highlight what we will cover. First we use a very simple example to go through some of the main principles and methods for the risk management of retirement portfolios. We tie back the principles of risk management to the familiar view from the capital markets line. We discuss the notion that by limiting losses, risk management may lead to a drag on expected return. However, since close monitoring enables more risk to be taken, the net impact of risk management depends on whether the adviser takes advantage of the increased scrutiny.

We extend our analysis to cover rules-based methods for managing the risk of retirement portfolios. Of particular interest is in creating rules that can be used to increment the floor when feasible. Our focus is therefore not just about putting money on the table but also in taking it off the table. We conclude with a discussion of what can and can't be done. What works well in an institutional setting may not scale down to work in individual portfolios. Finally, we cover some methods to avoid.

STATIC EXAMPLE

As a baseline example, let's first run through the dynamics of falling prices for at-risk assets in a static portfolio. For our example, let's assume that the allocation to flooring for this individual is 40 percent. Suppose that the owner of the portfolio is cautious and wants to lock in the flooring at inception; just set it and forget it.[3] Table 9.1 shows how allocations between flooring and excess change as the at-risk portfolio value changes.

Table 9.1 shows what happens to the functional allocations of a static portfolio as the index value of risky assets rises or falls. We assume that

TABLE 9.1 Dollars at Risk and Portfolio Allocations in a Static Portfolio under Market Stress

	Dollar Values		Allocation Percentages	
Static Case	Flooring	At-Risk	Flooring	At-Risk
Index = 140%	$40.00	$84.00	32%	68%
Index = 130%	$40.00	$78.00	34%	66%
Index = 120%	$40.00	$72.00	36%	64%
Index = 110%	$40.00	$66.00	38%	62%
Initial price index for at-risk assets = 100%	$40.00	$60.00	40%	60%
Index = 90%	$40.00	$54.00	43%	57%
Index = 80%	$40.00	$48.00	45%	55%
Index = 70%	$40.00	$42.00	49%	51%
Index = 60%	$40.00	$36.00	53%	47%
Index = 50%	$40.00	$30.00	57%	43%
Index = 40%	$40.00	$24.00	63%	38%
Index = 30%	$40.00	$18.00	69%	31%
Index = 20%	$40.00	$12.00	77%	23%
Index = 10%	$40.00	$6.00	87%	13%
Index = 0	$40.00	$—	100%	0%

the portfolio starts with a 60 percent allocation in risky assets and a 40 percent allocation to flooring. As the value of the risky assets falls, the allocation to flooring rises, but we do not rebalance away from flooring. As the risky asset values rise from their initial level, the allocation to risky assets increases and the portfolio becomes a candidate for rebalancing.

For each index level, the allocation to flooring stays constant in dollar terms, reflecting that we locked it in initially. The market value of the at-risk assets declines as the index declines. The most important fact to note from this table is that the percentage allocation to flooring is rising as the prices of risky assets fall.

Some could argue that all one needs is a static portfolio (x% Lifestyle protection + (1 − x%) Discretionary wealth), with the discretionary portfolio's risk scaled up to achieve the same expected return as that which would be obtained if the entire portfolio were at risk. The thrust of the argument is that a "beta"-adjusted risky portfolio could achieve the same expected return as having the entire portfolio at risk. There are practical limitations to this approach.

The claim that the risk of the discretionary wealth portion of a static portfolio can just be scaled up can be most easily illustrated by using the notation of the Capital Asset Pricing Model (CAPM): $E[r_p] = r_f + \beta_p(r_f - E[r_m])$, where it can be read as the expected return on portfolio p, $(E[r_p])$ equals the risk-free rate (r_f) plus the beta multiple of the market risk premium $\beta_p(r_f - E[r_m])$. The essence of the claim is that by choosing the right beta of a static portfolio β_s, we can set $E[r_p] = r_f + \beta_p(r - E[r_m]) = x \, r_f + (1 - x)[r_f + \beta_s(r_f - E[r_m])]$

$$\rightarrow \beta_p \left(r_f - E[r_m] \right) = (1 - x)[\beta_s \left(r_f - E[r_m] \right)]$$
$$\rightarrow \beta_s = \beta_p / (1 - x)$$

The previous approach is probably the best way for simple one-time construction of transaction-oriented client portfolios. For transactional relationships with clients, it is extraordinarily difficult for an individual to dispassionately monitor their own actions and risk-manage their own affairs. As a single individual desiring to self-manage, it is advisable to lock in the floor and segregate risk by keeping it in the discretionary wealth portfolio.

For professionals managing money for clients, it is a different story. There are reasons to think that the static approach may not work for all service models or appeal to the entire universe of clients including the following:

- An optimal static portfolio would not be scalable to different individuals at different stages of the lifecycle. Even for similarly risk-tolerant individuals, as the allocation to flooring changes with age, the optimized beta of the discretionary wealth portfolio changes.
- For many people comfortable with their current portfolios, simply "having an out" if markets fall will be preferable to actually getting out when it is unnecessary.
- An optimal static portfolio would not maintain a static beta as an individual's allocation to lifestyle protection increases. The beta would still need to be managed.
- Since the static beta would always exceed the risk-managed beta, long-only constraints may negate many possible static solutions on suitability grounds. It may be difficult to keep shopping around to find practical portfolios.
- Real portfolios with different betas may have entirely different risk profiles, not conforming to the simplistic notion of riskier assets having merely wider distributions than less risky assets.

- Depending on market conditions and your relationship with your client, the curb appeal of "here's how we're going to protect your portfolio" may be greater than "here is how we're going to alter your portfolio."

THE VIEW FROM THE CAPITAL MARKETS LINE

Using the familiar CML representation, we can show how the principle of risk management can be applied to retirement income portfolios. Figure 9.1 shows two examples of risk tolerance. For the low-tolerance portfolio, we have relatively tight limits that are somewhat skewed toward locked-in flooring. Tight limits do not necessarily mean more activity, but they do indicate a lower tolerance for pain. The high-tolerance portfolio has a much wider range and will require greater management activity when markets decline. In Figure 9.1, we also show how the allocation is allowed a much wider range in the presence of active risk management. In this case, our goal is to maintain the capacity and wherewithal to lock in flooring without actually executing the purchase of flooring unless the market turns unfavorably. The allowable range that is set depends on the aggressiveness of the portfolio and the client's tolerance for accepting risk.

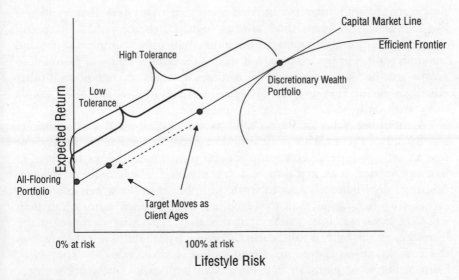

FIGURE 9.1 Active Risk Management for Security and Growth

RISK MANAGEMENT AND EXPECTED RETURNS

The object of risk management is not to generate higher returns for every path. A policy of buying lottery tickets and getting lucky with 10 wins in a row may work out to be the most profitable investment strategy—at least, after the fact. The point of risk management is to make high quality decisions before the fact, then protect outcomes. For most people, that would rule out the idea of rolling lottery winnings entirely into more lottery tickets. Even absent risk management, one can expect that increasing the risk of a portfolio will lead to higher average returns. However, absent risk management the volatility is two sided: You may win, you may lose. Our goal is to increase expected returns by taking more risk, but then give up a little bit of the potential gains to make sure that we are not endangered by the risk. It will only be known after the fact, but in the best paths, the drag on performance will be highest, and on the worst paths the positive value of risk management will be the greatest. The net average effect should roughly be given by the higher expected return from taking more risk, less the incremental cost of risk management activity.[4]

SIMPLE RULES: FOR PASSIVE AND ACTIVE RISK MANAGEMENT

Risk management is often surrounded by an aura of mystery. Risk managers like it that way, it keeps their salaries high. Often the practice is pretty straightforward and amounts to no more than using common sense and common tools. For the most part, it means thinking ahead and planning to act if a specified outcome occurs. Sometimes it means revising plans if other outcomes occur. They may be inelegant and suboptimal but often simple rules work quite well.

Mentioning Value at Risk (VaR) around experienced risk managers usually draws a sneer. VaR is a method that mainly focuses on the amount that a portfolio is expected to slop around some percentage of the time. In its simplest form, a normal distribution is used to find where the tails begin. A normal distribution is easy to work with, but in real markets the size of events are often larger than expected and they happen more often than would be expected under a normal distribution.[5] These disasters are usually labeled as "tail" or "fat tail" events. Putting a probability on the event in this context misses the point. The question is never what is expected to happen, but what plausible bad things can happen and how are we protected against them.

Passively Risk-Managed Investment Portfolios

For favorable market conditions, the risk management rule is to stay within the target allocation window. For passively risk-managed portfolios, the floor is always locked in, but positioned to allow for raising the floor. If the value of the discretionary wealth portfolio exceeds the upside limit on the window, a rebalancing occurs. The rebalancing is designed to bring the portfolio back inside the target allocation window. Whether this window is narrow or wide is based on personal preference. As discussed in Chapter 8, some individuals will prefer small but frequent increments to flooring, while others will be much more focused on incrementing flooring only when it leads to a step-change in lifestyle. In active trading, upside stops are often used to enforce discipline and take winnings off of the table without getting emotionally attached to a particular position.

Actively Risk-Managed Investment Portfolios

For portfolios that are meant as investment portfolios, there will generally be fixed rules on the downside; always protect the floor. For the upside, the answer depends on whether the portfolio has flooring partially locked in or is entirely at risk. For the portfolio entirely at risk, upside may trigger merely a revision of stops and purchase amounts, leaving the money at risk. For portfolios with flooring partially locked in, the choice will be to rebalance to maintain the partial flooring as a percentage of the overall portfolio, or to leave all of the gain at risk. In the first case, we raise our stops and purchase amounts proportionately. For the second case, we raise the stops proportionately and the flooring purchases by a greater proportion. We will tie most of this together later in this chapter.

Actively Managed Actively Risk-Managed Portfolios

For retail portfolios managed for active trading, there will most often be rules for concentration, upside, downside, and time. For example, if I expect ABC to double in the next two months, I may set stops at 95 and 220; if either outcome occurs, I will sell. I may also set a time limit on the position, after which I will either close out the position or reevaluate from scratch. I may close the position at any intermediate point if information warrants. Furthermore, my concentration limit will prevent betting the farm on a single position. It is okay to trade on what the market is expected to do, but risk management is undertaken based on what the market has the capability of doing.[6]

Passive or Active

The simplest rule for managing the risk of flooring is to have a series of stops set up to trigger action. In actively managed portfolios, stops are typically set up on both the upside and downside. On the downside, stops may mean selling into a falling market, but if the goal is protection of lifestyle, so be it. With a perpetual horizon, there will always be another whack at the cat and the world isn't about to end; riding out a storm may be a feasible tactic. In pure accumulation, the volatility helps to allow for taking advantage of dips in pursuit of the strategic goal of long-run performance. However, in retirement, the strategy is to protect lifestyle and there is only one whack at the cat. Don't confuse attempts at market timing for risk management. For a retirement income portfolio with simple rules, once you're out, you're out until and unless the remaining rump of the risk position claws its way back.

AN INELEGANT BUT SIMPLE PLAN

Suppose that we want to have a higher allocation to risky assets than a static model. Our purpose would be to protect a fraction of gains when feasible and avoid any degradation in lifestyle from losses. To focus on the downside for a moment, we may decide to set up some simple stops for moving gradually toward lifestyle protection if the value of risky assets begins to fall. For our example, we may set ad hoc stops based on 10 percent moves in the initial value of the portfolio. As before, we take the example where actual purchase of flooring would entail a 40 percent initial allocation.

Table 9.2 shows the effect of creating ad hoc downside stops that are designed to ensure lifestyle needs while maintaining a measure of exposure to risky assets in the event of a market recovery.

For this example, we set our downside stops so that lifestyle will be completely protected well before we reach the breaking point where we can't switch into flooring. For purposes of illustration, we set our stops to increment at 10 percent of initial portfolio value. This is a good place to introduce the notion of measuring the portfolio's cushion. The cushion measures the difference between the portfolio's market value and the dollar amount of flooring that is needed to fully protect lifestyle; it tells us how far we are from the floor. We start fully invested in risky assets, but each time that we hit one of our four stops we will buy $10 worth of flooring. Our at-risk portfolio immediately, after hitting a stop, is the value of the at-risk assets when we hit the floor less $10 for the flooring purchase.

TABLE 9.2 Naïve but Effective Risk Management (setting downside stops based on initial $100 portfolio value)

	Cushion	Flooring in Place	At Risk	Next Stop	Value of At-Risk Assets if Stop is Hit	Flooring Allocation
Initial price index for at-risk assets = 100%	$60.00	$0.00	$100.00	$90.00	$90.00	0%
Index = 90%	$50.00	$10.00	$80.00	$80.00	$71.11	13%
Index = 80%	$41.11	$20.00	$61.11	$70.00	$53.47	28%
Index = 70%	$33.47	$30.00	$43.47	$60.00	$37.26	47%
Index = 60%	$27.26	$40.00	$27.26			70%
Index = 50%	$22.72	$40.00	$22.72			64%
Index = 40%	$18.17	$40.00	$18.17			69%
Index = 30%	$13.63	$40.00	$13.63			75%
Index = 20%	$9.09	$40.00	$9.09			81%
Index = 10%	$4.54	$40.00	$4.54			90%
Index = 0		$40.00	$0.00			100%

HIGH-WATER MARK FLOORING

On the upside, we do not immediately allocate to flooring, but we do raise the notional level of the floor. We raise our floor by raising our stops and the amount of flooring that we will purchase at each stop that we hit. To keep it simple, we simply scale our stops and our flooring purchases to maintain the portfolio's floor at 40 percent of the portfolio's maximum value. In principle, high-water marks may be measured continuously or discretely. In practice, high-water marks should only be incorporated at frequencies and step sizes for which the new floor will be appreciated and action can be taken if the market reverses course. Presumably, you will want to maximize the mileage out of a rising floor through communication with the client.

Table 9.3 is a small table meant to illustrate how our stops and flooring purchases will be adjusted if the portfolio rises. Starting from an initial portfolio of $100, we have four stops in place. If the portfolio value rises to $110, we raise our stops and our purchases of flooring proportionately. Similarly, if the portfolio rises to $120, our stops and the notional floor will again be adjusted.

TABLE 9.3 Extending Naïve Stops for Raising the Floor: Rising Portfolio Values and Security for a Higher Lifestyle

Portfolio = $100		Portfolio = $110		Portfolio = $120	
Stops	Flooring	Stops	Flooring	Stops	Flooring
$90	$10	$99	$11	$108	$12
$80	$20	$88	$22	$96	$24
$70	$30	$77	$33	$84	$36
$60	$40	$66	$44	$72	$48

In the example just presented, our rule puts stops every 10 percent. This means that the stops were becoming further apart, percentagewise, as the portfolio value fell.[7] Looking at the measure of the cushion, we can get a better way to set up sensible combinations of limits and actions. This means we want the limits and actions to be as coarse or refined as our business model dictates. For some, this will mean very tight limits with frequent action and for others the limits will be set wider apart for greater portfolio stability.

THE CUSHION

As previously mentioned, the cushion measures the difference between the portfolio's market value and the market cost of the notional amount of flooring that is needed to fully protect lifestyle. Neither the floor nor cushion is a fixed amount: The floor can be thought of as a sequence of zero-coupon bonds either in spirit or in fact. Once the floor is chosen, each day that passes brings the pieces of the floor closer to maturity. This means that the present value of the floor will be tending toward par as time passes. On some days, rates may rise and the PV of the floor fall, but the inexorable trend will be that the PV of the floor will be rising. Depending on how the risky assets perform, the cushion may shrink, stay the same, or rise.

The problem is no harder for a client who is partially annuitized or has longevity insurance. Here we simply redefine the cushion as the difference between the portfolio and the cost of flooring not yet in place. If the client has a lifestyle costing $180,000 per year and has already purchased an annuity to provide $60,000 per year, then the remaining flooring need is $120,000. Similarly, if the client has a longevity policy that pays in 2050, then the fixed-term flooring needs to truncate in 2049.

Suppose for now that stripped bonds exist for all maturity dates and lifetimes are certain. We also know that Smith has a floor of $120,000 per year for 40 years and plans to retire at the beginning of 2015. Matching maturities with the appropriate strips allows setting up a position monitor showing the portfolio value and the cost of flooring.

Do I Have to Use Strips?

No. Strips are a great way to measure the maximum cost of the floor since they are government issued and contain no credit spread enhancement to the yield. As a practical matter, it is difficult to build corporate ladders that contain the same constituents on different days. Strips are observable, liquid, and almost always available. So, even if not used, they make a great benchmark.

What to Do If Not All Strips Are Trading

There are two possible problems; each has a slightly different solution. The first problem is if there is a gap. Suppose that I lay strips out at six-month intervals and can find strips for 8/15/2019 and 8/15/2020, but I can't locate any inventory or find a price for 2/15/2020. By bracketing the 2/15/2020 with higher allocations to the 8/15 strips for 2019 and 2020, I can take advantage of bond convexity and expect to safely trade out of the two August dates and into the desired February strip when available. The second problem is what to do if the maturity needed exceeds the available issuance. In this case, the typical conservative approach would be to "stack and roll" the position with or without adjustment. Currently, I can observe strips trading out to 2038, but for Smith we'd need to find zeroes out to 2055. The most conservative thing to do would be to cover the gap between 2038 and 2055 by stacking strips on the 2038 maturity, $18 \times 120 \times \text{Strip price}_{2038}$. Having a position in a bond that matures in 2038 with a face value that approximates the funds necessary to buy the strips in 2038 may be an attractive alternative to a stack. If one opted for the stack method, the stack would be rolled down each year until all strips are observable and tradable. Instead of stacking N times for an N-year gap, in principle one could refine this slightly by discounting the unobserved dates at the longest observed rate but to the correct maturity; this has a small element of inherent pricing risk.

Depending on data feed availability, we can set up a real-time monitor for Smith's entire retirement and keep close tabs on the cushion. For multiple clients with similar portfolio components, it is a straightforward task to create a single spreadsheet to monitor many portfolios against cushions.

By using the strips as our proxy for the flooring costs, the natural pull to par will be reflected as the flooring costs rise over time. Once we have set up a framework for monitoring portfolios against cushions, we can now move on to risk rules.

RISK RULES—PERIODIC REBALANCING

Suppose that our goal under normal market conditions is to only rebalance between flooring and the risky portfolio on a quarterly basis.[8] If one objective is to trade infrequently, then the risk needs to be kept low enough to avoid missing big moves where the cushion might disappear or go negative. We also want to take into account that the floor is likely to be higher by the next rebalance.

The amount to put at risk depends partly on the maximum fall in the risky portfolio that is possible in a quarter, partly on the cushion, and is between 0 percent and 100 percent. Suppose, for example, that we want to be prepared for a maximum fall of 50 percent. Suppose further that the cushion is 30 percent of total portfolio value.[9] The resulting allocation would allow us to put (Cushion)/(Maximum drop) = 0.30/0.50 = 60% at risk; the other 40 percent would be put into flooring right away. Using $100 as a base, we start with a static allocation of $70 flooring and $30 at risk, but put more at risk per our rule $40 flooring but $60 at risk. If the market falls by anything up to 50 percent then we will have at least 0.50 × $60 = $30 with which to secure our remaining flooring. If, on the other hand, the value of the risky portfolio rises faster than the natural rise in flooring, the end-of-period cushion will have grown. Upon rebalancing at the end of the period, the cushion is recalculated and the next round begins.[10]

Where's the Risk?

There are two risks in this approach. The first is crash risk. Crash risk is the chance that the portfolio can fall through the floor before a rebalancing occurs. That means that it is important to set the maximum loss with an eye on the planned interval between rebalancing. Even if you're willing to rebalance daily, the October 1987, 22 percent one-day crash should point you to think big when it comes to bad things. The other risk is that by goosing up your exposure to risky assets, you will lose your cushion faster if markets tumble. This means that if you set the risk too high, say a 10 percent maximum drop, even a small correction could wipe out your cushion leaving no opportunity for participation in a recovery. I would be comfortable offer-

TABLE 9.4 Keeping the Risk Proportionately Constant

Time	BOP[a] PV of Floor PV(F)	BOP Cushion Max ($P_{t-1}-F$,0)	BOP Risky Assets Min (4C,P_{t-1})	BOP Risk-Free Assets	Risky Return	EOP[b] Risky Assets	EOP Risk-Free Assets	EOP Portfolio (P_t)
1	$78.35	$21.65	$86.59	$13.41	11%	$96.11	$14.08	$110.20
2	$82.27	$27.93	$110.20	$0.00	−10%	$99.18	$0.00	$100.76
3	$86.76	$12.42	$49.66	$49.51	12%	$55.62	$51.99	$107.61
4	$91.10	$16.51	$76.05	$41.56	−20%	$52.84	$43.64	$96.48
5	$95.65	$0.83	$3.30	$95.65	0	$3.30	$100.44	$103.74

[a]BOP = Beginning of period.
[b]EOP = End of period.

ing 50 percent, but not much lower as the potential for a major bear market is too great during the long window of retirement. Clients will like it when their lifestyle floor is raised, but will often be less than enthused about losing market participation even with a higher lifestyle.

Table 9.4 provides an example of protecting a single payment. In this example, we set the maximum drop too low and lose participation. We set the maximum drop at 25 percent. With 1/0.25 = 4, our cushion, the natural exposure to the risky portfolio, will be multiplied by 4. The initial floor is 100 and the discount rate is assumed to be 5 percent per period.

T = 1 Beginning of Period

Our initial $100 floor was $78.35 to floor so that we could construct an initial passive portfolio by placing $78.35 in flooring and $21.65 in risky assets. The $21.65 is our cushion. What we do is take our cushion and with a multiplier m = 1/(Maximum drop), we make our initial equity exposure $86.59, with $13.41 in flooring (in our example m = 4).

T = 1 End of Period; T = 2 Beginning of Period

Equity went up 11 percent, so our end-of-period portfolio is now $14.08 in flooring and $96.11 in risky assets P_1 = 110.20.[3] Our floor has risen to $82.27, and our new cushion is $27.93 (110.20 − 82.27). This time we have more cushion than we need (4 × 27.93 = 111.72). We only have $110.20 and we will not take on leverage, so we put the entire $110.20

into the risky portfolio, but we also make a note of the $0.38 difference between $27.93 and $110.20/4, adding $0.38 to the $T = 3$ PV of the floor, raising it to $86.76 from $86.38. I leave most of the rest of the table to the reader to follow. The only other point to note is that at the end of the fifth period, we have secured $100.44 in flooring because we had raised our floor after the strong showing that occurred in period 1.

We therefore suggest four practical steps to taking prudent risk and ensuring that the portfolio will maintain continued participation in upside even after a significant market drop.

1. When it comes to setting a tolerance on the maximum drop, the bigger the percentage the less chance of crash risk and the lower the chance of being tapped out when a recovery occurs. Peak to trough markets can and do fall by amounts approaching 50 percent. This is a technique to carry clients through many years and not just next week. There is a good chance that there will be another gut-wrenching bear within 20 years. Bears can also come on quickly. Remember the fall of 2007 the SPX hit a new high and talking heads were proclaiming that the credit problems were behind us; they've repeated the same thing in 2008: July, September, November, and so on.

2. Whenever the ratio (Cushion)/(Maximum drop) > Portfolio value, raise the floor and push the ratio back down. Raise the floor until the cushion shrinks to a point where (New cushion)/(Maximum drop) ≤ Portfolio value.

3. Expect the floor to rise. Take the estimated cushion and discount by an amount appropriately timed for the next rebalance. You don't need to be precise; $1/(1.0125)$ will usually work.

4. Plan to keep some powder dry. If contributions are still being made, then it is less of a concern because they can always be used to revive the risky portfolio. But if contributions are no longer being made, then subtract 5 percent from the cushion to act as a last-ditch source of participation if knocked into flooring.

RISK RULES—MORE ACTIVE REBALANCING

Fisher Black was a god of Finance. Among his many accomplishments, he is remembered for Black/Scholes pricing of options, the Black/Derman/Toy model of interest rates, and constant proportional portfolio insurance (CPPI) by practitioners. He is remembered for these and he is remembered by academics for a host of scholarly articles.

The main idea behind CPPI is described in the previous section—that one can protect a minimum portfolio value while taking more risk than a static allocation permits. One difference with our example and CPPI is that the CPPI portfolio allocations move smoothly between flooring and a risky portfolio. In practice, CPPI rebalancing occurs daily. If the volatility of the risky portfolio is constant, probability of a crash through the floor is constant.

CPPI is a very flexible tool. We have already shown how to incorporate the concept of ratcheting the floor upward in the event of success. We can also incorporate different levels of risk taking at different times including a move back to a static allocation if ever desired.

Many financial firms have issued short-term and medium-term notes using the CPPI methodology. Along with offering a CPPI management style, the issued notes typically come with high risk and a protection feature. The notes typically start with a cushion of around 20 and to make it sexy, that is, offering 100 percent initial risky exposure, they have a maximum drop of 20 percent ($m = 1/.20 = 5$). By having such a high value for m over a long period, these notes often lose all of their participation.[11] What is advocated here is not very sexy; it adds the potential for upside but adds little risk to the portfolio. With the risk levels advocated here, the market value of protection, if it were to be offered, would be nil. With a low-risk approach and using common components, for flooring and risk it is possible to build a scalable business, complementary to static retirement and accumulation accounts.

Figure 9.2 illustrates a point about moderation in risk using historical backtest results. The starting value of the portfolio is $100, the term is 20 years. The floor ratchets whenever the cushion exceeds the amount necessary for 100 percent exposure to the at-risk assets. The at-risk portfolio is SPX (total return) and the risk-free asset is implied by Treasuries. Rebalancing occurs quarterly. The lines on the graph correspond to the percentile of paths at or below the line as the risk of the portfolio increases. Furthermore, at $1 \times$ Cushion, the portfolio is a static construct with flooring always locked in and the risky asset allocation made up entirely of discretionary wealth. As the risk is allowed to rise, flooring is placed at risk in an attempt to capture higher returns. In this historical simulation, once the risk exceeds 2, implying an ability to weather a 50 percent decline in the risky portfolio without completely losing participation to at-risk assets, the gains from taking incremental risk are reversed. In short, a high-risk portfolio is not compatible with protecting lifestyle but becomes self defeating. Taking a little risk may enhance expected returns but with a lot of risk, the likelihood is far higher that a market downturn will push the too-aggressive investor into a pure flooring allocation. For someone with aggressiveness consistent with a cushion greater than 2, the best bet would be to

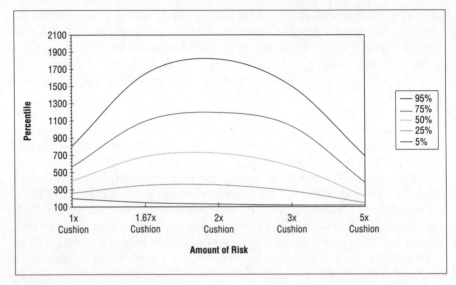

FIGURE 9.2   Managing Risk in Retirement Allocations: Historical Backtest (data from 1948–2007)

lock in the flooring and increase the risk of the at-risk portfolio; never mixing the two.

CPPI AND VOLATILITY

In options parlance, the CPPI methodology implies that the client becomes short volatility. The higher the volatility, the higher the probability that the portfolio will fall to the flooring amount; leaving the investor without the prospect of retaining exposure to upside. Frequently, this is most easily dealt with by considering underlying risky assets with dampened volatility. Using a balanced portfolio as the underlying risky portfolio managed by a CPPI methodology is just such a case. Using a lower volatility, underlying generally trades off expected return for a lower likelihood of hitting the flooring amount. However, if done improperly, the volatility reduction may have no impact on the probability of hitting the floor.

Buy/write portfolios[12] are sometimes used as lower volatility underlyings in CPPI notes and processes. There is a problem with using buy/writes as a lower volatility underlying in CPPI. A buy/write portfolio does have a lower volatility than a portfolio and without the short call overwrite. However, the volatility reduction is all on the upside. Realized downside volatility exposure remains unaffected. In short, the buy/write portfolio trades off upside in exchange for enhanced yield, but has no impact on the likelihood of a CPPI process ending up entirely in flooring assets.

TAXATION AND ACTIVE MANAGEMENT

Often active management is considered to be less tax friendly than static portfolios. This is not always the case. Naturally in tax deferred or tax preferred accounts the issue is moot. But even in fully taxable accounts, the impression of taxes and management is not always true.

Static portfolios that rely on securities such as bonds, notes, and other securities that guarantee a substantial (i.e., > 70%) return of principal are subject to ordinary income treatment.[13] This may even be true for structured notes with large equity components. If a structured note (static strategy) is created that guarantees a minimum value above 70 percent of principal, then the entire note becomes subject to ordinary income even if the note is comprised of roughly 30 percent equity. In other words, the note ends up converting a capital gains asset into an ordinary income asset. Again, most notes with guarantees are subject to ordinary income treatment.

On the other hand, in a portfolio that is actively risk managed, the assets will bifurcate into their component types. This remains true over many active strategies that may protect the portfolio in exactly the same way as certain guaranteed structured notes. There are caveats to this regarding effective monetization or defeasance of risk which can trigger gains so care must be exercised, but the following example should help to illustrate the possibilities.

As previously discussed, there is both the CPPI methodology and CPPI notes. CPPI notes almost always guarantee a return of principal. Although there are possibilities for tax savvier future constructions, the CPPI notes that are issued by many firms are subject to ordinary income treatment. This is true even if the note stays fully invested in capital gains instruments for its entire tenor. In other words, if your client buys a CPPI note that starts out and remains fully invested in equity for the entire term of the note, then the note will still be subject to ordinary income treatment. The double whammy here is that the ordinary income is taxable as it accrues and not just at maturity.

On the bright side, as a methodology rather than a note, CPPI allows for bifurcation of assets. To the extent that the portfolio remains invested in capital gains assets, those assets will remain eligible for capital gains treatment. The assets that are ordinary income assets will of course be subject to ordinary income treatment. To the extent that the portfolio remains invested in capital gains assets, the treatment will remain capital gains. If the risky portfolio declines sufficiently for the portfolio to convert into pure flooring then the flooring assets will be subject to ordinary income. The transition of assets from risky to flooring will trigger a taxable event that may entail recognition of either gains or losses.

Total active management can mean better management of both risk and tax liabilities than passive strategies allow. Notes that actively manage risk may be treated more onerously than the strategies that underlie the notes. For clients in the high-net-worth and ultra-high-net-worth categories, tax and risk strategies will be seen as more important.

LOCKING IN FLOORING: LONG END VERSUS SHORT END

Even if a portfolio is being run with lifestyle risk, perhaps using one of the methods described above, partial flooring may be required. For example, a static flooring allocation may call for a 70 percent allocation to floor, but the portfolio may currently be set at 50 percent floored, 50 percent risky. Leaving aside the issue of rebalancing, there is an open question about how to structure the flooring that is required. One approach would be to fill the floor for the earlier years first, leaving the latter years unprotected. Another approach would be to level the flooring and add or subtract across the board as the cushion changes.

One argument that won't be made here is that it is sufficient to fund the early part of the floor and leave the latter floor to be acquired at a later date. (See Chapter 15 for a fuller debunking of this myth.) Absent risk management of the style described in the previous sections of this chapter, that is an argument of hope over reason. Flooring the first few years of retirement to get over the hump is not a strategy that ensures a lifestyle floor. If the goal is to lay the floor down as the portfolio rolls through the floored window, the effect is equivalent to engaging in a drawdown approach, with no greater likelihood of success. However, using active risk management techniques, if the allocation to risky assets implies that only part of the flooring allocation be acquired, then laying the front of the flooring first may be sensible. The point being that the concept of the cushion applies to the flooring that is not yet locked in. As long as there is cushion available, it doesn't matter (in a financial sense) whether the cushion is spread evenly through the retirement period or back loaded toward the latter period of retirement.

With the techniques described thus far, a volatile market means that the cushion will also be volatile. To some extent the flooring allocation may rise and fall each quarter. In that case, the liquidity of the flooring that is being traded to manage the account becomes important. Liquidity is usually higher and trading costs are usually lower for the nearer term segments of the floor. Some could also argue that the long end of the curve provides more opportunity for taking a view, but the point of this discussion is purely agnostic to expectations.

A QUICK NOTE ON USABILITY, SCALABILITY, AND APPROACHES OTHER THAN LIABILITY MATCHING

All of the approaches that have been discussed fall into the category of managing around an asset/liability match. There are other approaches that could be taken with high probabilities of success that have been ignored. Part of the reason for this is space considerations and complexity. I have omitted some other solid techniques for managing risk to achieve one of my primary goals—to provide solutions that are scalable, to some degree. If managing a single portfolio, then there are many good approaches. But scalability requires that the techniques must apply to a large number of portfolios simultaneously.

With adherence to the self-discipline that requires action without senti-ment, these are safe practices. For a technique to be scalable, it needs to rely on common components, common tools, and a simple template. The recipe has to be simple, robust, and reliable regardless of the cook. The methods described in this chapter will work quite well for some business models, but they may not work as well for purely transaction-driven models. Also, for those who are managing their own portfolios, the emotional sepa-ration and dispassionate discipline that risk management requires will be difficult if not impossible. If someone wants to manage their own portfolio, then encourage them to construct a static portfolio. If someone wants a risk-managed portfolio, then let a neutral party—that is, an adviser— execute their plan.

PLAYING WITH FIRE IN A RETIREMENT INCOME PORTFOLIO

In the structuring/structured products arena prior to the crash of 2008, the focus on creation of enhanced yield was the rage. Except for the methods focusing on tax efficiency, the techniques for yield enhancement were akin to risk enhancement. There are no free arbitrages available in the retail market and enhancing yield is never free. Auction rate securities were but one case where the enhanced yield came about by the client perhaps unwittingly writing a binary put on auction failure. Enhanced yield products need to be scrutinized carefully before they are included in retirement income portfolios. The source of risk that drives the enhanced yield should never be taken lightly.

Many of the techniques for yield enhancement are popular but require extra caution when used in retirement income portfolios. Many of the strategies for yield enhancement leave the client short the market, short implied volatility, and short realized upside volatility. Even the volatility overlays that promote products to neutralize clients' volatility exposure have their place in the market and in portfolios, but they need to be used carefully.

Many of the structured products on the market offering enhanced expected returns such as autocallables, accelerated return structures, and even simple buy/writes are equivalent to a position where the client explicitly writes an in-the-money put—that is, insurance on the market—and in exchange for a fee, the client takes downside risk. If the downside doesn't materialize, which historically has been true more often than not, then the client retains the fee for writing protection. These products often back-test well, implying that, on average, they work. However, the downside risk that the client bears in exchange for enhanced yield can be extreme and binary, as it was for auction rate securities. Often sold as "enhanced cash," these securities offered a few extra basis points of yield over traditional money market products until the auctions began failing and they became completely illiquid or reverted to long-dated (often discount) bonds.

To illustrate the point about the equivalence between many enhanced-yield products and enhanced risk, consider the simplest yield enhancer, the buy/write, illustrated in Figure 9.3. As you can see, the rub is that the buy/write—that is, Long stock + Short out of the money call—is equivalent to having a client sell a fully funded in-the-money put. In other words, your client could probably do better by writing puts directly. It is generally true that selling protection on the market is nominally a moneymaker, but a portfolio based on selling protection is a dangerous thing if it is on autopilot. Another issue is that with the buy/write, the client becomes short implied volatility. If implied volatilities rise, then a client who needs to close out the position may have to pay more to buy back the call than was initially received for writing it, even if the underlying price is lower than when initiated. Other structured products like accelerated return notes are variations on the buy/write theme. In almost all cases, they are sold as enhanced yield but the client is really engaged in writing puts on the market. There is no free lunch.

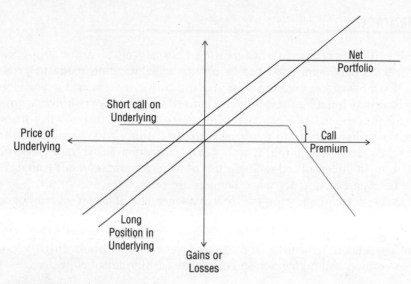

FIGURE 9.3 Buy/Writes

With a buy/write, the client who is long an underlying asset begins selling short-dated calls that are just out of the money. In exchange for the call premium received by the client, the client foregoes all upside participation if the underlying rises above the strike price on the call. In terms of terminal payoff, this usually looks fairly attractive.

As a final thought on active management for portfolios in general and retirement income portfolios in particular, I briefly mention the three-tier liquidity hierarchy that has been used at major firms. With luck, this will help frame the standards for caution in creating retirement income portfolios. The first tier of liquidity is the fostered "organic liquidity" that exists in exchange markets. Exchange markets actively seek to keep buyers and sellers engaged and liquidity is virtually always assured. Your clients may not like the price that they paid or received, but in exchange markets they can always get in or out of a position. The second tier of liquidity is the "hybrid liquidity" of well-functioning markets with multiple market makers. This would include most OTC markets. Liquidity is maintained by having multiple participants trading a relatively commoditized product. The third, and dangerous, kind of liquidity is usually called "inorganic liquidity." It is the liquidity that is maintained at the discretion of one or only a few parties. This third type of liquidity covers auction rate securities, hedge funds with gates, and many alternatives.

SUMMARY

Active risk management allows creating a business model around the notion of seeking maximum exposure to upside while standing ready to protect the floor. Instead of creating static portfolios for retirement income, some advisers may build business models centered on the active risk management of client accounts. Even clients who prefer to make their own portfolio decisions can benefit from someone who can monitor and more importantly act when action is required. Whether in a transaction-based or discretionary account, an underutilized selling point of financial professionals is that they can be counted on to act when triggers are hit.

Several techniques for the risk management of client portfolios are discussed within the chapter. The rules for risk management can vary from naïve simple stops to more fluid techniques for managing risk. The important concepts to remember from the chapter relate to monitoring the portfolio cushion and taking action before the cushion falls below zero.

Making It Happen

CHAPTER 10

The Transition Phase

Objectives

Moving clients from an accumulation portfolio into retirement income portfolios

Keeping clients on the path to their goals

Making it all fool natural

I magine a client who has been with your practice for 20 years. You have always known that they would retire in 2009 and that they would require a retirement solution. Throughout the 1990s, you were able to help them take advantage of market volatility. Their window of opportunity for taking advantage of volatility has closed. Volatility was an ally, but now it is an enemy. Moving them steadily from equity to fixed income wasn't sufficient. A disaster for you and your client was 2008. Diversification changed the probabilities but it didn't meaningfully change the set of possible outcomes. A 20-year relationship ends up needlessly strained. Does it matter if no one saw it coming? Rapid, unforeseen plunges have happened before, the possibility was out there. The expected outcome is useful for averaging portfolio outcomes, but retirement income is about robustness across outcomes.

Transitioning helps to avoid danger for client and adviser alike. Transitioning is about the simple things that you can do with the client to position the portfolio for secure outcomes at minimal cost to upside potential. In other words, the transition is about making small changes that can have a large impact.

In this chapter, we want to cover what the transition is about. It is hoped that you will come away knowing how to make the transition seem natural and how to avoid difficult transitions. Making the transition a seamless process, from accumulation to retirement income, is not as difficult as it seems at first blush. With an orderly process, it all seems natural to the client and during the transition the changes are subtle.

Of course, not all of your clients have been there long-term, and sometimes the circumstances of your clients change dramatically. You need to be prepared for the clients who walk in with new funds. Capturing *money in motion* is an important part of any adviser's business. But telling a client what you can do with the money works best when you can offer a concrete objective and show how it can be met. So, for this chapter, we want to focus on the natural evolution of portfolios and avoid sudden transitions that often create resistance and engender mistrust.

WHAT THE TRANSITION IS ABOUT

The transition is about moving from a posture of a singular focus on accumulation to a position of planning for both accumulation plus maintaining lifestyle after retirement. When done properly, the transition is a natural and seamless progression of the portfolio management problem. The focus is changing as the portfolio tilts toward lifestyle protection, but the portfolio feels as before. The client retains a sense of control and comfort. Even if the client ultimately ends up in a packaged, magic-bullet-bundled product that covers all needs, the transition begins a change in focus and direction that creates options for both the adviser and client. The goal is to take the accumulation portfolio and gradually move to a focus on protecting lifestyle. When done properly, it is a natural part of the relationship with the client that can work across the spectrum of business models that are in use.

It may well be the case that we see the ultimate destination for the client's assets as a product class or even a specific product. The goal of the transition is to move the client from focusing exclusively on the portfolio as a financial construct to a focus on the portfolio as a source of funding for lifestyle security. As shown in Figure 10.1, the transition gives us the opportunity to move the client's portfolio in the direction of the ultimate solution while retaining several key attributes:

- Retains familiarity with the current portfolio—small changes to start
- A strong sense of progress that the portfolio is beginning to be shaped up for retirement—changes that make sense in the context of the ultimate goal
- Demonstrates competence on the part of the adviser—can execute in all market conditions
- Reversibility in the event of sudden and unforeseen client needs—no major costs for a midcourse correction

Retirement Income Planner – Needs for Retirement Income

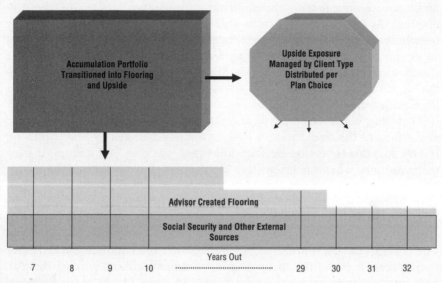

FIGURE 10.1 The Transition from Accumulation to Retirement

- Encourage rollover distributions from sponsored plans into an IRA. This is especially useful when rollover distributions can be used to help shift the focus of the portfolio from accumulation in the generic sense to a portfolio that is customized to the client's specific needs.
- Scalability and simplicity for the adviser

Let's approach the transition by putting some of the language in an alternative framework. In accumulation, the focus is on finding the right combination of expected return and volatility that works best for the client. For the adviser, this place becomes comfortable once the practice is set up because the portfolios can be manufactured en masse. What we're trying to do for the transition is twofold: First, we need the transition to be as scalable as before, meaning the change has to be as simple as changing a lightbulb. Second, for the client, we change the focus from volatility to outcomes. That is, we want roughly the same risk profile as before, but we want to make sure that the client's one roll of the dice has limited downside. There's an expression in structured trading: "Buy your hedges when they're cheap, when you don't think you'll ever need them." A good example of the reasoning behind this maxim can be illustrated by an example: An electricity trade was undertaken where my firm was agreeing to act as a producer and deliver of electricity, "electrons" in the jargon, to a major hub. To satisfy the requirements of that power region, all we had to do was find a source for capacity (the ability to produce) and electricity (the production). At the time that the trade was undertaken, capacity was essentially free. Instead of locking in capacity at the time of the trade, a bad decision was made to just buy it on the fly as needed. After all, capacity was always cheap. Hedging, it was argued, would mean leaving money on the table— that is, net about $100,000. Guess what? A hot summer and a cold winter later, with a few facilities out of service and needing repair, capacity costs went stratospheric. The price we would receive for the electricity was fixed at the time of the trade, and we hedged the basic electricity price up front, but the loss due to leaving capacity unhedged was over $60 million. During the transition, when the hedges are very cheap, don't wait, buy them.

THE ORDER OF TRANSITION

The order of the transition is important because the hallmark of the transition process is to set the client up for retirement without forcing them to lock into anything before they are ready. This is why the main theme of the transition is focused on capital markets where changing course creates little deadweight loss. With that in mind, the following ordering of transition is provided:

1. Fixed income allocation → flooring allocation
2. Cash Allocation → precautionary allocation
3. Equity allocation → mostly remains allocated for upside potential (risky assets)
4. Equity allocation → some allocated for purchase of lifestyle insurance

The first allocation from fixed income to flooring is generally a straightforward transition, but it is the most important step. You want to refocus the fixed income component of the accumulation portfolio from constant maturity to defined maturity. It generally has the same volatility-dampening impact on the portfolio as before, but it begins to provide a sense of income security.

For clients it is an appealing prospect. Instead of taking a $1 million portfolio and offering the hope of $4 million in 20 years, you can offer the same hope but with a failsafe or fallback that retirement income will not fall below $40,000 per year out to age 90.[1]

The second transition is from cash to precautionary. While this at first may seem straightforward, the uncertainties of retirement are different than during the accumulation years. Furthermore, depending on the rigidity of their final retirement portfolio, they may need to hold more in precautionary reserves to make up for a lack of flexibility in their ultimate plan. Some product solutions are so rigid that if your client has an event that requires even $1 more than the maximum payout allowed for a particular period, then it triggers a reset of all future periods based on the then prevailing market conditions. For example a GMWB offering a maximum payout of $50,000 may reset down to $40,000 if your client happens to need to exceed the withdrawal cap by even a tiny amount during a major down market. This is not meant as a knock on the product. It is an argument to recognize that the precautionary needs of the client will vary based on the rigidity of their ultimate retirement portfolio. As a rule of thumb, a client with a fully tradable retirement portfolio can probably get by with as little as 5 percent in excess cash, while a client with a rigid retirement contract may want to have at least 10 percent in precautionary reserves.

The third part of the transition is that having the flooring in place creates a freedom in the upside portfolio that was not previously there. What was previously a purely equity component of a portfolio becomes a miniature portfolio where accumulation remains the focus. Volatility is a friend of discretionary wealth, the upside component of the portfolio. Almost every client aspires to a better future. A conservative approach to managing the discretionary wealth component of the portfolio is to reintroduce the fixed income components that were transitioned away when the initial flooring was created. A more aggressive approach would be, with flooring in place, to move up the risk spectrum in this subportfolio to seek higher expected returns.

The final part of the transition is to put the protections in place that will keep the lifestyle secure in the face of the retirement risks that can be properly and best laid off through insurance products. This final phase of the transition, when the style of the ultimate portfolio becomes clear, is the time to secure the precise features of the retirement plan. There is no need to secure the capital markets "transition" flooring with longevity insurance if the capital markets flooring is ultimately going to be sold off in favor of an annuity.

What Changes from Before?

For the most part, the feel of the portfolio remains unchanged. If you were working predominantly in the capital markets domain, then a few transactions are all that are required. Most of the assets remain untouched. The following sentence can't be overemphasized. Proposing large and sudden changes can unnerve clients. You want to make sure that you put a proposal in front of them to begin making the first, small steps. Stress that the first step is small, but it is a crucial piece of the puzzle. When you first transition the fixed income component, everything else remains the same.

What you may find is that the biggest changes are in the client and the nature of the relationship. Some clients will become interested in seeing how much flooring they can add. That is fine, particularly if you can encourage them to do it through tax-advantaged rollovers rather than adding flooring funds outside of their retirement umbrella. The other change is that, flooring in place, they may become much more interested in your thoughts and ideas for potential upside.

What About Clients Who Come into Money?

Clients who come into money are often ideal candidates for transitioning portfolios into retirement income. There is a wealth of anecdotal evidence that one of the major sources of retirement funds that Americans count on is their parents. On the one hand, this is money that has already been earmarked for the future, rather than current needs. On the other hand, as a social issue, it sounds odd and unnerving. Odd and unnerving as this may sound, this question is how to manage it properly if the client is correct.[2]

Usually the funds come in at stepped-up basis but confer no other tax advantages. Since these funds tend to come in outside of any tax-advantaged account, you need to be careful about the uses that you put the funds. To repeat, most of the useful components of capital markets flooring create phantom income. Discount securities, as a rule, best fit in tax-deferred accounts. To take the tax considerations properly into account, the funds can be handled in either a direct fashion or an indirect fashion.

Handling the funds directly means finding a tax-advantageous vehicle to transform the funds into retirement income. The most efficient way to shelter such wealth is through an insurance product. Again, since this was money that the client has already mentally earmarked for retirement, this client is more likely to be amenable to insurance solutions.

The indirect approach is a second-best solution. For this approach, the client rolls over an equivalent amount of 401(k) assets into an IRA and the rollover funds are turned into flooring. With the funds from the 401(k) turned into flooring, the legacy funds that started this ball rolling are natural candidates for being placed in assets that qualify for treatment as long-term gains.

A DIFFICULT TRANSITION

In everything, from diet to politics to business, abrupt or radical change is a hard sell. Before talking about seamless transitioning, I digress to talk about transitions that are considered difficult and go through some of the reasons that make them tough. I focus on a simple example, but the story could apply to many of the first-generation products that are on the market today, products that are designed to be the magic bullets of retirement. The first-generation products often suffer from the same faults of trying to solve every part of the retirement income as a one-shot fix.

Annuities and their more complex brethren often face initial client resistance even when it is clearly a client who would be most likely to derive a benefit from monetizing their mortality (e.g., single and without heirs). I'm not talking about those who are not disposed to annuities, but those who will probably benefit from them. Why is it so tough to get them to make the leap? Part of the reason is that it is a leap and not a step—and a few factors can put hurdles on the way to the sale.

First, there are psychological factors. Annuities are generally purchases that engender cognitive dissonance on the part of the client. They are being asked to change their portfolio orientation from stocks and bonds to an insurance contract. The questions that people ask are why? Why now? Was what I was doing before wrong? Clients also can take the transition to an annuity as a tacit reminder of their mortality. Some view it as a surrender of portfolio control. Others feel they are intimidated by the complexity of the contract, even if the terms of the annuity are quite straightforward.[3]

Second, there are economic factors of annuities, in general, that require more forethought on the part of the client. Almost anyone considering an annuity will perform the mental calculus of the net value of the annuity for different possible life spans. This means that the client once again is forced to confront the cheery thought of their own death and its possible specific circumstances. Many people will imagine a possibly devastating visit to an oncologist. Then what? For example, once purchased, most annuities are expensive to surrender. One would expect to pay an exit fee since the act of surrendering an annuity is correlated to the client having private information about impending mortality. Essentially, the insurance company wants to keep people who have shortened life expectancies in the pool, and wanting out of the pool strongly signals the possibility of private information. This means that people often want to think about their likelihood of long-term survival and whether the value of mitigating the risk of running out of money too soon is sufficient to overcome the expected deadweight loss if surrender is required.

For some advisors, annuities mean either dead money or assets are going away to the insurance company. To overcome this seller resistance, a trailer is generally built into the annuity. The trick for the annuity producer is to devise a trailer that is high enough to induce the seller while at the same time not so high as to dissuade the client from making the purchase.

These factors and others make the decision to annuitize a decision that tends to be an abrupt change in portfolio composition. Even if the ultimate goal is to make the client secure with an annuity, and even if the client is ultimately willing to annuitize, the very abruptness makes for a difficult transition. We now focus on the goal of finding a transition that is an easier sell for client and advisor alike.

WHEN TO TRANSITION

As a rule of thumb, people start to think about retirement at age 40, fret about retirement when they reach 50, and panic about their retirement after age 60. By working with clients on transitioning their portfolios around the time that they begin to fret, panic can be avoided.[4]

Assuming retirement at 65, there isn't much that can be done for people before age 35.[5] Fixed income securities rarely trade beyond a 30-year window. So for a client who is more than 30 years from retirement, the best advice may simply be to keep saving money and take advantage of the volatility in markets by buying into down markets. Once inside the 30-year window, it becomes possible to act, but it may not yet be necessary. At the end of this chapter, I discuss the value of a business model that includes a retirement income focus from inception.

Different clients will want to transition themselves at different times. It is therefore important to put some structure around transitioning to avoid excessive dissimilarity among client types and their portfolios. To be able to offer competitive services, you need to make the customization that you offer for different clients very inexpensive for you to manage. One way to do this is with a fixed transitioning that can be used across clients and client types.

When constructing accumulation portfolios, it is common to work with a listing of five types of investor risk tolerances and hold different allocations usually in stocks, bonds, and cash for each of them. For the sake of clarity, I'll focus on the typical moderate 60/30/10 allocation. For a conservative investor, the allocation to bonds will be higher; for the aggressive investor the allocation to bonds will be lower. When discussing retirement income, the risk tolerance is mostly a concern for the discretionary portfolio. The concept of risk tolerance has no real meaning when discussing the floor.[6]

The natural point to transition is when the fixed income allocation that you are providing to your client becomes approximately equal to the flooring allocation given by your flooring allocation tables. To illustrate this point, I reproduce the allocation tables from Chapter 7 in Table 10.1, which

TABLE 10.1 Tables of Portfolio Allocations for Different Lifestyles, Ages, and Anticipations of Inflation (percentages)

Allocations for Flooring to 85 Nominal Values, 0% Anticipated Inflation					Allocations for Flooring to 90 Nominal Values, 0% Anticipated Inflation				
Age	Flooring	Longevity	Cash	At Risk	Age	Flooring	Longevity	Cash	At Risk
30	12%	1%	10%	77%	30	11%	0%	10%	79%
35	15%	1%	10%	74%	35	14%	0%	10%	76%
40	19%	2%	10%	69%	40	17%	1%	10%	72%
45	25%	2%	10%	63%	45	22%	1%	10%	67%
50	31%	3%	10%	56%	50	28%	1%	10%	61%
55	40%	3%	10%	47%	55	36%	1%	10%	53%
60	51%	4%	10%	35%	60	46%	2%	10%	42%
65	65%	5%	5%	25%	65	59%	2%	5%	34%
70	73%	7%	5%	15%	70	65%	3%	5%	27%
75	81%	9%	10%	0%	75	73%	3%	5%	19%

2% Anticipated Inflation					2% Anticipated Inflation				
Age	Flooring	Longevity	Cash	At Risk	Age	Flooring	Longevity	Cash	At Risk
30	28%	3%	10%	59%	30	26%	1%	10%	63%
35	32%	4%	10%	54%	35	30%	2%	10%	58%
40	37%	4%	10%	49%	40	35%	2%	10%	53%
45	43%	5%	10%	42%	45	40%	2%	10%	48%
50	50%	6%	10%	34%	50	47%	2%	10%	41%
55	58%	7%	10%	25%	55	54%	3%	10%	33%
60	67%	8%	10%	15%	60	62%	3%	10%	25%
65	77%	9%	10%	4%	65	72%	4%	5%	19%
70	82%	11%	10%	−3%	70	77%	4%	5%	14%
75	88%	12%	10%	−10%	75	82%	5%	10%	3%

3% Anticipated Inflation					3% Anticipated Inflation				
Age	Flooring	Longevity	Cash	At Risk	Age	Flooring	Longevity	Cash	At Risk
30	43%	6%	10%	41%	30	41%	3%	10%	46%
35	47%	7%	10%	36%	35	45%	3%	10%	42%
40	52%	7%	10%	31%	40	50%	3%	10%	37%
45	57%	8%	10%	25%	45	55%	3%	10%	32%
50	63%	9%	10%	18%	50	60%	4%	10%	26%
55	69%	10%	10%	11%	55	66%	4%	10%	20%
60	76%	11%	10%	3%	60	73%	4%	10%	13%
65	84%	12%	10%	−6%	65	80%	5%	10%	5%
70	88%	13%	10%	−11%	70	84%	5%	10%	1%
75	92%	14%	10%	−16%	75	88%	6%	10%	−4%

provide allocations for flooring, longevity risk, precautionary cash, and risky assets. These tables provide for annual flooring at 5 percent of initial principal for the set designed to last to age 85 and flooring at 4 percent per year of initial principal for the set designed to last to age 90.

You want to be careful about one aspect of the tables that will be impacted by your flooring choices. Strictly speaking, the tables create allocations based on the cost of putting down a string of Treasury principal strips or zero-coupon bonds to secure income once it's needed, but not before. If you are working exclusively with taxable funds, then you may want to use a ladder of ordinary bonds so that the annual income yield can defray the expected taxes. Otherwise you can take the opportunity to talk with your client about the important advantages that can come with holding assets in a tax-deferred account like an IRA or an exempt-on-the-way-out account like a Roth IRA. Laying down lifestyle flooring is a great reason for rolling assets from a 401(k) to IRA. If possible, you want to avoid the client feeling blindsided by a tax liability for phantom income that they weren't expecting and don't fully understand. Finally, note that since the tables use flooring based on U.S. Treasury securities, it is the most costly flooring to buy— there's no credit risk.

Again note that the entries with negative or miniscule allocation to at-risk assets represent allocations where building capital markets flooring is infeasible.

The point of reproducing the table is to highlight that the flooring allocations are rising through time, much as the fixed income asset class rises in the traditional accumulation portfolio context. This provides us with a key to selling and managing client transitions: when their flooring allocations begin to rise to the level of their model portfolio, fixed income allocations. In such a process, the transition becomes a yes/no proposition that can be presented to the client, taking the onus off of the adviser. As retirement income becomes increasingly utilized, the documentation trail for encouraging transitions will become more important.

MAKING THE TRANSITION SEAMLESS

Making the transition seamless means two things. The first is proposing the familiar concept of allocation to clients who are now rising in age to where their fixed income allocations equal the proposed flooring allocations; the transition becomes a natural part of the client-service proposition. The other way to making the transition seamless is that you want retirement income to be a natural enhancement to your existing practice, not a repudiation of past practices. Both the timing of the transition and the integration of transition services into an existing practice are important.

The first phase of transition transforms only the fixed-income component of an accumulation portfolio. What you are accomplishing here is in setting a floor under the client's retirement lifestyle.

The allocation tables provide a natural way and a natural time to have the client portfolio begin to switch over; you do not want to propose a major change in direction. The transition is simply the point in time that you and the client recognize the horizon and start taking consideration of the maturity structure of the client's fixed-income components. Without endorsing a specific product set, the generic version would entail beginning to move the client away from a constant-maturity fixed-income component to a defined-maturity income component.[7] It is a subtle change that begins to lay down basic, but easily reversible, flooring in with roughly the same allocation to fixed income as before.

As bonds near maturity and their prices tend to par, their volatility is decreasing. What you are doing is trading away the constant expected volatility profile of the previous fixed-income funds for an amortizing volatility profile of the flooring component. The flooring component is heading to par and that is a floor.

If the transition is started early, then the transition can be described as beginning the process of building a road for retirement. For the early starter, only a small part of the usual fixed-income window of 30 years will cover retirement years. In this case, the advisor has three options:

1. For a client who is expected to have a steady stream of income over their remaining working life, building the road steadily through time is generally appealing. Using discount securities tends to be viewed favorably when the notional payout amounts are significantly higher than the current market values. The client has the ability to see the road being built. By being directly able to impact the lifestyle through additional deposits, the transition is likely to appeal to the goal and task orientations of many client types. As just a fraction of client assets, the road isn't an upper limit on lifestyle, only a lower bound. The client knows there is discretion that can be exercised if building the road needs to be interrupted; it can be resumed at will. In case of disaster, the road can be dismantled without incurring large transactions costs.

2. For a client with an irregular income stream, the adviser may simply leave some of the bond funds unconverted, with only a portion of the fixed-income assets transitioned at each point in time.

3. A younger client with a substantial portfolio but with irregular contributions may benefit from a stack-and-roll transition. In the stack-and-roll transition, the fixed-income portfolio is transitioned into a stack of securities that only cover the near-term end of retirement. As

time progresses and it is possible to lock in future income components, part of the stack is sold off and the maturity is rolled out to cover a new segment of retirement.

If the transition is started late, then the transition involves laying down a wider swathe of flooring from the outset. For the late starter, it becomes harder to build sufficient flooring in an IRA without a rollover distribution from a 401(k). In this case, it is best to show the client the benefit of retirement income transitioning and show them what you can do with their current assets. Whatever the approach used for selling your services and gathering assets, the value of a rollover distribution that can be turned into transition-period flooring is a straightforward concept. With the rollover, the only onus put on the adviser is to execute on the flooring purchase.

One of the important aspects of the transition is that it should be portrayed as part of the natural evolution of client portfolios. There may be a point in time when the portfolio is transformed completely into a product-centric solution, but that is the endgame not the transition.

CREATING A BUSINESS MODEL THAT INCLUDES A NATURAL TRANSITION

Most clients have more than one financial service provider, but that usually translates into one adviser, one mutual fund company, and a number of 401(k) plan administrators corresponding to different employers from the client's work history. That said, the adviser has the best opportunity to make a compelling case to the client for consolidation. Suppose that you have a raft of clients and you want to include an automatic transition process for transforming the portfolio into a retirement income focus that can be handled without much effort or the need for intervention. Your goal is to bring in sticky assets that leave open the possibility for a deeper relationship when the client has a willingness to transfer meaningful assets. To do this, you demonstrate that you are the one out of the three with the most ability to customize for the client.

The value proposition that you provide is the current and future ability to customize their portfolio for their specific needs. Without going into a lot of detail about the mechanics of the business, you add value because you do something that the other guys can't do. If the client is able to grow as you'd hoped, then you will be well positioned to become the primary adviser and attract some of the away assets.

Creating a pitchbook that helps you help clients prepare for retirement that differs—by its concreteness—from the pitchbook presentations of other asset administrators is a worthwhile endeavor.

SUDDEN TRANSITIONS

Sudden transition—it's kind of an oxymoron. However, the issue can come up, particularly with a client who has just suffered a life-changing event. Here's where reversibility of the transition portfolio becomes important.

For the client with a simple lifestyle, where the post-event lifestyle remains simple, a sudden or unexpected transition is not that big of a problem. By definition, these people are overfunded relative to their needs. In such a case, the issue usually becomes a modest change in planned harvest schedule for discretionary wealth and the precautionary cash is sufficient to get over the transition hump.

Typically such sudden transitions require revamping the plans for retirement. It is more expensive to renegotiate contracts than to create a set of exchange transactions. The goal of the transition is to position assets without having them be irretrievably committed in the wrong place. By choosing transition assets that are flexible and liquid, you are prepared for when clients suffer a setback in retirement timing.

SUMMARY

Transitions can be abrupt or prolonged. The earlier in a client's life that the portfolio is tilted toward retirement income, the easier it is to create a retirement portfolio—or begin the process of preparing the client for a product geared to retirement rather than waiting and trying to sell the unwanted to the unwilling. This chapter shows how to avoid abrupt changes and turn the transition "problem" around to create a natural evolution that strengthens your client relationship.

CHAPTER 11

Putting Together
the Proposal

Objectives

Creating proposals to transform from an accumulation focus to a retirement income focus

Making the transformation a natural extension of business

For advisers serving longtime clients, the material contained in Chapter 10 on transitioning from accumulation to retirement income will provide the right set of tools and themes for the job. For advisers working with clients, this is an opportunity to show them what can be done. New clients may or may not already be oriented to thinking about retirement income. If not, then this is a great opportunity to introduce them to the concepts and signal your competence in the area.

This chapter is designed to help you lay out your client's assets to show current status with a retirement income view. The idea is to help you take the current portfolio and show where the biggest impact can be made with the smallest effort. The idea is to conduct the financial equivalent of minimally invasive surgery. Thus we want to help you create a proposal for reconfiguration.

Clearly your proposed configuration will reflect the lifestyle of the client and the flooring types that are mainstays of your platform. Depending on your licensing you will have a preference for using particular accumulation plan types and allocations. Finally, depending on your business model, you will want to think through the proposal in regard to passive or active risk management.

LAYING OUT CLIENT'S ASSETS TO SHOW CURRENT STATUS

Naturally the first place to start is with a portfolio status report. The main thing here is to look at the portfolio and start to create a view useful for retirement income with a device to guide the discussion along a path that is practical and consistent with what you and the client are comfortable doing.

A typical view of a portfolio usually includes a rollup by type. As an example we take an individual with the following hypothetical assets and rollup, shown in Table 11.1.

For retirement-income purposes, this is not a very helpful view. The first step is to take the information in Table 11.1 and convert it into a more useful and usable way to steer the conversation. To that end, we take the portfolio and spread out the assets along a time line. See Figure 11.1, which presents a graph laying out the assets by market value according to the dates that cash flows are scheduled to occur. Since most of the assets have no specified payment date, they are put into a bucket labeled uncommitted.

We now want to focus in on the bond and strips from the fixed-income component of the portfolio and look at the notional amounts that are expected by date. We show these data in both Table 11.2 and Figure 11.2 (which focuses on the fixed-income components to highlight the coupon and notional payments by paydate year).

TABLE 11.1 Hypothetical Client Statement

Fixed Income	
ABC Co 6.25%, 2025, Annual	$796,426.53
US Treas Prin Strip 2016	$54,147.15
US Treas Prin Strip 2017	$25,784.36
US Treas Prin Strip 2018	$24,556.53
US Treas Prin Strip 2019	$23,387.17
US Treas Prin Strip 2022	$40,405.44
XYZ Bond Fund	$350,000.00
Total Fixed Income	*$1,314,707.17*

Equity	
LSMFT Passive/Aggressive Fund	$1,750,000.00
Total Equity	*$1,750,000.00*
Total Market Value	*$3,064,707.17*

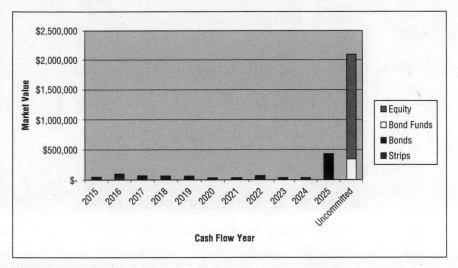

FIGURE 11.1 Laying Out Current Holdings: Market Value

TABLE 11.2 Focus on the Fixed-Income Portion of Client Portfolio

Notional Fixed-Income Cash Flows, Existing Portfolio			
Year	Strips	Bonds	Bond Funds
2015		$62,500	
2016	$80,000	$62,500	
2017	$40,000	$62,500	
2018	$40,000	$62,500	
2019	$40,000	$62,500	
2020		$62,500	
2021		$62,500	
2022	$80,000	$62,500	
2023		$62,500	
2024		$62,500	
2025		$1,000,000	
Uncommitted			$350,000

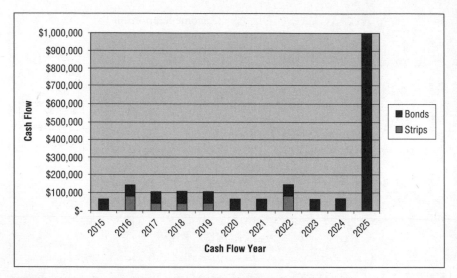

FIGURE 11.2 Laying Out Current Holdings: Bond Payments

As a last point, this is a good juncture to show them why pure drawdown schemes create the possibility of running out of money. Even a 4 percent drawdown rate, which always *seems* like it ought to work for at least 25 years, becomes risky if there is a down market in the early years of retirement.

MINIMALLY INVASIVE SURGERY: RECONFIGURATION PROPOSAL

The portfolio described in the previous section may have been designed for some purpose, but it is not well suited to retirement income needs. Even before knowing anything about the individual other than the desire stated when the individual walked in, to prepare for retirement income we can offer some ideas. For example, to illustrate the concept of readying for retirement, we can show the impact of taking the bond fund and setting up a more level income profile than implied by the layout of current bond holdings shown previously. For Table 11.3, I used hypothetical prices for strips, assuming a flat 5 percent yield curve, and smoothed out the income profile, which is also shown in Figure 11.3. As shown in the graph, the first part of the proposal is to smooth out the income stream by reformatting the existing fixed-income portfolio to conform more closely to retirement income needs. The final bond notional can be used as longevity protection. Similarly, in an insurance context,

TABLE 11.3 Arbitrary Fixed-Income Subportfolio Transformed for Retirement Income

Year	Strips	Proposed Notional Amounts After Redistributing Bond Fund	
		Bonds	Bond Funds
2015	$90,000	$62,500	
2016	$90,000	$62,500	
2017	$90,000	$62,500	
2018	$90,000	$62,500	
2019	$90,000	$62,500	
2020	$90,000	$62,500	
2021	$90,000	$62,500	
2022	$90,000	$62,500	
2023	$90,000	$62,500	
2024	$90,000	$62,500	
2025		$1,000,000	
Uncommitted			$(306.33)

one could construct a hypothetical sale of fixed-income assets replaced by an annuity.

By laying out the portfolio and showing a simple example of what can be done to create a secure floor, you have accomplished two things. First, you have helped to convey the idea behind what retirement income is all about. Second, by providing an example with the existing portfolio, you have

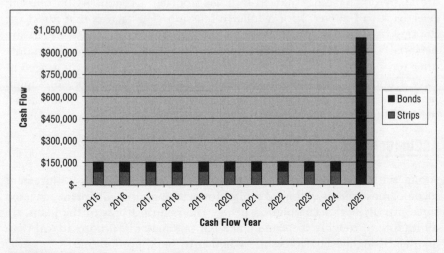

FIGURE 11.3 Proposed Bond Reconfiguration by Notional

provided an anchoring to the real world that will help to shape future discussions and set realistic expectations for managing the entire portfolio. In other words, you have helped to frame the problem and potentially averted a difficult conversation about what is desired and what is feasible.

LIFESTYLE AND FLOORING TYPES

Not all securities professionals are licensed to sell insurance products or offer advice, and not all insurance professionals are licensed to sell general securities or offer advice. However, after providing the concept of what needs to be done and an example of what can be done, it is time to get a better handle on needs and wants.

Using either top-down or bottom-up versions of needs, current wealth, and accumulation path, it is possible to get a good handle on the type of flooring most appropriate to the lifestyle type. Chapter 3 went through ways of estimating flooring needs and ascertaining sufficiency of wealth to fund the desired lifestyle by wealth. Underfunded lifestyles where annual lifestyle exceeds 7 percent of wealth are natural need-based candidates for monetization of mortality. Hybrid flooring candidates have lower lifestyle needs as a percentage of wealth and pure capital markets candidates are those who live the simplest lifestyles relative to wealth. Only for those with lifestyle needs below 3.5 percent does the flooring discussion become superfluous. When it comes to flooring candidacy, the important point to get across is that it is the lifestyle relative to wealth and not just the wealth level that matters for a flooring recommendation.

Sustainability is a concern, but it is not the only concern. Clearly there are many other factors that go into the flooring decision. Again one can refer back to Chapter 3 for a fuller discussion. The factors that affect the flooring choices are myriad. Some of the factors are objective.[1] Others are personal.[2] Many, who ultimately purchase insurance annuities, do so only after retirement. Even if the individual is below 60, there is still a need to have a flooring plan in place, but the tradability and liquidity of capital markets products means that it is easy to move someone from capital markets flooring to insurance-based flooring at a later date.

ACCUMULATION PLAN TYPES

Along with transitioning a portfolio from accumulation to retirement income, most clients will need a plan for accumulation. Chapter 6 covered three prototypical accumulation plans. The main features of the plans are all leading to roughly the same place but one may offer more appeal than another. Roughly the choices are whether to build up flooring:

- Within a fixed window (brick layer)
- By sliding the window further out every year (track layer)
- To a maximum amount within a window before sliding the window further out (surge maker)

If we take the desire to switch from accumulation to protecting income in retirement as a given, it becomes a practical engineering problem to find a transition solution. Every professional will have a preferred set of tools and products for moving clients from accumulation to retirement income. Even with two parties needing to stay in their comfort zones while engaged in the transition, there are a great many products that can be used to effect the change. There are many equally good ways to make the transition that conform to best practices. The only thing that is relatively certain about transitioning is that drawdown plans for accumulation-style investing are rapidly falling out of favor as part of best practices for retirement income.

ALLOCATIONS

Chapter 7 provided formulas and tables for determining allocation percentages based on sustainable floors. Fortunately, many of the allocations are quite close to the rules-of-thumb allocations that are useful in accumulation plans. One important point to keep in mind with the allocations provided in the tables is that they are engineered tables based on given draw rates and time horizons. They are not derived allocations based on a model of optimal behavior for a particular set of preferences.

One of the first tasks for matching lifestyle assets with liabilities involves estimating the lifestyle liabilities of the client, including realistic expectations about inflation. In this regard, context is everything. Estimates are often constructed in nominal dollars, essentially ignoring the effects of inflation. Even if the floor will be built with inflation-protected securities, it will be advisable to show how the assets and liabilities match up against one another. With it one can also help to construct a floor that adjusts for anticipated inflation. If not using TIPS or inflation-protected flooring of some type, then the nominal liabilities shown in Table 11.4 will not work in the presence of inflation.

For either a nominal floor or for a floor made up of inflation-protected securities, Table 11.4 tells us the number of units of income in today's dollars that we need to match against or propose to match against the needs shown in the table.

With an adjustment for expected inflation, we can adapt flooring with nominal securities to diminish the impact of inflation. Table 11.5 shows how we expect the dollar cost of lifestyle needs to rise over time due to

TABLE 11.4   Lifestyle Needs in Nominal Amounts Will Underestimate the Cost of Retirement

Real Lifestyle Needs for Each Year of Retirement by Current Age

		Age at Withdrawal					
		65	66	67	68	69	70
	30	$10,000	$10,000	$10,000	$10,000	$10,000	$10,000
	35	$10,000	$10,000	$10,000	$10,000	$10,000	$10,000
Age Today	40	$10,000	$10,000	$10,000	$10,000	$10,000	$10,000
	45	$10,000	$10,000	$10,000	$10,000	$10,000	$10,000
	50	$10,000	$10,000	$10,000	$10,000	$10,000	$10,000
	55	$10,000	$10,000	$10,000	$10,000	$10,000	$10,000
	60	$10,000	$10,000	$10,000	$10,000	$10,000	$10,000
	65	$10,000	$10,000	$10,000	$10,000	$10,000	$10,000

inflation. The table shows the lifestyle needs are rising, but almost as importantly, it provides a roadmap for constructing the asset profile of flooring products to match the liabilities.

We can now connect the schedule of lifestyle needs given in Table 11.5 with prices of the Treasury strips as shown in Chapter 5. As with Chapter 5, we use indicative prices for October 9, 2008. Table 11.6 and Figure 11.4 were constructed by simply matching the price feed to the client worksheet.

TABLE 11.5   Adjusting Amounts for Expected Inflation

Adjusted Lifestyle Needs for Each Year of Retirement by Current Age, 3% Expected Inflation

		Age at Withdrawal					
		65	66	67	68	69	70
	30	$28,139	$28,983	$29,852	$30,748	$31,670	$32,620
	35	$24,273	$25,001	$25,751	$26,523	$27,319	$28,139
Age Today	40	$20,938	$21,566	$22,213	$22,879	$23,566	$24,273
	45	$18,061	$18,603	$19,161	$19,736	$20,328	$20,938
	50	$15,580	$16,047	$16,528	$17,024	$17,535	$18,061
	55	$13,439	$13,842	$14,258	$14,685	$15,126	$15,580
	60	$11,593	$11,941	$12,299	$12,668	$13,048	$13,439
	65	$10,000	$10,300	$10,609	$10,927	$11,255	$11,593

TABLE 11.6   The Cost of Meeting Lifestyle Needs with Treasury Strips

	Lifestyle Needs	Notional of Strips to Purchase	Market Value of Assets
2024	$15,580	$15,000	$7,579.50
2025	$16,047	$16,000	$7,844.96
2026	$16,528	$16,000	$7,399.20
2027	$17,024	$17,000	$7,604.27
2028	$17,535	$17,000	$7,338.39
2029	$18,061	$18,000	$7,534.26
Totals	$100,775	$99,000	$45,301

The graph in Figure 11.4 matches assets to liabilities, using a time frame (October 2008) when the cost of secure flooring was at a substantial premium to typical markets.

PASSIVE VERSUS ACTIVE RISK MANAGEMENT

Periodic rebalancing is required and desirable even in portfolios set up for passive maintenance of lifestyle. One aspect of rebalancing along the functional dimension is that it's not the purely mechanical rebalancing of an accumulation portfolio. Rebalancing to raise the lifestyle floor is a happy

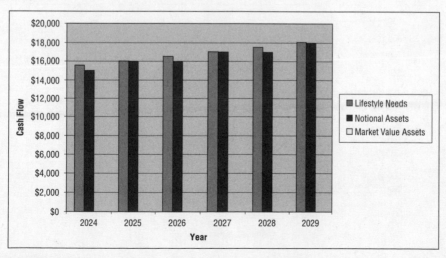

FIGURE 11.4   Asset/Liability Match, October 9, 2008

occasion. For the self-directed, it is a time to reflect on lifestyle goals and for the professional adviser a great opportunity to interact with the client about the redirection of the funds.

Whether actively managing portfolio risk as in Chapter 9 or simply trying to maintain the portfolios functional balance, the notion of cushion also encountered in Chapter 9 is a great way to motivate the discussion about rebalancing. Aside from its uses as a risk-management tool, the cushion tells us the amount of slack in the portfolio that could be directed to risk or raising the lifestyle. There may be a desire to maintain the cushion as a percentage of the overall portfolio or as a dollar amount.

The results of Chapter 9 show that historically speaking, taking a small, repeat small, amount of risk in an actively managed portfolio leads to improved outcomes for the client. In all cases, the outcome was floored to protect a predetermined minimum of lifestyle flooring. The results show the additional importance of being prepared for big bear markets. Perhaps most important is to work with the client to let them know how much flooring can be purchased and where you will take them out of the market if things don't go as planned. Remind them that part of your value to them is that you help craft portfolios designed to perform, and another part of your value to them is that you know what to do if the plan, no matter how good a plan, begins to go awry. Remember it is only feasible to take money off of the table when the money is there.

Figure 11.5 shows backtest results from using the risk management methods discussed in Chapter 9. The data are historical from 1948 through

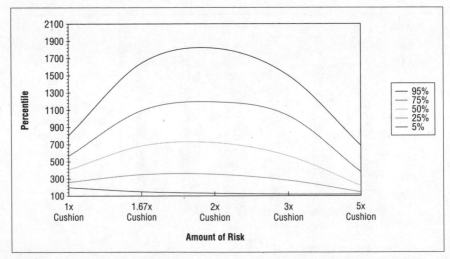

FIGURE 11.5 Managing Risk in Retirement Allocations: Historical Backtest

2007, using both Treasury data and SPX total returns. Figure 11.5 has five lines representing the 1st, 25th, 50th, 75th, and 95th percentiles of the 240 quarters. On the left column, we see portfolio dollar values corresponding to an initial investment of $100 and an initial floor of $100. The floor is allowed to ratchet upward whenever there is excess cushion. The right-hand column shows the percentage of the portfolio allocated to the discretionary wealth portfolio of risky assets. The picture is tiny, but it shows that from a static portfolio starting point, as risk rises the terminal values move higher for low levels of risk (Risky allocation <3× Cushion). But at higher levels of risk the gains reverse.

Figure 11.5 shows that adding a small amount of risk to a lifestyle-protection portfolio may indeed outperform a static fully locked allocation. That said, historical backtest results indicate that adding a small measure of risk, if monitored and managed, is beneficial on average. Standing ready to act if necessary is of vital importance.

It is not right to interpret that risk management is holding the portfolio back. The right interpretation is that some paths would recover and others would not recover. Before the fact we did not know which path we were on and that the best practice is to protect the lifestyle floor for each individual and not just protect "on average."

SUMMARY

This chapter focused on taking a traditional portfolio construct and positioning a proposal to transform the portfolio into a retirement income portfolio. The adviser needs to make sure that the transformation is backward compatible in the sense that this is an improvement over something that was already good. The natural place to start is to show that the fixed-income component of the original portfolio can be transformed to provide a customized solution for the client—one that also scales easily for the adviser who needs to serve many clients.

CHAPTER 12

Market Segmentation

Objectives

Show how to match clients with product types by market segment

Show segmentation for retirement portfolios

Illustrate segmentation differences between retirement income portfolios and accumulation portfolios

K nowing the right products for a particular client or demographic cohort is an important part of an adviser's knowledge base. The products with the greatest appeal to a mass-affluent base differ from the products preferred by a base comprised of clients with high net worth. In accumulation, the segmentation is based on risk tolerance and wealth. Risk tolerance is notoriously difficult to pin down, leaving the bucketing of clients often owing more to concerns related to the potential for suitability complaints than any solid measure of risk tolerance.

This brief chapter is designed to help producers and advisers understand client segmentation for retirement income. For producers, it is an opportunity to think about their product offerings in a different light, possibly triggering ideas for new products. For advisers, it provides a better understanding of what will work and for whom. With a retirement income focus, the segmentation becomes cleaner and more objective than in accumulation. With a more objective way to evaluate clients, the potential for suitability mismatches diminishes.

The organization of the chapter is to start with the familiar segmentation for traditional accumulation portfolios. With the standard framework in place, it is easy for us to shift our emphasis to segmentation for retirement income.

SEGMENTATION FOR TRADITIONAL PORTFOLIOS

Building a business around retirement income requires being able to effectively segment different clients and their different needs, and doing so in a way that can be scaled up to a large size. Fortunately, the requirements for segmentation relevant for retirement income are simple, measurable, and intuitive.

In accumulation, the segmentation is typically by wealth and level of risk aversion. As a concept, risk aversion is simple. Unfortunately, as a delineator for segmentation, the degree of risk aversion is imprecisely measured and often a poor measure for crafting a successful proposal. Whatever its drawbacks, the standard model uses five categories of risk aversion and four categories of wealth. The result allows firms to standardize off-the-shelf portfolios directly or through targeted sleeving as depicted by the buckets in Table 12.1.

Many firms organize themselves to specialize in particular wealth classes or individual niches. Product offerings for the upper end of the wealth spectrum are high margin, creating a natural gravitation for firms to seek to cater only to the high-net-worth and ultra-high-net-worth segments. Often the notion of the exclusivity of products and services is used as a selling point.[1] It is unclear how this business model will fare in the aftermath of the 2008 meltdown where many of the high-margin offerings for registered investors fared poorly and anecdotal evidence indicates that wealthier investors weighted more heavily to illiquid alternative assets may have suffered more than the mass affluent.[2]

Slotting the clients into the matrix is not as easy as it may seem to an outsider. The difficulty lies in understanding the client's risk tolerance. Most

TABLE 12.1 A Traditional Segmentation Grid

	Mass Market W < $250,000	Mass Affluent $250,000 < W < $2 Million	High Net Worth $2 Million < W < $10 Million	Ultra-High Net Worth W > $10 Million
Conservative				
Moderately Conservative				
Moderate				
Moderately Aggressive				
Aggressive				

firms rely on a small, inane, and poorly designed set of questions that seem less designed to elicit information and more to protect the firm from arbitration and lawsuits. Protecting the firm is a different goal than making the most out of the client/adviser relationship. With a retirement income focus and a commitment of a part of the portfolio to building a lifestyle floor, the adviser's exposure to suitability concerns becomes lessened and largely confined to the discretionary-wealth subportfolio.

SEGMENTATION FOR RETIREMENT INCOME PORTFOLIOS

To an adviser, the most useful and yet simplest piece of information for creating retirement income portfolios is in knowing the years until planned retirement. With that single datum, both transaction-oriented and fee-based representatives can create scalable retirement income portfolios that look and feel like traditional portfolios with the exception that the fixed-income component has a defined maturity facet rather than the constant maturity facet in traditional portfolios.

For firms creating product and generic universal diversified portfolios to feed into the distribution channels, a more thorough segmentation is required. In what follows, I develop an approach leading to market segmentation for retirement income. The ultimate goal is to show how a firm can reconfigure segmentation in a straightforward and immediately usable fashion.

For any starting level of wealth, the ending distribution of possible outcomes widens for a risky portfolio. A longer investment horizon has a wider distribution of possible portfolio outcomes. In the typical model of accumulation, returns are assumed to be normally distributed, and the volatility of the returns over any horizon will grow at roughly the square root of the length of the horizon. Using traditional assumptions as a rough gauge means that the cumulative return at a four-year horizon will have twice the volatility of returns over a one-year horizon.

When switching from accumulation to retirement income, the endpoints begin to take on greater importance. In the retirement income context, the endpoints denote wealth levels at each of the dates for which consumption will need to be funded. The minimum amount that the client will need at each of these dates is the consumption floor.

Do they have enough? A natural consequence of using a retirement income framework is that the first level of segmentation is based on whether the client's assets are more than sufficient (excess funding) to meet the floor without risk, barely sufficient to meet the floor (constrained) without risk, or insufficient to meet the floor without risk (underfunded).

Open-ended investment strategies and speculative end-point strategies may be appropriate and comfortable to use for long-term planning. However, optimized portfolios may be less resilient to surprises than outcome-based portfolios.[3] Creating specific end point and minimum income end-point strategies may make for more resilient portfolios.

Figure 12.1 provides a dimension along which client segmentation falls naturally out of the analysis. For a portfolio of risky assets that starts at time $t = 0$, we construct an arbitrary confidence band. The lines of expectation and the line of risk-free growth refer to the portfolio growing respectively according to the expected rate of return and the risk-free rate. In Figure 12.1, the flooring needs below line A have excess funding; the flooring needs above line B are underfunded; and between lines A and B, choices are constrained. Aside from the segmentation, what we can take away from the picture is that the lower the floor the more tolerance there is for unfavorable outcomes.

Note that at this point, risk aversion is not yet in play. The primary issue is whether there are sufficient assets to fund the consumption floor. Only after the flooring is secure does the issue of risk aversion come into play; risk aversion matters only to the extent that the portfolio has capacity to allow the client to seek upside potential on top of the floor.

Many advisers find it easier to discuss retirement income in terms of the retirement date portfolio yield required to maintain lifestyle. The picture in Figure 12.1 roughly translates to the following draw rates:

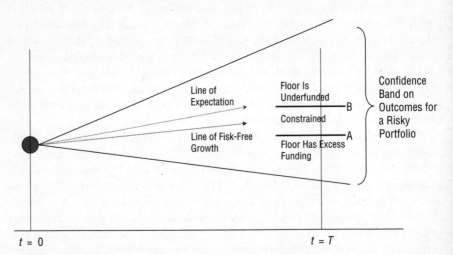

$t = 0$ $t = T$

FIGURE 12.1 Segmentation: Floor Relative to Wealth

- Excess funding ≈ draw rate ≤3.5%
- Constrained ≈ 3.5% < draw rate ≤7%
- Underfunded ≈ draw rate >7%

Table 12.2 presents a simple segmentation of retirement income clients that clarifies the targeting of product sets that are combined into the solutions to the client's retirement income portfolio problem.

The difference between Tables 12.1 and 12.2 shows up in the first column. Instead of relying on notions of client risk aversion, retirement income segmentation relies on the client's ability to fund lifestyle during retirement

Notice that the base segmentation does not rely on ersatz risk aversion classifications. The degree of risk aversion is only relevant to the degree that it influences the construction of the upside subportfolio. The upshot is that with a bona fide floor, the risk and possibly liability inherent in guessing suitability can be lessened. Even if actively managed, absent malfeasance, misjudging an upside portfolio has less potential for catastrophe than misjudging a traditional, unsegregated portfolio.

Another way to view the segmentation is to follow the stylized description shown Figure 12.2. Here you can see how the market segments typically are matched with products. The typical business model followed by financial firms recognizes that time has value and it is costly to service clients. The necessity is to spend as little time as possible with the low-wealth clients and devote resources to the higher end of the spectrum. At the low end, the products need to be simple and intuitive; they need to sell themselves. At some firms, even the mass affluent are too costly to service profitably. They may get call center service or online guidance, but very little can be profitably personalized. There are other firms that specialize in creating efficient, personalized service for the mass affluent. Regardless of the service level, the products aimed at the mass affluent tend toward relatively clean, if not trivially simple, products.

TABLE 12.2 Base Segmentation for Retirement Income

	Mass Market $W < \$250,000$	Mass Affluent $\$250,000 < W < \$2$ Million	High Net Worth $\$2$ Million $< W < \$10$ Milllion	Ultra-High Net Worth $W > \$10$ Million
Underfunded				
Constrained				
Excess Funding				

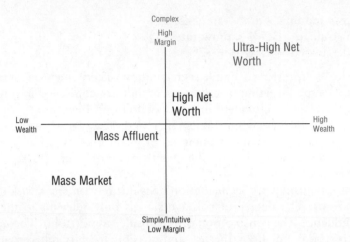

FIGURE 12.2 Stylized Description of Products by Client Type

Many of the largest firms focus on the high-net-worth and ultra-high-net-worth clients, with the higher margin complex products pushed toward the ultra-high-net-worth clients. For many of the big name firms, with high overhead and large sales-support forces, this is really the only client base that they want to service. Members of these groups are often pushed toward becoming registered investors. Once registered, the suitability requirements are lowered and both the client and the firm are freer to engage in more esoteric transaction types.

Figure 12.3 uses the same axes to show stylistically how to place specific products along the axes of client wealth and profit margin. Here, products are placed in the context of target market and the gross margin contained in the products.

While an imperfect guide, Figure 12.4 puts together the products by their client lifestyle cohort—that is, where the products combine with the lifestyles and the wealth of the clients. The underfunded clients have the fewest choices, while the simple lifestyle clients are unconstrained in their choices. The picture is meant to be illustrative rather than definitive.

For the simple client with a simple lifestyle, the financial world is their oyster. Little is out of reach; desire is a different issue. For the constrained lifestyle, the choices are somewhat but not severely limited. Unlike the simple case where all was feasible if not desirable, for the constrained case that which is desirable may not be feasible. This constraint becomes more severe for the underfunded case. In the underfunded case, the appropriate product choices become even more constrained; fewer options are available for meeting the lifestyle needs of the client.

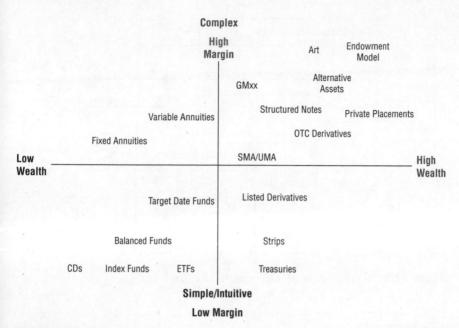

FIGURE 12.3 Product Overlay

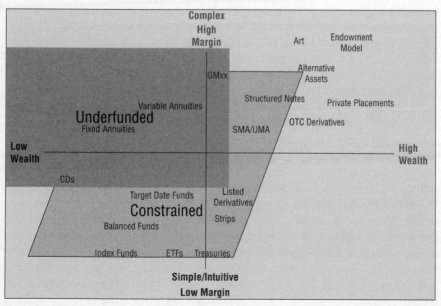

FIGURE 12.4 Products, Lifestyles, and Wealth

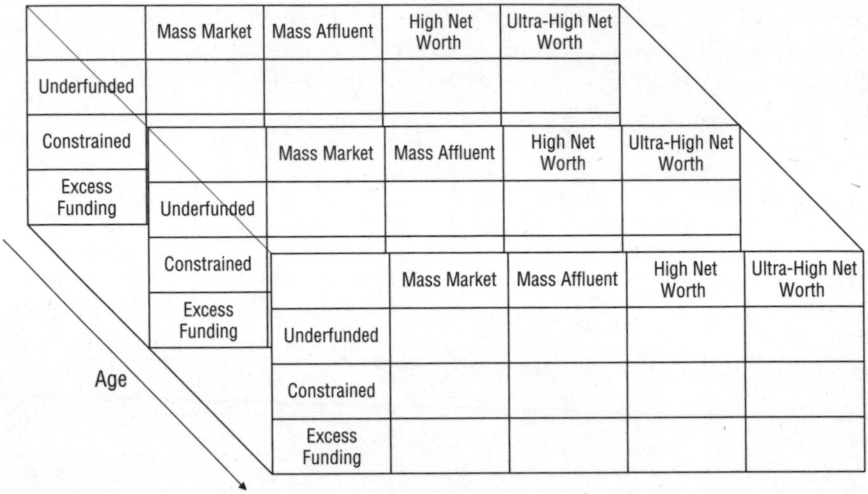

	Mass Market	Mass Affluent	High Net Worth	Ultra-High Net Worth
Underfunded				
Constrained				
Excess Funding				

(Second layer)

	Mass Market	Mass Affluent	High Net Worth	Ultra-High Net Worth
Underfunded				
Constrained				
Excess Funding				

(Third layer)

	Mass Market	Mass Affluent	High Net Worth	Ultra-High Net Worth
Underfunded				
Constrained				
Excess Funding				

Age

FIGURE 12.5   Segmentation by Lifestyle, Wealth, and Age

The two-dimensional representation in Figure 12.4 is useful but incomplete. If followed naively, it would lead to unsatisfying dilemmas where a 40-year-old could be shown fewer options than a 65-year-old. Looking beyond the base two-dimensional segmentation, the third dimension for segmentation is age. Even for a 40-year-old client categorized as underfunded today and probably to remain underfunded forever, the adviser may be confident that the pipe will lead to an annuity; but a portfolio heavily weighted to laddered treasury strips may be more satisfying to the client, leave options open, and ease the likely transition.

Figure 12.5 provides a picture for what has been discussed over the course of the book. As individuals age, they may transition within the same wealth/lifestyle box or migrate to different wealth and lifestyle combinations.

The cube in Figure 12.5 is not quite as daunting as the picture would indicate. There may be some migration into different categories by clients; but for most clients age differences imply allocation differences rather than wholly separate portfolios. The challenge that the remaining firms in the industry will face will be to fill the cube with as *few* portfolios as possible. Filling the cube means matching products and guidance to be somewhat seamless across the wealth and funding ability dimension and sensibly consistent by client age groups. In my view, this is the area where the industry has fallen flat. Most of the current product-oriented approaches to retirement income are in the form of a magic-bullet product that is supposed to solve every problem simultaneously. These product solutions typically involve abrupt and dramatic changes in portfolios that clients do not find compelling. The task is to create portfolios that evolve without requiring a spasmodic revolution.

SUMMARY

Traditional accumulation portfolios rely on a segmentation designed to differentiate based on the amount of volatility that the client is willing to tolerate. Low-volatility or volatility-reduction schemes are, by themselves, insufficient for retirement income portfolios. They don't appreciably lower the probability of drowning, but they increase the probability that if drowning occurs, it will be in a shallower pool.

Segmentation for retirement income rests in one dimension on the observable level of client wealth relative to the present value of the client's desired lifestyle. The other dimension for client segmentation in retirement income is the easily observable age of the client. Mapping products into the segmentation structure then becomes a straightforward and natural process.

CHAPTER 13

Products and Example Portfolios

Objectives

Provide a categorization of products by type

Provide example portfolios for the commonly served segments

Show examples of how the product choices tend to change by segments

Whenever advisers get together, the discussion eventually gets around to two topics: specific portfolio constructions and compensation structures. Here we'll stick to our knitting and limit the topic to portfolio constructions. Whether discussing asset classes, fund families, fund managers, or individual securities, the conversation about portfolio construction helps advisers share pointers about what is working best at the time.

For retirement income, we want to follow in the spirit of a discussion about construction with specific client types in mind. Both the techniques and products are a little different for retirement portfolios, so we begin with an overview of product types and how they fit into a retirement income framework. We also present a ballpark way to estimate the requirements to help you manage the client's expectations. Finally, we move on to a rather lengthy list of example portfolios that should help you to create portfolios, each with appeal to specific subgroups of your clients. We show examples for appeal to different wealth levels, different lifestyles, and for different age groups.

OVERVIEW OF PRODUCTS OFFERED

This section is intended to provide a view inside the toolkit that we use for our sample portfolios. In the current marketplace, there are both modular products and bundled products.

Functional Definitions

For our purposes, products are defined and categorized by their functions:

- *Flooring products.* Flooring products have this property: They guarantee to pay at least $X per period for at least Y periods. Some amount of credit risk is permissible, but the guarantee is what makes it a floor. Flooring is the basis for protecting lifestyle. Products that do not specify a guaranteed minimum payment do not protect the level of lifestyle. Products that do not guarantee payment for at least a minimum length of time do not guarantee a protected lifestyle through time. Products that do not meet either or both requirements may be fine for decumulation of discretionary funds but they are not sufficient for what can reasonably be described as securing lifestyle.
- *Longevity protection.* Longevity protection is important because an individual's life expectancy is an average for life spans and there is a substantial probability of surviving past the date of life expectancy, possibly by decades. In our definition, longevity protection provides flooring protection for an uncertain lifetime. There are flooring products that embed longevity protection, but longevity protection may also encompass a method, as mentioned previously, and not just a product. We split out flooring products from longevity products partially to highlight their importance and partially to recognize that longevity products are but one method of dealing with the risk.
- *Precautionary holdings.* Precautionary holdings are meant to cover unexpected and immediate needs. They need to be liquid enough to access instantaneously and safe enough to be considered a ready store of dry powder. They may be held for both defensive and offensive reasons.
- *Upside.* In a sense, we could define upside as that which is not flooring, longevity protection, or precautionary balances. But it is preferable to think of upside as the risky subportfolio that is generally close in spirit and construction to accumulation portfolios. In the absence of needing a floor, lifestyle protection, and precautionary balances, we would be back in the traditional world of Markowitz. Upside is where aspiration resides subject to risk tolerance.

Basic Building Blocks

Table 13.1 is a listing of product types for basic flooring. Table 13.2 provides a listing of basic product types for longevity protection. Table 13.3

TABLE 13.1 Basic Flooring Product Types

Product	Comments
Government bonds	Safe and liquid, but generated income may not be needed prior to retirement.
Treasury principal strips	Solid and highly liquid. No credit risk. Very easy to string together for an even floor out to 30 years.
TIPS	Risk-free real flooring—no credit risk, increases in principal tied to CPI (urban, not seasonally adjusted, three-month lag)
Savings bonds	Sold direct to retail, not tradable. No credit risk.
Noncallable corporate debt	May include corporate bonds and corporate zero-coupon bonds. These products contain credit risk, so they are less costly than government issues.
Municipal debt	Municipal securities have federal tax exemption, but usually contain credit risk
Annuities	Contain credit risk and mortality credits that make the flooring less costly than government securities. Most annuities include longevity protection.
Guaranteed minimum structured products	Structures may be used for flooring, but are generally short dated. With structured products care is required when choosing since most are topical punts, better for upside, rather than the guaranteed payments required for flooring.
Risky asset + derivative	Risky assets may be used as flooring when combined with direct hedges, that is, no basis risk. This often works for clients who have concentrated stock positions that want to liquidate over time.

TABLE 13.2 Longevity Protection Product Types

Product	Comments
Annuities	Annuities that provide lifetime payments have embedded longevity insurance.
Deferred annuities	Provide longevity insurance for coupling with finite-length capital markets floors.
Long-term (LT) care insurance	Though not longevity insurance strictly speaking, LT care insurance is more important for those who achieve longevity. Ironically, it is often those who are healthiest at retirement who end up needing long-term care.
Longevity insurance	A pure-play bullet payment on longevity. Not widely provided at present time.

TABLE 13.3 Precautionary Assets

Product	Comments
Treasury bills	Short dated, ultra liquid, and no credit risk.
Insured bank deposits	Short dated and ultra liquid. In the event of bank failure, the only potential problem is the extremely rare event of waiting for the FDIC to settle. Depending on form of deposit may be required waiting period and/or penalty for early withdrawal.
Insured money market deposit accounts	Short dated and ultra liquid. Withdrawal notification period may be contained.

provides a listing of basic product types for precautionary assets. Table 13.4 provides a listing of basic product types for upside assets. All of the tables break out a few specific product subclasses due to their special topical interest for retirement income. This listing is not intended as a full catalog of specific products and no endorsements are intended.

Bundled Products Directed at the Retirement Market

All products decompose into simpler instruments. Often firms will want to take the simpler instruments and combine them into bundles that can be sold for their appeal as "one-stop" products. Table 13.5 provides a listing of bundled products commonly proposed for use in retirement portfolios.

There are many products offered in the retirement market that attempt to serve purposes of both flooring and upside. On the producer side the lure to try to find the magic bullet that serves all of the retiree's financial needs is substantial. The simplest of these bundled products is the variable annuity. Variable annuities are contracts that are simple combinations of fixed annuities with mutual funds.

The decomposition of variable annuities is straightforward. A fixed annuity that offers fair-market yields but is deferred will sell essentially with a discount as a forward starting bond. By charging par, the amount Par—Deferred annuity value can be placed in a subaccount fund. The payout that a client will receive will be the yield on the fixed annuity plus the market value of a fraction of the subaccount, where the fraction of the subaccount that is liquidated is based on life expectancy. Voilà, the client has a product that bundles floor and upside.

The variable annuity construct has appeal and is a viable product. Objectively it faces two hurdles that stand in the way of ubiquity: credit risk and inflexibility between the flooring and upside allocations. Insurance

TABLE 13.4 Upside Assets

Product	Comments
SMA/UMA	Upside may be completely bundled in a separate or separately managed portfolio.
Investment companies	Both open- and closed-end mutual funds, UITs, ETFs, and other investment companies subject to the Investment Company Act of 1940.
UITs, ETFs	These investment companies are somewhat special because they have a static or algorithmic construction that makes them both lower cost and more widely eligible for accounts where self-dealing is prohibited.
Target date funds	Combination of stock funds with bond funds that rebalance through time to a higher weighting on the bond component. They are balanced funds that evolve to become more conservative.
Managed payout funds	Funds that follow a planned disbursement schedule. This may be a preferred option for a retiree with a desire to draw down their upside portfolio on a fixed schedule. Less a product then a distribution mechanism for upside.
Structured products and notes	These are generally sold as topical derivative and enhanced yield products for clients. In note form, the embedded derivatives skirt past the need for a signed options agreement.
Fixed income securities	These can be used in an upside portfolio either as a stabilizer (highly rated debt) or as a speculative component (below investment grade).
Equity claims	Historically, equity is the strategic bedrock of an upside portfolio.
Currencies	These often serve as a way to take temporary or speculative bets on relative currency values.
Commodities	These often serve as a way to take temporary or speculative bets on a particular subclass of commodities: energy, metals, or agricultural products. While recently popular, there is no credible academic evidence of enhanced long-term portfolio performance or risk reduction obtained by using commodities.
Derivatives	Can be used for both speculative and hedging purposes within a carefully monitored portfolio. Many options and futures are highly liquid and trade with relative depth.
Unregistered securities	Generally only found in portfolios of registered investors, these securities generally offer higher expected return as compensation for liquidity premia. Often it is useful to think of the buyer of an unregistered security as being long an asset and short a recession put (when liquidity dries up).

(Continued)

TABLE 13.4   (*Continued*)

Product	Comments
Partnerships	Particularly in limited liability form, these are often popular components of the portfolios of registered investors.
Real estate	This may be comprised of formal components of a financial portfolio (e.g., REITs), or as an informal component (e.g., secondary housing).
Hedge funds	The greatest value of these funds is when they provide access to a class of trades that individual investors cannot obtain directly (e.g., credit trading). The frontier enhancement often claimed by sales-oriented organizations is something that has yet to be rigorously scrutinized.
Business ownership	Direct ownership is often a source of pride, accomplishment, sustenance, identity, and enslavement. While some are happy to sell on retirement, many will continue engagement as long as possible.
Marketable art Gems and precious metals Numismatic and philatelic items Other monetizable collectibles	A passion for some, real assets provide both financial return and usually more meaningful consumption return. They provide mostly enjoyment and offer less as pure investments. Assets with higher consumption return, over the long run, will have lower financial return. Financial performance trades off with enjoyment. With these assets, pure financial return is not a reason to include them in a portfolio. But for the aficionado they can provide a wonderful way to obtain psychological upside and remain engaged during retirement.

companies have made efforts to offer a wide variety of mutual funds as part of the variable annuity bundle. Variable annuities can be a great complement to retirement income portfolios for a wide variety of clients; but, in practice, it is rare that they are the sole product for the client's needs.

GMAB, GMIB, and GMWB products are generally offshoots of the variable annuity construct offering a put option as protection on the payouts or value of the subaccount. The idea behind all of the GMxx's was that the weakness of the variable annuity was in its market exposure. The cost of such guarantees is discussed in Chapter 15. To understand these products it is easiest to focus on their decomposition as Annuity + Mutual fund + Long put.

Many capital markets financial advisers do not like to sell insurance-related products. Depending on the adviser's compensation structure, they are either considered dead money or assets that have gone away. Insurance

TABLE 13.5 Combined Flooring/Upside Products

Product	Comments
Variable annuities	Annuities with embedded mutual funds. Generally offering a wide array of fund choices. Payout is typically a minimum value plus a percentage of the attached subaccount (fund).
GMABs	Guaranteed minimum accumulation benefits. Variable annuities with embedded guarantees on performance of the subaccount over some horizon. Roughly, Annuity + Fund + Long-in-the-money put.
GMIBs	Guaranteed minimum income benefits. Variable annuities with embedded guarantees on payments regardless of the performance of the subaccount once payment starts. Roughly, Annuity + Fund + Long-in-the-money put.
GMWBs	Guaranteed minimum withdrawal benefits. Variable annuities with embedded guarantees on payments that cannot fall once payment starts. Roughly, Annuity + Fund + Long forward starting the lookback put.
Insurance-wrapped portfolios	Relatively new idea that attempts to detach the management of the insurance from the management of the underlying assets. The idea is to allow advisers to keep assets under management with the insurance funding the only part that "goes away."

wrappers are an attempt to circumvent the problem of "lost" assets. With the insurance wrap, a client can keep their familiar portfolio while enjoying the benefits of a GMxx-type structure. To the adviser, other than the insurance premiums, the assets remain in place. The client who engages in a wrap does assume some measure of credit risk and possible constraints on trading.

The set of basic products shown in Table 13.5 can be used to construct myriad types of retirement income portfolios.

A Note on Reverse Mortgages

The topic of reverse mortgages comes up quite often. With a reverse mortgage a homeowner receives payments for the remainder of life and is allowed to remain in the home; in exchange the issuer of the reverse mortgage receives the value of the home upon death. The three aspects that make this interesting are longevity, timing of cash flows, and incentives.

Since the issuer of the reverse mortgage is providing income for life, a reverse mortgage should be considered as a type of fixed-payment immediate annuity. Reverse mortgages almost always offer payment for life so the longevity risk is borne by the writer just as with a life annuity. However, unlike a typical annuity, the writer receives payment at the back end of the trade, upon death of the homeowner.

The third aspect that makes reverse mortgages interesting is what is termed the incentive effect. While the homeowner will have an incentive to keep the structure safe and minimally habitable, there will be no incentive to make improvements or provide nonstructural upkeep within salable standards. The combination of potential longevity and the incentive effect means that the valuation of the home by the writer of the reverse mortgage will be pushed toward the actuarial present value of the land without the structure.

To make a comparison that is relevant to the homeowner one should compare the purchase of an annuity funded by an outright sale of the home with an annuity offered through a reverse mortgage. The homeowner should also be clearly notified about any clauses that may be contained in the contract about maintenance, insurance, inspections, or other constraints.

For a client with a strong or overwhelming desire to remain in "their own house," a reverse mortgage may be a good solution; but there are aspects that make reverse mortgages a product that needs to be handled carefully.

MANAGING EXPECTATIONS AROUND OUTCOMES

To provide a little more flavor to the discussion of allocating to flooring, the following example is presented. Table 13.6 shows the cost of securing $10,000 in flooring purchased at the age given in the left column. The flooring in all three columns runs from age 65 to 100. Three columns labeled 5%, 6%, and 7% are presented. These three columns are meant to roughly—very roughly—illustrate the cost of the flooring stream using Treasury strips (5%), corporate bonds (6%), and an insurance annuity (7%). One can read this as the risk-free cost (Treasury), the credit-risk cost (corporate), and the credit-risk-plus-mortality-credits cost (annuity). As one can see, the cost of flooring rises dramatically as the client ages. It should also be noted that the relative difference in flooring costs declines through time.

This table illustrates the possibilities, but it requires some work to put into effect. While there are insurance companies that will sell deferred annuities for such a purpose, creating a floor using corporate bonds or

TABLE 13.6 Present Values of $10,000 Nominal
Payment Streams by Discount Rate and Age
at Purchase

Age at Purchase	Cost Per $10,000K Annual Payment; Stream from Age 65–100 Nominal Values, 0% Anticipated Inflation		
	5%	6%	7%
30	$31,169	$19,995	$12,976
35	$39,781	$26,757	$18,200
40	$50,771	$35,808	$25,526
45	$64,798	$47,919	$35,801
50	$82,701	$64,126	$50,213
55	$105,550	$85,815	$70,427
60	$134,711	$114,840	$98,777
65	$171,929	$153,681	$138,540

Treasury strips would require stacking up a large number of bonds at the furthest practical end of the available curve, 30 years out, and then rolling some of those bonds out to cover the needed dates when the tradable curve marches out sufficiently to cover those dates. The procedure of stacking and rolling is easy to do, but it does require a commitment to future action.

EXAMPLE PORTFOLIOS

The goal now is to present a brief catalog of example portfolios to provide an idea of ways to address different client types and to provoke thought about how to tailor some of the examples for a particular client service practice. The outline presented here follows the segmentation material presented in Chapter 12. Many samples are provided below for each of four wealth categories:

1. Mass market
2. Mass affluent
3. High net worth
4. Ultra-high net worth

We cover the following three sets of lifestyles:

1. Simple lifestyle
2. Constrained lifestyle
3. Underfunded lifestyle

For many of the portfolios, we also distinguish with separate examples those clients who are at the point of retirement from those who are still in the process of accumulating and planning for retirement.

First, to get the most out of these examples, you are best served if you read all of the neighbors rather than simply the exact match for the wealth and lifestyle of any particular client. Second, the goal in presenting these examples is to focus on the retirement income part of construction that differs from accumulation. This book is about helping clients and extending your business model without upsetting the entire framework that you have been using thus far.

The Mass Market as a Group (Financial Wealth <$250,000)

The mass-market category includes a vast number of Americans in a variety of occupations. Some are low earners who are nonetheless thrifty, some have done well but faced one of life's harder knocks, while others have higher wages but are profligate consumers. For one reason or another they have insufficient financial wealth to combine with their Social Security income to have their net retirement income rise much above the poverty level. For those who own their own homes, this is less dire than it may sound, but this is the group that needs to budget carefully and avoid surprises.

As a group the mass market tends to favor simple, no-frills solutions that have a higher probability of success. Low-cost solutions that seem somewhat risky will generally be less preferred than higher-cost solutions that have a long track record of performance. In short, this is a group that will pay the price to stick with tried-and-true solutions. The gravitation for the mass market is often characterized by certificates of deposit, fixed annuities, and low-cost mutual funds.

Example 1: Mass Market—One Choice   For many people, the fact is that they were unable to save much over their working lives. Many will feel compelled to continue working long past their legal retirement age. Social Security is pegged at roughly two-thirds of the level of income defined as the poverty level. For people with little put away to supplement their Social Security, the choice is whether to apply the funds to flooring or upside.

Generally for this group the choice is between the following:

1. Fixed immediate annuity
2. Mutual fund (either intermediate-term bond or equity-income fund)

Capital Markets   Generally, an equity income mutual fund that provides *some* income and *some* potential upside seems to be the preferred mass-market solution. Having the dividends paid out and capital gains reinvested provides some stable funding and a small measure of progress. Gauging the client risk tolerance properly is important and a bond fund may be preferable. The income-generating capability on $50,000 will generally be a couple of hundred dollars per month for the bond fund and a couple of hundred dollars per quarter for the equity fund.

Insurance   Another possibility is a fixed immediate-start annuity. For a client who owns around $50,000 in assets, an annuity may provide a few hundred dollars a month in supplemental income.

Annuities are popular for specific groups, but without sufficient funds to keep as precautionary assets, people may feel boxed in.

It's very difficult to base a practice on the mass market, but the value of your services to the mass market is often magnified by the fact that small differences in portfolio choice can have a large impact on the well-being of mass-market clients.

The Mass Affluent as a Group ($250,000 < Financial Wealth < $2 Million)

The mass-affluent category incorporates many small business owners, but it is predominantly made up of white-collar professionals. The bulk of the group includes managers, educators, lawyers, accountants, and most financial professionals. This is the group for whom the retirement income portfolio begins to resemble a bond plus call. That is not meant in the literal sense—that would be hideously expensive. It is meant that figuratively the shape we seek is floor plus upside; this would resemble the payoff of a bond plus call construct. The differences across portfolios are in what is used to comprise the floor portion and what is used to construct the upside.

The mass affluent are generally one step away from parents of more moderate means. As a rule, they grew up in houses that are smaller than the ones in which they now live. They know where they came from and they don't want to go back. They are often well educated but lack the fearlessness required for entrepreneurial undertakings;[1] as a rule they ascribe to the dictum that it is better to consistently hit singles than to swing for home runs and strike out. They often retain the fear of falling back to the mass market and ending up losing ground. But they are often able to separate their intellectual from their visceral feelings. They generally have the capability to understand simple financial products and portfolio constructs. They prefer products that they feel they can understand and processes that they feel they can influence.

While too many have portfolios that are overweight with company stock, the mass affluent generally participate in well-diversified retirement plans, hold portfolios outside of the retirement "umbrella," and are amenable to value-added products such as variable annuities and managed mutual funds.

Example 2: Mass Affluent—Simple Lifestyle at Point of Retirement   We've loosely defined the simple lifestyle as having flooring needs relative to wealth below 3.5 percent. There may be rare instances where it is not possible to have a yield-based portfolio achieving 3.5 percent without drawdown, but it is generally possible. For a simple lifestyle, the main difference between the mass affluent and the high net worth is the desire and tolerance for sophisticated products.

For the mass affluent who have simple lifestyles, the two options that seemingly resonate best are the following:

1. Yield-based capital markets portfolio with upside potential.
2. Annuity/variable annuity at the level of needs plus precautionary balances and maybe a small upside portfolio geared toward risk taking.

Capital Markets   With a simple lifestyle, the yield-based portfolio needs to be robust enough to survive downturns that may persist. The yield must be coupled with preservation of principal or there should be a fallback plan to lock in flooring in the event of a major market catastrophe. Since they are by definition overfunded, they can bear a shock that may impact their financial plans without impacting their retirement lifestyle plans.

Insurance   On the other side of the coin, an annuity or variable annuity with a minimum withdrawal (even one that does not ratchet) coupled with a separate upside portfolio may provide mass-affluent clients with a preferred bifurcated solution. This solution is appealing because, even though the lifestyle is simple, splitting funding of needs from the bulk of aspirational wealth allows a more confident posture for handling market cycles.

Example 3: Mass Affluent—Constrained Lifestyle with a Transition   We've defined the constrained lifestyle as having flooring needs relative to wealth between 3.5 percent and 7 percent. It is almost always the case that for this group, wealth will be drawn down over retirement. However, by starting early and having a transition, this group will be able to retire comfortable and securely. This group may comprise the bread and butter of your practice.

Generally, for this group, although many options are available, the two that resonate best seem to be the following:

1. Capital markets floor coupled with longevity protection, precautionary cash balances, and an upside portfolio. As the client increments the portfolio with annual contributions, the proportions are held constant.
2. Annuity/variable annuity/GMxx at the level of needs plus precautionary balances and maybe a small upside portfolio geared towards risk taking.

Capital Markets   For the capital markets solution, the following two tables illustrate the cost of basic flooring. Table 13.7 shows the rough cost for each $10,000 in required flooring under different allowances for anticipated inflation. This first table is most useful for the client who knows how much they want to live on and wants to get an idea of how much it will cost to secure their lifestyle.

Note that in all cases shown in Table 13.7, the entries are increasing with age up to age 65 and decreasing thereafter. Ages 70 and 75 are lower because the flooring will begin to roll off as the remaining years dwindle.

TABLE 13.7 Incorporating Inflation Expectations into the Cost of Flooring Based on Age at Purchase (cost per $10,000 annual payment from age 65 until age 90 at 5% discount rate)

		Anticipated Inflation	
Age at Purchase	Nominal Value	2%	3%
30	$26,828	$65,418	$102,226
35	$34,241	$75,621	$112,544
40	$43,701	$87,416	$123,903
45	$55,775	$101,050	$136,409
50	$71,184	$116,810	$150,177
55	$90,851	$135,029	$165,334
60	$115,951	$156,089	$182,022
65	$147,986	$180,434	$200,393
70	$130,853	$153,987	$167,630
75	$108,986	$123,415	$131,560

Generally, the earlier that a client's portfolio can be refocused toward retirement income, the easier it will be to make their lifestyle secure. From the examples in Table 13.7, we can see $10,000 of nominal flooring covering ages 65 to 90 would cost a 30-year-old $26,828. For a 35-year-old who anticipates a 2 percent inflation rate over the horizon, each $10,000 of flooring that grows at the 2 percent anticipated inflation rate will cost $75,621. As the gap between nominal yields and anticipated inflation shrinks, there is less direct rate of return advantage to locking in early; there is no free lunch. The nonreturn advantage, which may still be a very real client preference, is a way of reducing lifestyle risk. Although it is not shown in the table, if there is a risk of high inflation that the client is unwilling to bear, then flooring with TIPS will provide a high degree of inflation protection.

Table 13.8 shows similar information but conveyed differently. It shows the required allocation to flooring per 1 percent of wealth that the floor represents. For example, the allocation required to floor at 1 percent of current wealth is 2.68 percent. This means that for a 50-year-old creating a floor of 4 percent of then-current wealth would require an allocation of 28.48 percent (4 × 7.12%). Feasible flooring allocations must add up to less than 100 percent. However, once flooring allocations exceed 60 percent, it doesn't leave much room for the other components of a retirement income portfolio.

TABLE 13.8 Percentage of Portfolio Allocation to Flooring Required Per 1 Percent of Wealth Yielded (allocation to flooring per 1% of initial wealth; payment age 65 until age 90)

Age at Purchase	Nominal Value	Anticipated Inflation	
		2%	3%
30	2.68%	6.54%	10.22%
35	3.42%	7.56%	11.25%
40	4.37%	8.74%	12.39%
45	5.58%	10.10%	13.64%
50	7.12%	11.68%	15.02%
55	9.09%	13.50%	16.53%
60	11.60%	15.61%	18.20%
65	14.80%	18.04%	20.04%
70	13.09%	15.40%	16.76%
75	10.90%	12.34%	13.16%

Each entry in Table 13.8 shows, in terms of the percentage of initial wealth, the cost of creating a 1 percent yield stream covering ages 65 to 90. The columns represent how the flows will differ to keep the inflation-adjusted flow constant per 1 percent of initial wealth. The different rows represent cost differences for clients by age at time of purchase.

Suppose that for our example here the client is a 50-year-old who would like a floor at 5 percent of current wealth. The client would like to be prepared for a 2 percent average inflation rate. For this client, using our 5 percent assumed discount rate applied to flooring, the allocation required would be 58.4% = 5 × 11.68%. Longevity protection would be expected to cost another 3 percent.[2] With 10 percent set aside in precautionary balances, the subportfolio for upside assets would have an allocation of 28.6 percent.

With regard to location, the flooring needs to be in a tax-advantaged retirement account. If the precautionary funds can accrue interest, either tax-deferred (IRA) or tax-free (Roth IRA), that is the best location. The upside portfolio benefits less from residing in a tax-advantaged account since it will likely consist of capital gains and dividend producing instruments. The longevity protection comes with an automatic tax deferral as an insurance product; and deferred annuities have their own headaches in tax-deferred accounts, so it is usually best to locate the longevity protection in a taxable account.

Insurance For clients who transition later in their life, or have higher ratios of their lifestyle expenses to wealth, insurance will start to be a preferred solution. As lifestyle costs rise relative to wealth, it becomes harder to support lifestyle and retain exposure to upside without at least a partial monetization of one's mortality.

Instead of a capital markets solution, the client may want to opt for a flooring solution that takes greater advantage of mortality credits. Mass-affluent clients often find the value-added features of variable annuities and GMxx's to be attractive. While there is some evidence that annuity solutions tend to be most popular in the first market downturn after retirement,[3] the pricing of market-linked annuity solutions can make them attractive components of retirement income portfolios prior to retirement. As with all flooring, the overriding concerns are stability and security. This means that a significant portion of clients may be happiest ameliorating credit risk with fixed annuities from more than one source.

A benefit of insurance-based flooring is that it almost always contains longevity protection as part of the package. This means that on top of the insurance-based floor, the adviser needs only to think about creating precautionary balances and, to the extent not included in the annuity, upside.

Precautionary reserves need to be higher as a greater portion of the portfolio is embedded in insurance products. Insurance is a contractual asset rather than a traded asset. This means that insurance can be somewhat more constraining and harder to unwind in part or in whole. Precautionary reserves are there in part to avoid having to make costly changes to other parts of the portfolio. We use a baseline of 10 percent for precautionary reserves. Once the allocation of insurance products in the portfolio crosses 50 percent, a ballpark rule of thumb is to increase precautionary reserves by 2 percent for each 10 percent increase in the allocation to insurance. This means that if the allocation to insurance rises to 60 percent, then the precautionary balances would rise to 12 percent (i.e., $10\% + 2(60\% - 50\%)$).

While insurance companies have made great efforts to create products that allow clients to cross the financial spectrum, they are still primarily viewed as, well, insurance companies. This, even in the absence of credit risk, often makes pure insurance solutions a tough sell. Of course, many of the insurance companies have affiliates, subsidiaries, or revenue agreements with fund families. This generally makes it possible for an affiliated insurance representative to offer and provide a unified portfolio view.

Example 4: Mass Affluent—Constrained Lifestyle at the Point of Retirement

For the mass affluent who wait until the point of retirement before transitioning their portfolios to a retirement income posture, the options dwindle. The constrained lifestyle is defined here as lifestyle cost to wealth ratios covering the range from 3.5 percent to 7 percent. At point of retirement both capital markets–based flooring and insurance-based flooring are still feasible. However, the capital markets solutions become less attractive as the flooring allocation begins to preclude allocating sufficient funds for a meaningful upside subportfolio.

Our goals for retirement income are to create secure flooring for maintenance of lifestyle plus retain the ability to take aspirational risks. The richer solutions take both of the factors into consideration in a balanced fashion. Point of retirement portfolios for the constrained class of mass affluent tend to skew more toward combination flooring and upside products. The adviser should be aware that there may be cyclical aspects to preferences over types of annuities. During robust markets variable annuities that link to capital markets are likely to be more popular than in down markets when market fears may skew preferences toward fixed annuities.[4]

In general, the insurance-based flooring dominates the pure capital markets solutions when creating retirement income at point of retirement.[5] In this case insurance-based flooring can liberate funds for upside exposure. This transformation is not free of course. It means that the client needs to be willing to monetize their mortality. However, there may be personal reasons like dependent children or shortened life expectancy that make insurance a less attractive solution for this group.

If there is personal information that the expected life will be considerably shorter than average, then it is reasonable to do without longevity protection. If other reasons combine to make insurance undesirable for a particular client, then it is still technically feasible to create a capital markets solution. Capital markets products have the added benefit in this case because they can be quickly liquidated if new information creates a desire for spending down more quickly.

For this client, simple Treasury strips, although expensive relative to instrument with credit risk, are highly liquid and easy to blitz quickly. If the flooring need is less than 5 percent of wealth, then there is still about 30 percent left over for precautionary balances and upside. For the upside in this case, much will depend on the personality of the client. With limited allocation to upside, the client may desire to take more risk and may even desire a consumption benefit from more active transactions. The other end of the spectrum is that a client may have a plan in mind for use of the funds allocated to limited upside and will tend toward more conservatism. In any case, the client's preferences quickly become clear.

Example 5: Mass Affluent—Underfunded Lifestyle with a Transition

Underfunded lifestyles come in two types—the temporary and the permanent. Everyone is underfunded as a child and generally while in school. The permanently underfunded lifestyle is more prevalent after age 30 when lifestyles and earnings capacity begin to stabilize. With the occasional exception, these are the people who have a very low rate of saving that stays low even when their income rises. In general, for these people starting early provides some latitude in creating solutions, but not all that much.

For an underfunded preretirement lifestyle, the small latitude that remains means that there is still an opportunity for upside; but here is a case where combination products dominate. By starting early enough, all of the combinations of variable annuities or GMxx's are feasible. With an underfunded lifestyle, the client needs to recognize that lifestyle security can be purchased, but at the cost of monetizing mortality and yielding control of their assets.[6] The choice set is constrained; but an earlier start helps to collar the client both in terms of your ability to secure his or her lifestyle and expectations for retirement.[7]

One possibility is that at preretirement the client can be shown the flooring costs and given a target to aim for. In the preretirement phase, there are some, when shown the amount of flooring that they can currently purchase and at what cost, whose saving behavior may be favorably affected. Don't expect miracles. However, for certain clients, a feasible endpoint can become a goal. Like an athletic coach, you may be able to motivate your client to alter the current course and final outcome.

Example 6: Mass Affluent—Underfunded Lifestyle at Point of Retirement For an underfunded lifestyle at the point of retirement, what little latitude there was is gone. For some, this will mean delaying retirement. For others, it will mean a secure lifestyle and little more. The better off—that is, the less underfunded—can still lock in a floor with a fixed ratio of upside such as a variable annuity. With a variable annuity, the excess that is available each year will vary with the performance of the subaccount. For those affected by the constraint at the extreme, a fixed annuity will be the only feasible solution.

High Net Worth as a Group ($2 Million < Financial Wealth < $10 Million)

The majority of high-net-worth individuals are not legacies. Many come from the ranks of the professionally educated. But the real glue that seems to bind this group is an entrepreneurial spirit, meaning optimism, self-confidence, and, in some cases, a willingness to take risk. Unlike the mass affluent, for whom the need of security trumps the desire for striking out in a new direction, the high-net-worth client may have seemingly identical backgrounds but strikingly different outlooks and far less fear.

It is not useful to speculate on whether the high-net-worth client's rewards owe more to luck or skill. The image that many hold of high-net-worth individuals is that they have made it and have no worries. Unfortunately, this is not the case. As wealth rises, lifestyles tend to rise. What we end up with is the same trichotomy of types for the high net worth as for the other groups: simple, constrained, underfunded. The things that differ between groups are the products pitched and the products desired.

The product desires differ for the high-net-worth individuals primarily because their time is more valuable. Such clients don't always want to delegate, but many must delegate their financial affairs in order to concentrate on their true interests. Just as dairy farmers may love their lifestyles but be chained to their farms, the entrepreneur or skilled professional is often similarly rewarded and tethered. They are much more likely to be interested in wrap accounts and other managed solutions than the mass affluent. They will also be more receptive to enhanced solutions.[8]

For high-net-worth individuals, taxes and the location of assets becomes more important. They almost certainly will have more financial assets than can be contained in tax-deferred and tax-advantaged accounts. They will be much more interested in strategies that recognize and minimize their potential tax liabilities. For many, retirement will keep them in high marginal brackets making municipal securities relatively more attractive. The strategies that work best will include location and may include structured products,[9] vehicles and other solutions that allow for borrowing against assets rather than realizing gains.

In the high-net-worth category intergenerational transfers of wealth also begin to become more of an issue. Uncertainty about the existence and level of estate taxes on death means that this group is generally in the free-fire zone that divides taxed and untaxed estates. One does not need to take political sides on this issue to recognize that whatever the merits of the estate tax, or any tax for that matter, for some avoiding the expected tax payment for any amount less than the potential tax payment will be seen as a worthwhile endeavor.

Example 7: High Net Worth—Simple Lifestyle For the high-net-worth client with a simple lifestyle, both managed portfolios and static yield–based portfolios may be broadly possible. Whether active or passive, this suggests a multiproduct, fee-based package of the unified managed account (UMA) type. The trick, in this case, is not creating the portfolio or doing so in a way that is simple for the advisor to implement, the trick is in having a solution that the client understands and feels confident that it is a wise and appropriate solution.

For a simple lifestyle in a high-net-worth client, the following portfolios are worth considering:

- Yield-based portfolio with a view toward tax-efficient estate transfer
- An actively managed portfolio designed for yield and growth
- Variable annuity/GMxx combined with upside portfolio geared toward aspiration and legacy planning

Capital Markets For the yield-based portfolio, there are a multitude of fixed-income choices that are available for creating sufficient yield appropriate for sufficient yield and the client service required of a high-net-worth client. There are both transactional and fee-based approaches that will be suitable for such clients. A three-layer approach may be the most appealing. The top layer would contain sufficient yield-based instruments for meeting the client's lifestyle needs. The layer below that would be oriented to moderately conservative growth, providing some upside but also a buffer in case of a partial failure of the top layer. The bottom, and thinnest, layer would be more aggressive and might possibly contain more sophisticated instruments or alternative assets.[10] In this layer, having capital gains assets with a basis that will step up upon death may be useful. While on the cusp of estate taxes, this client may benefit from a small, whole-life policy.

Active Management Active management of a portfolio for a high-net-worth client is also a feasible choice. In this case, it is probably worthwhile to set a notional floor well above the hard floor given by the present value of future needs. If the client is paying for active management, he or she probably expects better downside protection. For the high-net-worth client with a simple lifestyle, using a balanced fund as the risky underlying to manage is an attractive option. The balance will diminish portfolio volatility and the fixed-income component will help provide the necessary yield for funding the client's lifestyle. Furthermore, a simple lifestyle usually correlates somewhat with a desire for a portfolio that has greater clarity and intuitiveness.

Insurance Annuitization may also be an attractive option to this type of client. The most popular of the guaranteed products, particularly in this cohort, is the GMWB. The GMWB, funded to provide slightly above an inflation-adjusted floor, may provide comfort to the client and allow more freedom of movement with regard to positioning the remainder of the portfolio for aspirations or legacy planning. If the client perceives the GMxx to be too complex an instrument, then its simpler brethren can be used with equal success. If a fixed annuity is chosen, then an inflation-protected annuity is always preferred.[11]

As always, taxes are important. Locating assets in the proper accounts can have important ramifications. In addition, for those whose postretirement income is sufficiently high that it will keep them in a higher tax bracket, municipal securities will be more important.

Example 8: High Net Worth—Constrained Lifestyle with a Transition As always, we define the constrained lifestyle as having at retirement flooring needs relative to wealth between 3.5 percent and 7 percent. Generally, this group can be counted on to draw down assets. However, starting early and having a transition can help the process by preparing the portfolio and by focusing the client on the need to save for retirement. The constrained group will probably be the largest segment of your business and there is much that you can do to help.

Since they are high-net-worth clients, and there is still plenty of time, this leaves three broad approaches that we can take:

1. Static approach of a capital markets floor coupled with longevity protection, precautionary balances, and an upside portfolio. For many of those, the best description would be to say that they are accumulating in proportion.
2. Actively managed portfolio designed to build up the floor over time through gains and further accumulation.

3. Build up temporary flooring with the purpose of final transition to GMxx; building precautionary balances and maybe a small upside portfolio geared toward risk taking.

Static Capital Markets For the high-net-worth client, a capital markets floor can be built using standard products like treasury strips or in borderline cases a bespoke ladder.[12] For the high-net-worth investor, income is usually high enough to place the client in a high-tax bracket. If at all possible, this should be undertaken in a tax-deferred account or in a Roth IRA. In some limited cases, part of the floor may be sourced by using municipal strips outside of the tax-preferred accounts, but this is not a solution that can be readily relied on and is hard to scale.

Protection against inflation is another important consideration. Inflation does not move all prices in lockstep; but the constrained lifestyle is somewhat sensitive to differences in inflation rates. Since prices do not move in lockstep, clients retain the ability to substitute activities and consumption goods. The ability to substitute goods means that the headline CPI often overstates the impact of inflation. However, overstated does not mean unimportant. Referring back to Table 13.8, we focus on securing against 2 percent inflation.

If our client is a 50-year-old who would like a floor at 5 percent of current wealth, he or she should be prepared for a 2 percent average inflation rate. For this client, using our 5 percent assumed discount rate applied to flooring, the allocation required would be 58.4% = 5 × 11.68%. Longevity protection would be expected to cost another 3 period.[13] With 10 percent set aside in precautionary balances, the upside portfolio would have an allocation of 28.6 percent.

With flooring in place, the high-net-worth client often requires a more complex upside portfolio. The complexity may take the form that requires creating a separately managed subaccount or using more complex products in the portfolio.

At the risk of being repetitive, the flooring needs to be in a tax-advantaged retirement account. If the precautionary funds can accrue interest, either tax-deferred (IRA) or taxed-up-front (Roth IRA) options are the best location. The upside portfolio may need to be in a fully taxable account. Clearly, municipal securities belong in a fully taxable account. The longevity protection comes with an automatic tax deferral as an insurance product, and deferred annuities have eligibility problems in tax-deferred accounts, so it is usually best to locate the longevity protection in a taxable account.

Actively Managed High-net-worth clients are solid candidates for actively managed portfolios. The tightrope to walk here is that simpler underlying assets are easier to actively manage but high-net-worth clients often have an expectation of more complex portfolios. As any Wall Street firm will attest, it is sometimes difficult to actively risk manage in markets where liquidity is dependent on a small number of liquidity providers. It would be very difficult, for example, to actively risk manage a portfolio based on the endowment approach.

On the bright side, a straightforward portfolio protection methodology, overlaying a portfolio of highly varied but liquid asset types, would be quite workable. An underlying portfolio of stocks, bonds, commodities, currencies, and other trading assets would add no complications. The point to be made is that the process is not the issue, choosing the right underlying portfolio is the issue.

Insurance   Insurance-based flooring may be the ultimate destination of the client. However, an accumulation to insurance transition may be too abrupt and jarring for a client. In that case, a detour through a temporary Treasury floor may work well. It is difficult to annuitize early when needs are not estimable with any confidence or clarity. Contractual solutions such as annuities work best when the conditions, under which the contract was entered, prevail as the contract is being honored. The issue is to move the client from accumulation to retirement income. Both a long transition and an intermediate step that keeps options open to achieve the right client solution.[14]

Ultimately, with normal longevity expectations and few dependents, the client may opt for a flooring solution that takes advantage of mortality credits; dependents and possible early death can be addressed with death benefit riders. High-net-worth clients often expect the value-added features that are contained in variable annuities and GMxx's tend to be the most popular versions of these products. There are also insurance wrappers over traditional portfolios that are available and may provide an attractive alternative. Again, since insurance contracts contain credit risk, multiple issuers are preferable to a large, concentrated, single policy.

The insurance-based flooring will most likely embed the longevity protection as part of the insurance contract. Precautionary balances need to be a little larger when there is a greater allocation to insurance. Emergency withdrawals above the contracted maximum annual withdrawal can trigger major resets in GMxx's. Breaching the maximum in a down market may trigger a disastrously lower withdrawal reset.

Aside from the upside contained in the insurance, if not a wrapped contract, the high-net-worth client may have a desire for an additional upside portfolio. The upside that is embedded in the insurance or insurance wrapper will generally be a balanced but vanilla portfolio. Of course, it is dependent on the client's preferences and adviser's practice, but a high-net-worth client may desire to round out the portfolio with nonvanilla products.

The rule we follow is to use a baseline of 10 percent for precautionary reserves, increment by 2 percent for each 10 percent increase in the allocation to insurance-based flooring. This means that if the allocation to insurance rises to 60 percent, then the precautionary balances would rise to 12 percent (i.e., 10% + 2(60% − 50%)).

Example 9: High Net Worth—Constrained Lifestyle at Point of Retirement For the high-net-worth clients who wait until the point of retirement before creating a retirement income plan there are fewer options. As per our usual definition, a constrained lifestyle has lifestyle cost to wealth ratios covering the range from 3.5 percent to 7 percent. At point of retirement, both active and static capital markets–based flooring and insurance-based flooring are still feasible. Whatever the solution the constrained lifestyle coupled with the late-stage planning mean that there will be fewer resources to devote to creating the potential for upside.

Static Capital Markets Without a lot of time to source corporate ladders and municipal strips, at the point of retirement, flooring with Treasury strips is the easiest road to take. If the client balks at the low yield in government securities, it can be truthfully argued that the floor is a place for security and this will afford a greater opportunity for risk taking in the upside portfolio. If those arguments aren't well received, then static capital markets flooring may not be the best bet for the particular client.

Once again, it is important to protect the client against inflation. Whether by using TIPS or creating a floor that steps up, it is important to provide the client with some degree of inflation immunization.

Once the flooring is in place, the constrained high-net-worth client still requires precautionary balances, probably longevity protection, and an upside portfolio. The complexity may take the form of creating a separately managed subaccount or using more complex products in the portfolio.

To return once more to the tax issue, flooring needs to be located in a tax-advantaged account. If the precautionary funds can accrue interest, either tax-deferred (IRA) or tax-free (Roth IRA) options are the best location. The upside portfolio may need to be in a fully taxable account. Clearly, municipal securities belong in a fully taxable account. The longevity protection comes with an automatic tax deferral as an insurance product and deferred annuities have eligibility problems in tax-deferred accounts, so it is usually best to locate the longevity protection in a taxable account.

Actively Managed Even constrained high-net-worth clients are solid candidates for actively managed portfolios. The difference is that there is less room to maneuver as constrained lifestyle manifests itself with a relatively higher floor and less cushion. The art is in choosing the underlying portfolio of risk that will be actively managed. A portfolio constructed of ETFs and traded futures can be made sufficiently rich in structure to provide low volatility and the potential for upside while remaining attractive to the high-net-worth client. Remember, the key to success in active risk management is that the underlying must be liquid enough to be able to neutralize the risk quickly.

Insurance   At point of retirement, insurance-based flooring is often seen as a better solution than capital markets solutions. As insurance company executives like to claim, insurance-based flooring can liberate funds for upside exposure; in this case it is more than mere hype. For the solution to be seen as the right one, the client needs to be willing to monetize their mortality and accept the trade-off of "more if alive in exchange for less if dead too soon." There may be other personal reasons like dependent children or shortened life expectancy that make insurance undesirable for a particular client.

With normal longevity expectations and few dependents, the client may opt for a flooring solution that takes advantage of mortality credits; in many cases dependents and possible early death can be addressed with death benefit riders. High-net-worth clients often prefer the features that are contained in variable annuities and GMxx's. The insurance wrappers over traditional portfolios may provide another alternative. As has been repeated before, insurance contracts contain credit risk so multiple issuers are preferable to a large, concentrated, single policy.

With the constrained lifestyle and late start if an insurance wrapper is chosen, there may be some room for unfettered upside within the account but essentially outside the wrapper. However, if a GMxx is used, there will probably be little left over for a traditional separate upside portfolio.

Example 10: High Net Worth—Underfunded Lifestyle with a Transition   One of the major benefits of an early start is that it allows the opportunity to change behavior thus changing the path and thereby changing the outcome. A client faced with the prospect of a dismal future may take steps toward greater saving and actively work on building up their retirement floor. For many of the self-made, high-net-worth individuals, their attitude and spirit can be awakened by the challenge and they will rise to meet the challenge. In such a case, there may be both static capital markets builds and the full panoply of insurance opportunities.[15] Aside from inducing a higher rate of saving, another avenue is to delay retirement or plan for a partial retirement. A delay or a deferral in retirement can have a dramatic effect on the client's ability to fund the later stages of retirement. To put it in a bond context, a 50-year-old client expecting to retire on the last day of his or her 65th year, and having a level flooring need out to age 90, by delaying retirement by three years, or about 12 percent of the retirement span, the present value of funding costs[16] decline by nearly 20%. This reflects the fact that the early years of retirement take up a greater share of the retirement funding needs.

For those clients who are underfunded and unable to meaningfully alter their situation, the outlook is less rosy. They may end up happily covered by an annuity; but there is little to offer in the way of alternatives if they are not amenable to insurance solutions. With an underfunded lifestyle, the client needs to recognize that lifestyle security can be purchased by monetizing mortality and yielding tactical control of assets. Their choices are constrained, but the transition period may be an effective time for you to begin the drip of information pointing them toward accepting the steps that they will ultimately need to take.

Example 11: High Net Worth—Underfunded Lifestyle at Point of Retirement

The better off—that is, the less underfunded—will still be able to lock in a floor with some potential for upside such as a variable annuity. With a variable annuity, the excess that is available each year will vary with performance of the subaccount. For those who are affected by the constraint at the extreme, a fixed annuity will be the only feasible solution. For the extreme case, the result is that a high-net-worth client ends up living on an allowance. Before shedding too many tears, an underfunded high-net-worth lifestyle is different from abject poverty, but it does suggest a client whose retirement goals will remain unfulfilled.

You may be thinking that it is possible to take more risk in the client's portfolio. That possibility is discussed more fully in Chapter 14. To foreshadow, there may be a few clients for whom that is an appropriate strategy, but in general it is a gamble with the potential to leave the client worse off.

Ultra-High Net Worth (Financial Wealth > $10 Million)

We provide no generalized picture of the ultra-high-net-worth client. Partially because they are too idiosyncratic to type and partially because each one can afford personalized and customized attention. Most of these clients do not have retirement needs per se. It is true that some will want something to act as a fallback in the case of catastrophe, a floor of some sort. But their needs revolve around wealth management, tax-efficient transfers of assets, and legacies. To that extent they, as a group—examples like those provided previously—are unlikely to provide much insight to the UHNW adviser.

SUMMARY

This chapter has provided a survey of product groupings that are useful to advisers serving the retirement space. This chapter has also provided a small catalog of examples that advisers can use to frame their approaches to clients in the various segments described in Chapter 12.

CHAPTER 14

Preparing Your Client for a Retirement Income Portfolio

Objectives

Provide information that can be supplied directly to clients to help them understand the process of creating a retirement income portfolio

Help clients understand what information you need from them

Help clients understand what you will be doing for them

This chapter is addressed to the client—both real and hypothetical from the vantage point of the adviser. An adviser–client relationship is more than just a business relationship. Advisers get to know their clients and empathize with them. Relationships last longer than careers—they last lifetimes. An adviser has a real desire to create secure retirements for every client. To accomplish the goal of a secure retirement, your help is needed.

Portfolios are occasionally described as gardens to be watered, weeded, and pruned. Even if your portfolio were a garden, your portfolio isn't meant as a flower garden, but a vegetable garden. You probably didn't work hard and save money just to create something decorative. Most people save money to use it at a later date. Whether to fund boats, cars, weddings, college, retirement, or endow a legacy; your portfolio is not an end in itself, but a means to achieve your ends. In order to make the most of your portfolio, it is important to be clear to yourself and your financial adviser your reasons for saving money.

There are many aspects of retirement to which your adviser can add value. Many of you are probably familiar with the ability of an adviser to create trusts and estates. Those aspects are important, but they relate to the endgame of your retirement. Where your adviser can be of most help to you is by creating a portfolio that provides a floor for your lifestyle while recognizing that your aspirations don't stop when you stop working. What

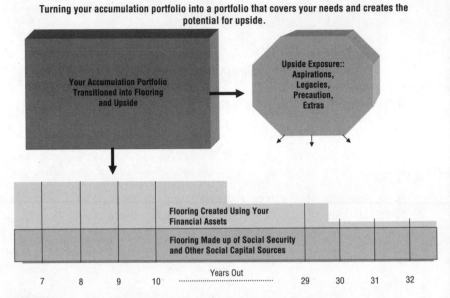

Turning your accumulation portfolio into a portfolio that covers your needs and creates the potential for upside.

Your Accumulation Portfolio Transitioned into Flooring and Upside

Upside Exposure:: Aspirations, Legacies, Precaution, Extras

Flooring Created Using Your Financial Assets

Flooring Made up of Social Security and Other Social Capital Sources

Years Out

7   8   9   10   29   30   31   32

FIGURE 14.1 The Transition from Accumulation to Retirement

your adviser will be trying to do is to create a portfolio that supports both your lifestyle and your aspirations. The right portfolio for you depends on your age, your wherewithal, your lifestyle, your plans, the risks you face, and your tolerance to risk.

A properly constructed portfolio for retirement income should be able to immunize your lifestyle against market and economic cycles. You should be able to sleep soundly in the knowledge that your lifestyle is secure. Figure 14.1 shows how the accumulated funds in a traditional portfolio are allocated to serve your needs. The flooring part is there to secure the minimum you need for *your* lifestyle, while the upside exposures are there to provide the things that make your lifestyle enjoyable. That's not to say that retirement portfolios are designed to be risk free. They are not. Your aspirations imply that you need to take wisely chosen and measured risks. Retirement portfolios are designed in a way to keep the risk in your portfolio separated from the funds needed to secure your lifestyle. We label the parts of retirement portfolios as either floor or upside components; the risk is in the upside component, not the floor.

If you have an established relationship with an adviser, your adviser has some of the information that is needed to create your retirement portfolio. But a fuller picture is needed to really create a customized portfolio that meets your specific needs.

As the recent market turmoil has painfully emphasized, a well-diversified portfolio is not always strong enough to withstand market downturns if the funds are needed in the near term. It may well be true that in the long run markets always come back but that is cold comfort to someone who will need to access their money in the near term. For someone in their 30s, who is fully able to take advantage of a market down cycle, volatility is a friend. For an individual at or near retirement, volatility is no longer a friend; watching as years of careful planning and thrift turn to dust can be heart wrenching.

For retirement you want to protect a lifestyle and ensure that the funds last for indeterminate and hopefully extended longevity. There are pitfalls. Constructed improperly, portfolios run the risk of being drawn down to rapidly and running out of money too soon. You don't want to outlive your money. Another pitfall is when fear drives people to preserve their resources too frugally until they are incapable of enjoying the fruits of their labor. These are the problems of ruin and missed opportunity. No one wants to die poor or with regrets for what they didn't do but could have done.

The good news is that there are steps that can be taken to ensure that your portfolio is there when you need it. There is a thicket full of problems that can trip up retirements, but there are a myriad of solutions. In fact, there are so many ways to address the problems that having someone to help navigate through the clutter and find the right solution becomes more helpful than ever. Your input is important so that your adviser can know what things are most important to you and your retirement.

Finding the right portfolio for your retirement is not simply a function of your wealth and risk tolerance. The right portfolio for *your* retirement depends not so much on your wealth as on the cost of your lifestyle relative to your wealth. Beyond the basic lifestyle need are the needs to protect your lifestyle against both the vagaries and risks that threaten your lifestyle and the need to create the potential for bettering your lifestyle. In a nutshell, your adviser's goal for your portfolio is the following simple rule: Build a secure floor and create upside.

To help you along in the process of understanding what you need to do for your adviser to be more effective in helping you to achieve a secure retirement, we start by walking through Figure 14.2 which shows the hub and spoke advisory process of the Retirement Income Industry Association (RIIA), a nonprofit organization that promotes adviser education, standards, and best practices within the retirement income industry (www .RIIA-USA.org). The client relationship is the heart of the wheel, while the spokes denote the steps for advisers to take to help secure the client's lifestyle and the client–adviser relationship.

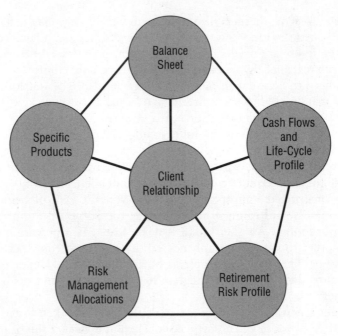

FIGURE 14.2   RIIA's Retirement Management and
Retirement Income Advisory Process

To create secure retirement income for clients, the first three spokes of
the RIIA process require the adviser to know the resources, listen to the
plans of their clients, and to evaluate the risks faced by the client. The last
two spokes involve combining products and techniques for implementing
the right portfolio for the client. While the adviser is an expert in the products and techniques useful for building a retirement portfolio, the client's
help and input is needed to appropriately customize the portfolio.

The wheel in Figure 14.2 illustrates the advisory process for retirement
income developed by RIIA. Once again, the RIIA advisory process can be
boiled down to the goals of building a floor and creating upside for clients.
The concept of building a floor refers to the level of consumption or lifestyle
that is to be maintained during retirement. The floor should be constructed
to be strong enough to support consumption in the face of a reasonable
array of needs, risks, and uncertainties. The RIIA process also recognizes
that aspiration doesn't end at retirement; RIIA encourages creating the
potential for upside, resources permitting, on top of the floor, for the client.

While the RIIA wheel helps to tell us what needs to be done, by itself
it doesn't stress the nature of the dialog that needs to take place between

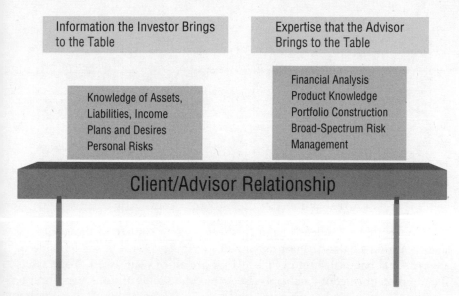

FIGURE 14.3 Important Actions and Interactions for Retirement Portfolios

you and your adviser as shown in Figure 14.3. The adviser needs information from you to create a portfolio that is properly tailored to your needs. With the right information, the adviser can create the right amount of the right type of flooring that is secure against most foreseeable risks and some unforeseeable events, and retain the maximum amount for potential upside. Generic portfolios are possible for clients who do not wish to share information, but they will be less efficient than tailored portfolios.

KNOW YOUR RESOURCES

The first spoke in the RIIA wheel is concerned with an estimation of your needs and your financial capabilities. Your assets, if properly measured, can give a good indication of your capability to support your needs. Your needs are, well, your needs. If we measure your needs against your capabilities then we know if there is any slack or if steps must be taken to either augment assets or reevaluate needs.

For many clients, the process of understanding their assets and flows is quite revealing. Just as corporations and businesses have balance sheets and income statements, so too do individuals. The individual's balance sheet is not defined as strictly as the legal reporting document that corporations maintain, but the concept is the same.

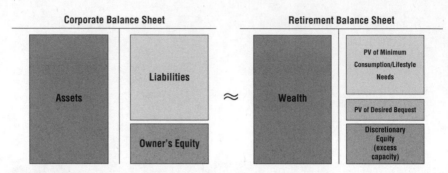

FIGURE 14.4   Retirement Balance Sheets

Conceptually, a client's balance sheet is quite similar to the notion of a corporation's balance sheet as shown in Figure 14.4. On the left side of the personal balance sheet in Figure 14.4 are all of your assets. Your assets include not only your financial assets, but the value of your cars, house, stamp collection, and other items that have monetary value. Depending on your age, the biggest component of your assets may not be your house, but the present value of your future earning power. In some frameworks, assets are categorized in three buckets as financial capital, human capital, and social capital.

Financial capital includes those things that can easily be turned into readily usable funds including financial assets and real assets: stocks, bonds, houses, cars, art collections, and the like. Human capital includes the present value of the remaining stream of your future expected earnings. Social capital includes the claims that you retain that are reliant on the payments of others as part of the social compact such as Social Security, Medicare, and Medicaid.

On the right side of the balance sheet are your liabilities including fixed debts like a mortgage and harder to pin down sums like the present value of your food bills. The liability section, in total, is the lump-sum amount that would be needed to fund your lifestyle for the remainder of your life. It may include the desire to leave something to heirs or charity after you die.

In the corporate context, when we compare the left side of the balance sheet, assets, with the right side of the balance sheet, liabilities, the difference between the two is a balancing amount known as owner's equity. When the assets exceed the liabilities there is positive owner's equity. When the liabilities exceed the assets, then a corporation has negative equity and is insolvent.

For an individual, the idea is similar. If your assets exceed your liabilities then you have excess capacity. In the retirement income world, the liabilities represent the present value of the cost to fund and insure your lifestyle; any excess capacity can be used to create the potential for upside.

So with regard to your balance sheet, what follows is a short list of some questions that you should think about.

Assets
- What are your earnings per year?
- Are you eligible for Social Security?
- Are you a veteran, or entitled to benefits from the V.A.?
- Are there any other governmental programs for which you are entitled to receive benefits?
- Are you covered by a defined benefit plan?
- Do you receive employee insurance benefits that will be retained in retirement?
- Are you self-employed or an employee?
- Do you ever earn money for work outside of your regular employment?
- Do you have outside interests that can be turned into an employment opportunity?
- Have you ever or ever thought of starting your own business?
- What do you have in retirement assets such as 401(k), 403(b), IRA, Keogh, and the like?
- What other financial assets do you own?
- Do you own any real assets?
- Do you own any other assets that could be sold or used as a source of funds?

Liabilities
- What is your mortgage balance?
- What do you owe on vehicles?
- How often do you replace vehicles?
- What are the monthly required insurance premiums?
- What are your minimally necessary annual needs?
- Are you expecting any large expenditures in the future like a child's wedding?

Some of the amounts that result from the above questions will be in the form of the total stock of assets (home, mortgage) while others will be rates of flow amounts per year (Social Security, annual needs). Your adviser can help to estimate present values of the flow amounts so that your balance sheet will present everything in comparable units.

TABLE 14.1 Understanding your Personal
Income Statement

Income	Expenses
Earnings	Household expenses
Other income	Work-related expenses
Portfolio income	Education expenses
Gifts	Taxes
	Other expenses

The other facet for gauging needs and capabilities looks at how current expenses are being financed. This will be an important part of helping to determine the best type of flooring for you since it indicates a measure of how your lifestyle measures up against your income. The individual income statement gives a pure flow to flow comparison. See Table 14.1.

Note that your expenses will change when you retire. For example, work-related expenses including commuting and wardrobe costs may go away, decline, or be replaced by new expenses once you retire.

LIFESTYLE AND LIFE CYCLE

The assets, liabilities, and income statements are important pieces of the puzzle but more information from you is needed. Only you know, or have an idea of, when you want to retire, how fully you intend to retire, and how you want to spend your retirement. And how do you decide what to do? Figure 14.5 shows that while most people plan for a single-career path, there is wide variation in the interesting paths that individual careers may take, some with multiple work and retirement cycles. In the traditional view of the life cycle, you acquire skills during your youth, work a full career, and retire to a life of complete leisure.

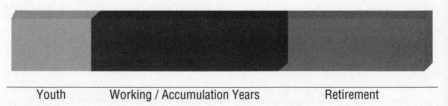

| Youth | Working / Accumulation Years | Retirement |

FIGURE 14.5 In a Traditional View, Where Are You?

Conveying your plans, goals and desires to your adviser helps to craft the right kind of portfolio for you. Sometimes what people plan can be surprising:

> *At the market where I used to shop on 74th Street in New York City, one of the full timers was Mr. B. Over the course of time, we had a long running conversation. He had worked at the store for about 30 years and made an average of $30,000/year. He'd been born in British Guiana (now Guyana) but had lived in New York from an early age. One day he told me it was his last. He and his wife (a nurse's aide) were retiring to a beach house in Guyana that they'd bought and paid for. I was astounded when he said that their finances were comprised of about $300,000 in Treasury inflation-protected securities (TIPS) and a small amount in an index fund. The yield would give them more than enough to live their retirement dream. Their lifestyle needs were simple and their resources ample for the task. Their case was simple. I fervently hope that they remain happy and healthy.*

Not everyone expects or wants a traditional life cycle. Some will not retire. Some will ease into retirement, others will treat retirement as an opportunity to take life in a new direction. Whether you expect to retire fully, open a small shop, or take on a whole new career, knowing where you are in your life cycle and what you want for your lifestyle during retirement are important considerations for creating the right portfolio. Below is a set of questions that are designed to elicit basic information.

A Basic Set of Planning Questions
- How long until you/your spouse expect to retire?
- If applicable, how old are your children?
- If applicable, do you expect to support your children after they reach majority?
- Do you/your spouse expect to retire fully or partially?
- Do you have any entrepreneurial ambitions for retirement?
- What are your annual contributions to retirement accounts?
- At what rate does your employer match or fund retirement contributions?
- How much per year do you save outside of your retirement accounts?
- What amount of living expenses that you currently incur, in total, do you expect to carry into retirement?
- What are the major lifestyle changes you expect or want for retirement?

- Where do you plan to live during retirement?
- Do you have hobbies or avocations that you plan on pursuing during retirement?
- How much and what type of travel do you anticipate during retirement?
- How likely are you to decide to spontaneously but meaningfully change your plans?
- Do you consider your planned legacy a need or a desire?

RISKS TO YOUR RETIREMENT LIFESTYLE

Knowing the risks to you lifestyle are important for two main reasons. First, by knowing what the risks are we can take actions to avoid the consequences of those risks being realized. Much as buying collision insurance for a car protects you against the adverse consequences of an expensive auto repair bill, many of the personal risks we face in retirement are insurable. Second, for those risks that aren't directly insurable we can either hold some extra cash to cover the small events or try to design a floor that has the right amount of flexibility for you.

It is relatively easy for your adviser to set up a band of funding that guarantees a stream of payments for either a definite or indefinite period during your retirement. The trick is to make that stream secure against events that can cause you to change your lifestyle. There are both capital markets and insurance products, things like bond strips and annuities that can easily be used to create a basic floor. Then you want to make the flooring robust to risks and uncertainties. Threats to your lifestyle can come from personal events, from your investments, or from wider public phenomena.

While your adviser may be an expert at finding the right assets for your portfolio and protecting them against investment-related risks, protecting against both public and personal risks can be most effectively accomplished with dialogue and coordinated planning (see Table 14.2).

The personal risks that we are concerned with are those events that have economic consequences to individuals like health, fire, and flood but do not, in general, relate to business risks or public policy events. Many personal risks can be neutralized with insurance. The list of personal risks that are typically insured is long and includes longevity, medical care, long-term care, property, and casualty. Other personal events that can upset planning arise when, for example, grown children require assistance. With the right types of insurance or planning, the likelihood of needing to make unintended portfolio changes can be minimized. Even if you choose to leave

TABLE 14.2   Knowing Your Risks is Your First Defense

Personal Risks
Home/fire/flood
Auto
Property
Theft/fraud
Personal liability
Acute health care
Longevity
Long-term care
Offspring

Investment Risks
Market risk—market swings
Credit risk—bonds that fail to pay
Operational risks—mistakes

Public Policy Risks
Inflation
Changes in tax law
Takings
Repudiation of sovereign debt
War

---

yourself exposed to particular negative events, there are still ways to minimize the impact on your portfolio. You can't insure yourself against every possibility, nor should you. By carefully considering your personal risks, discussing those risks with your adviser, and learning the cost of protection, you can prioritize your individual risks, and decide which risks that you will protect yourself against and which risks you will bear.

The business and investment risks that you face include the risks of stock declines or bond defaults. Your adviser should be well versed in helping you avoid investment risks in a way that is comfortable for you. For many, the typical ways to minimize investment risks include diversification and maintaining a fraction of assets in government-protected securities. For others who feel comfortable doing so, there are ways to protect assets using options and other derivative securities. Whatever your level of financial sophistication and risk tolerance, advisers are adept at handling investment risks to avoid the downside of bear markets, corporate bankruptcies, and other bad events that befall individual companies or industries.

Public policy events range from the straightforward but dangerous problem of inflation that is always in the background to the downright stupefying changes in tax law that seemingly come out of left (or right) field but have an impact on your entire planning strategy. For retirees, the potential for changes in laws regarding privatization of Social Security, Medicare, and tax deferral for IRAs and 401(k)s mean that the adviser must prepare and remain vigilant on behalf of the client to avoid the client ending up on that well-known road paved with good intentions.

The two simplest ways to secure your lifestyle fall into the broad categories of precaution and protection. Precaution is as simple as having a cash reserve in case a negative surprise occurs. Thus, precaution can be thought of as a way to self insure. Protecting your lifestyle means having contracts and/or plans in place to mitigate the risks faced by the client. In the realm of personal risks, protection may involve insurance for likely risks and catastrophic outcomes. For the business and investment risks, there are usually allocation strategies and traded instruments that allow for this class of risk to be avoided.

Approaches for Handling Risks
1. *Precaution.* Government securities and government-insured deposits
2. *Diversification.* Stock and bond mutual funds to avoid having all of your eggs in one basket
3. *Risk pooling.* Insurance contracts
4. *Hedges.* To offset risk usually through options and futures

For the basic flooring stream, it is important to know whether plans are likely to change to require a reconfiguration of the flooring; some types of flooring are harder to alter than others.

LIFESTYLE AND FLOORING TYPES

When it comes to planning for retirement income, the absolute level of your lifestyle is less important than your lifestyle relative to your wealth. As your wealth rises, it becomes easier to support a particular lifestyle.

Earlier in the chapter, I had mentioned the anecdote of Mr. B. By most standards his lifestyle would be considered simple. Both he and his wife were retiring to a small beach house in Guyana. They had no children, no out-of-pocket medical costs; on a breezy beach so near the equator that their house required little in the way of heat. Coupled with the Social Security payments they are entitled to receive, their bond portfolio provides both a bridge until they become eligible to receive Social Security and a buffer on top of their Social Security thereafter.

For most people with families or the comfort of familiarity and community ties, moving to a low-cost foreign country is not a viable option to consider. Still, there are differences in relative lifestyles that can have important implications for how to construct portfolios for retirement income.

Previously, we had talked about the concept of a balance sheet and how to convey information about your personal balance sheet to your financial adviser. We now want to focus on the difference between your wherewithal (wealth) and your requirements (consumption plus desired bequests). In brief, the discretionary equity box measures the amount of dry powder that you have for creating upside, funding impulse purchases, or absorbing negative uninsured shocks.

Figure 14.6 illustrates the importance of your balance sheet in securing your retirement lifestyle and keeping your aspirations. Advisers and clients need to understand the resources (assets) and requirements (liabilities) that are captured in a client balance sheet in order to craft the portfolio that best serves the client's needs. Of importance in determining the kind of flooring that you need, and the availability of excess capacity to take advantage of your aspirations and desires, is the relative size of each of the boxes.[1] We categorize individual lifestyles into three lifestyle types. Remember that these lifestyle types are relative to your wealth and not simply related to your absolute wealth.

Figure 14.7 is a stylized illustration of how a client's lifestyle affects the options for creating portfolios for retirement. This figure shows how the cost of maintaining a lifestyle needs to be compared to available wealth.

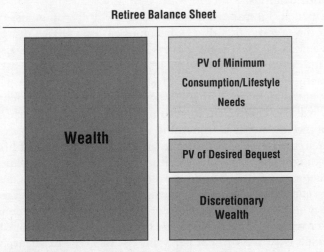

FIGURE 14.6 Your Retirement Balance Sheet

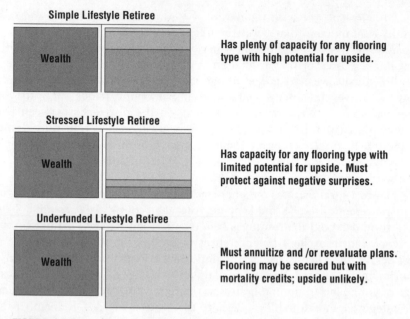

Simple Lifestyle Retiree

Wealth

Has plenty of capacity for any flooring type with high potential for upside.

Stressed Lifestyle Retiree

Wealth

Has capacity for any flooring type with limited potential for upside. Must protect against negative surprises.

Underfunded Lifestyle Retiree

Wealth

Must annuitize and /or reevaluate plans. Flooring may be secured but with mortality credits; upside unlikely.

FIGURE 14.7 Lifestyles and Flooring

Only a lucky few live simple enough lifestyles to fund their needs indefinitely. While few people plan to outspend their resources, some will and most must be cautious.

Often people fantasize about winning a lottery or amassing greater wealth. In the fantasy, life always becomes easier, worries disappear, and happiness increases. The reality, even for lottery winners, is usually less grand. Why? Usually the reality is less compelling because a change in wealth usually leads to a change in lifestyle. The full-bore type who spends as much as possible each year will not have more relative slack, but that individual will become accustomed to a new and higher lifestyle. This isn't an issue of morals, but it is something to recognize.

It is important for your adviser to get a feel for the type of lifestyle you will be leading relative to your wealth. It is a lot easier to plan the right portfolio beforehand than to adjust to reality later.

For the simple lifestyle retiree, the options are almost unlimited and the (financial) world is their oyster. The simple-lifestyle retiree is defined to be someone for whom the needed lifestyle that must be funded out of financial wealth doesn't exceed 3 percent per year. For this type of client, an adviser can build flooring of the following types:

- Insurance-based products such as annuities
- Capital markets products such as bonds or bond strips
- Yield-based strategies such as high-dividend funds

If you are in this category you are fortunate. This type of client is generally able to fund retirement for an indefinite period without having to draw down their capital. Depending on how low their spending to wealth ratio is they may be able to self-insure against most risks. The possibility of maintaining exposure to potential upside is not constrained in this case. This type of client is truly lucky. This type of client is extremely rare.

For the stressed lifestyle where there is little room for error, a few constraints on choices exist. The prospect of a yield-based plan for retirement is no longer feasible. However, as long as the required annual lifestyle is below 7 percent of wealth per year, there are still options available for building flooring and upside. This type of client can build flooring out of the following types:

- Insurance-based products such as annuities
- Capital markets products such as bonds or bond strips

If you are in this group you need to think through your plans carefully. This type of client has limited capacity to absorb shocks without the aid of insurances and precautionary balances. You're not alone. This grouping covers a wide swathe of clients. The good news is that there are solid solutions available for these clients. The caveat is that these retirement portfolios must be crafted wisely and monitored frequently.

For the underfunded lifestyle, there are few choices. Frankly, this is the most difficult prospect that one can face. It may still be possible to build a floor for clients who are willing to accept higher payments while alive at the risk of leaving little for survivors. The mortality credits—embedded in post-annuities—trade off more while alive for less after death. This type of client has extremely limited capacity to absorb uninsured shocks. There are of course alternatives open even to this type of client. The client may be able to delay retirement or possibly scale back lifestyle.

Many people like to make comparisons between themselves and their neighbors. Part of what Figure 14.8 shows is that, even within the same lifestyle group, variations in lifestyle relative to wealth can dictate different portfolio approaches and determine the best way to meet your retirement needs. The best portfolio for someone with a simple lifestyle may differ radically from someone who spends at a rate greater than their wealth can support through retirement.

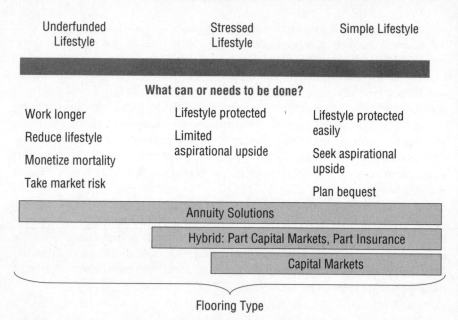

FIGURE 14.8   Segmenting Flooring Types

Each flooring type has its strengths and weaknesses. Choosing the right flooring is influenced by both financial and personal considerations; the personal component makes choosing the right flooring as much an art as a science. Much depends on the likelihood that your plans may undergo radical change at some point in the future.

To explore the differences between flooring types, we'll now take a little detour and discuss what we mean by insurance and capital markets. Then we will walk through some of the major differences in flooring that is based on insurance products and flooring based on capital markets products (for example, stocks and bonds).

One of the major differences is how the two types of products trade. Capital markets products trade as securities. Insurance products are based on individual contracts.

Capital markets products are financial instruments. The set of capital markets products includes stocks, bonds, currencies, futures, and options. Securities issued by the U.S. government are considered risk free.[2] All other securities are considered risky. Markets move up and down. Individual firms can flourish or fail. Diversification helps to limit the second risk, but often gets undue credit for mitigating the first risk.

Most capital markets instruments trade on exchanges. Exchanges act as auction markets. When a client decides to sell his or her shares of stock in some firm there are multiple potential purchasers bidding to buy the shares. The transaction is standardized in such a way that it doesn't matter who buys your shares, you'll get paid for them. By trading on exchanges, the products, terms of delivery, and terms of settlement are standardized.

The typical capital markets products used for flooring are bonds and bond strips. Bonds are essentially loans made by investors to companies. The simplest bonds offer a fixed payment for a specified number of years and repayment of principal at maturity. For retirement income, bonds are useful instruments for creating flooring. Even better are bond strips. Bond strips are created when a bond is pulled apart into its component payments. Once the payments are pulled apart they can be reconstituted to form a customized floor. For those with the very simplest lifestyles, equity dividends may be another source of flooring. Generally though, equities are considered too risky for creating reliable flooring. As traded securities, capital markets products are great for purchasing while still in the process of saving for retirement, particularly when ultimate needs and abilities are unclear.

Insurance products do not trade on exchanges. Insurance products sell as individual contracts that are generally not transferable.[3] For retirement income, the standard insurance-based product is the annuity. An annuity is essentially a bond issued by the insurance company where the number of payments depends on *your* longevity, and the amount of the payments depends on *average* mortality for those in your age cohort. In the simplest annuities, you receive payments as long as you live and nothing thereafter. The insurance company hopes to sufficiently issue many of these contracts so that the average annuity is profitable. Since lifetimes are generally uncertain, annuities and other longevity-related products are a great way to lay down flooring that will last as long as you.

Before we move on to the next section, I'll mention a few important points to keep in mind and bring up when discussing your retirement income portfolio. The major factors to keep in mind are the following:

1. Longevity
2. Issuer risk
3. Reversibility
4. Taxes

Longevity should be thought of as a benefit that comes with a risk that you might outlive your assets. Issuer risk is the potential that you may not receive all that you are owed. Incorporating reversibility into a plan is helpful for when fate changes your plans. And taxes matter during working years and they matter in retirement.

- *Bonds and bond strips cover a fixed term.*[4] A long life is usually thought of as a blessing. However, since the level of Social Security payments is designed to be roughly two-thirds of the level of income designated as the poverty level, longevity without resources is poverty without recourse. Bonds and bond strips are very simple instruments that are easily purchased and sold. They are versatile and can be easily tailored and customized to your unique circumstances. However, they only cover a fixed window of time. Life expectancy tells us the average age at death. A significant percentage of people live longer than their life expectancy.[5] One needs to either retain a cushion of funds for longevity or have insurance in the form of a longevity policy—either an annuity or pure longevity insurance.
- *Bonds and annuities have issuer risk.* When a corporate borrower, whether the borrowing is linked to bonds or other contractual obligations, has the potential to pay what is owed, the term is known as *issuer risk*. To the holders of obligations, whether bondholders, pensioners, or annuitants, issuer risk can devastate a retirement. Both bonds and annuities are obligations of companies to pay over time. One can think of annuities as bonds with a "mortality premium" attached. All bonds are subject to the risk that the issuer will be unable to pay. As mentioned previously, individual firms may flourish or fail. There are two protections for both bonds and annuities: diversification and rating. Diversification spreads the risks around and ratings give a snapshot view of the creditworthiness of the debt.[6] The only flooring that can reasonably be considered as risk free are U.S. government–issued or U.S. government–insured instruments.
- *Capital markets flooring is easily reversed.* Sometimes lives change suddenly and in ways that are unforeseen. Sometimes lives change for the better and sometimes not. The longer the planning horizon, the greater the value in making plans that are flexible. Plans that are irreversible can turn out to be costly even if the up-front cost made them look attractive. Reversibility is something to keep in mind. There may be circumstances where it becomes necessary or desirable to reduce flooring or shorten the length of coverage. Traded securities can be easily sold back into the market with little effort or cost. The price will likely have changed since purchase but it is an arm's-length transaction. Annuities can usually be sold back to the issuer, but the pricing is generally less transparent.[7]
- *Taxes matter.* What is your tax bracket? What is your view on future tax rates? Have you talked with your adviser about how your portfolio

is structured with regard to taxes? Taxes matter. There are ways, particularly by meshing your portfolio's funds across taxable and tax-advantaged accounts (such as 401(k), IRA, and Keogh) that let you make the most out of your retirement. Annuities create taxable income when the payment is received. Therefore, there is no advantage to purchasing an annuity in a retirement account that defers taxation like a traditional IRA. On the other hand, bond strips and TIPS can create phantom income that creates taxable income even when no cash flows are received by the client. Therefore, there is every advantage to keeping bond strips and TIPS in IRA-type retirement accounts. In general, the tax advantages conferred by retirement accounts should be used as fully as practicable and as wisely as possible.

WHAT THE ADVISER NEEDS FROM THE CLIENT

We've spent a lot of time discussing the pieces needed to put together the retirement plan that's right for you. Now we're going to switch gears a little bit and get to the end result.

Let's start at the floor. A good portion of the information that you need to provide to your adviser helps to figure out how much annual income that you need your portfolio to generate for you during retirement. The next bit of information that you provide helps the adviser provide some insulation around your lifestyle by a combination of actions to avoid, mitigate, or absorb shocks. The last pieces are put in place once your adviser understands your aspirations and any plans that you may have around the assets that you intend to bequeath to the future.

SUMMARY

Creating the right retirement portfolio for you is a job that requires you to provide your adviser with some information. You know your resources and your plans and the more completely you can convey the information to your adviser, the better the outcome that you can expect. The adviser will need to know a few things:

- About when you plan to retire
- How you want to be able to live
- Your willingness to save today for your goals tomorrow
- What you want to leave for future generations
- What the important risks are for you
- Your resources for meeting your goals

CHAPTER 15

Salvage Operations, Mistakes, and Fallacies

Objectives

Illuminate common mistakes and debunk some myths about long-run performance and long-run risk

Developing techniques and plans for helping clients recover from financial disaster

For the few who were already positioned for retirement income, 2008 was not a bad year. For those people, it was either a pretty good year or, at worst, a diminishment of discretionary upside. Positioned properly, the floor would be intact. For those whose flooring was already set up in Treasury strips, there were significant mark-to-market gains.

Unfortunately, most people were not positioned for retirement income. For them, 2008 was a disastrous year. In many straightforward cases, client portfolios are down by more than 35 percent. Some of the unluckiest were the multimanager UMAs and endowment plans where fees, illiquidity, and manager herding combined for declines in excess of 40 percent. For some clients, their plans will be changed forever. There is no shortage of anger and disappointment. Now, many advisers are fearful of losing clients. This book is about doing the right things for clients. To that end, we first cover two common mistakes and fallacies that are often promoted as ways to regain lost ground. We then move on to what can be done. To be clear, for many there is no way to regain enough ground to get back to the start line. The issue is to salvage the salvageable, take limited risk where prudent, and to accept that some of the loss is likely to be permanent.

The first part of this chapter covers what *not* to do if an accumulation portfolio falls sufficiently to become underfunded in the retirement income context, and what one *can* do to help get the client out of the hole. We'll get to the part about getting out of the hole, but we'll first take a detour through some mistakes and fallacies that are fairly commonly promulgated. The mistakes and fallacies are in some cases wrong and in other cases riskier than advertised. There may be a willingness to take some risk, but it should not be taken blindly.

Once we cover mistakes and fallacies, we cover things that can be done to help a client who has dug themselves into a hole. Our discussion will be general, but for those attempting to recover post-2008 it is also quite topical. We work on creating an action plan for recovery and what needs to be done to stay on top of the situation.

MISTAKES AND FALLACIES

There are many mistakes and fallacies that persist around retirement and retirement planning. Most are variations on the same theme—that it is not only possible to grow out of the problem, but that it is a safe bet. The ones that I want to highlight here are more pernicious because they have a measure of "truthiness."[1] They sound plausible, reasonable, have a certain face-value appeal, and seem provable but they are not. They are risky. They may be taking a client portfolio that is in a precarious position and creating catastrophe out of disaster.

Increased Risk Improves the Outlook

There are a couple of variations of this old chestnut. The most demonstrably wrong is that by taking riskier assets on the balance sheet the liabilities become eligible for discounting at a higher rate, thus making the client better off.

On a balance sheet, if safe assets are disposed and replaced by risky assets, the current asset value of the balance sheet is neither increased, nor is it decreased. The composition of the balance sheet changes but not the value. What does change is the probability distribution of future asset values. With riskier assets, the mean and the variance of the distribution of future outcomes will be higher. In a corporate context, higher capital would be required as a buffer against the probability of a shortfall in value where the obligation implied by the liabilities would not be met. If liabilities are backed up by risk-free assets, then there would be no probability of a shortfall, and no risk capital would be required.

The riskier assets may have a higher expected return, but they have a commensurately higher discount rate keeping the current balance sheet unaffected. In short, the riskier assets have a higher discount rate, but the liabilities do not. The riskier assets will however, require more capital to be posted. By taking on riskier assets there is the possibility of not having sufficient wherewithal to meet the liabilities. The greater the risk in the assets, the higher the probability of missing the amount needed to meet the liabilities; by a wider margin.

The Long Run Is Less Risky

The horizon doesn't matter. If the horizon did matter, then one would expect that over the long run the cost of insuring against earning less than the risk-free rate of interest would be declining.[2] But the forward value of any traded assets is given by the future value T periods ahead, growing at the risk-free rate.

In order to see the cost of insurance for a portfolio, we construct a simple, but realistic example in Table 15.1. Suppose that your client is long a basket of non-dividend-paying stocks. The client would like to hold the basket for T periods before selling. The client wants a minimum price to be guaranteed for the sale T periods from now when the shares are to be sold. We now show how the shares can be insured and how the guarantee price will be derived.

The trading desk that provides the guarantee agrees to buy the shares at a future date. Without wanting to be at risk, the desk will go out and hedge their position by selling the basket short today and carrying the short position until period T. At that point, they will take your client's shares and deliver them against the short position. The proceeds from the short sale will be deposited in a risk-free account. When period T arrives, the client delivers the shares, which are then used to close out the short position and the client will receive the proceeds of the funds that have been sitting in the risk-free account net of the costs associated with the guarantor having to fund the short position for T periods, known as the *borrow cost*.

TABLE 15.1 Hedging Guaranteed Stock Performance

	Today	Period T
Client	Wants to lock in Selling Price for period T	1. Delivers shares 2. Receives proceeds
Guarantor	Sells short an identical position and deposits funds in a risk-free account	1. Receives shares and closes out short position 2. Delivers proceeds

Without wanting to take risk, the most that the guarantor will offer is the forward price less the cumulative borrow costs, $F_T = S_t e^{(r_f - b)(T-t)}$, where F_T is the forward at future time T, S_t is the stock price in the present (time t), r_f is the risk-free rate, b denotes the rate paid to borrow shares for a short position, and e is the base for natural logarithms (roughly 2.71828) used for continuous compounding.

This forward value represents the cost of hedging. It tells us what is often described as "at the money, forward." Most people are familiar with the term *at the money*, denoting an option where the current price of the underlying asset equals the strike price of an option written on that underlying asset. At the money, forward is the point where puts or calls are of equal value.[3] In practice, the borrow costs are low; only a few basis points for liquid securities that are easy to borrow. The accompanying workbook shows the cost of a guarantee for a dividend-paying security.

What has just been described provides the solution for a guarantee where the client pays no up-front premium. Notice that expected returns on the portfolio had nothing to do with the answer. To the guarantor, the only questions are "How do I hedge and how much will the hedge cost me?"

If the client is willing to pay an up-front premium for the protection without engaging in a forward sale, then option solutions are a possibility. But again the forward price is the center of the distribution for an option of tenor T. This means that the risk-free return is always at-the-money forward. That is, the forward price is the strike value at which calls and puts will price equally.

It is true that if there are two put options of differing maturities but sharing the same strike price, the longer dated put option will be priced cheaper. But the relevant, apples-to-apples comparison would be if the longer-dated option were struck at a level grossed up by the risk-free rate accrued for the time differential of the strike prices. That is, for a strike of K, the strikes would need to be related by $K_2 = K_1 e^{r_f(T_2 - T_1)}$.

Now both options will be struck at the same time-adjusted *moneyness*, that is, they will both be the same relative distance from at-the-money for their respective maturities. With any two options of the same moneyness, a longer-dated option will be more costly. The cost of insuring a portfolio relative to risk-free performance is always increasing as the time horizon lengthens. The expected return of the stock, whether mean reverting or not, is unimportant—what matters is the cost of the hedge.

What we have just shown doesn't mean that the expected return on stock is given by the risk-free rate. The expected return is for a positive beta asset, which is higher than the risk-free rate. What the capital market is telling us is that the cost associated with the risk of underperforming the risk-free rate is not declining over time. Insurance is available, but insuring against any growth rate above the risk-free rate will mean buying puts that are in the money relative to the forward price.

There is a second version of this fallacy purporting that the volatility of a portfolio declines through time. This version is a simple case of confusing the volatility of an average with the volatility of a sum—average returns versus cumulative returns. It is true that the periodic volatility of average returns sampled over some window of time would be declining with the square root of the number of sample periods. However, the volatility of cumulative returns increases at the square root of the number of periods.

A typical example is that if the annual volatility is 30 percent, then the volatility over 16 years would only be 7.5 percent. Not only is this a fallacy, but it's also dumb. An implication is that if we run the problem in reverse, the shorter the interval the higher the volatility. If the annual volatility were 30 percent, then the implication of the fallacy would be that the volatility over one trading day would be about 480 percent.

In multiperiod analysis, it is easiest to calculate returns based on logarithmic changes (geometric returns) $r(t, t + 1) = Ln(P_{t+1}) - Ln(P_t)$. The return r is then decomposed into an average return μ, and a random component ε. $r \equiv r(t, t +1) = \mu + \varepsilon(t, t + 1)$ and the random component has a variance, $var((t, t + 1)) \equiv \sigma^2$. The rest is easy to show.

We start with an initial portfolio value of P_0. The cumulative return by holding the portfolio for T periods can be written as:

$$Ln(P_T) - Ln(P_0) = r(0, T) = \sum_{t=0}^{T-1} r(t, t+1).$$

The key simplification that this form buys for us is that by using log prices, the intermediate prices P_1, P_2, and so on cancel each other out, and we are left with the ending value P_T as our starting value plus the cumulative return: $Ln(P_T) = Ln(P_0) + \sum_{t=0}^{T-1} r(t, t+1)$ or $P_T = P_0 e^{\sum_{t=0}^{T-1} r(t,t+1)}$ (continuous compounding). To see the fallacy, we expand the component showing the sum of returns:

$$\sum_{t=0}^{T-1} r(t, t+1) = T\mu + \sum_{t=0}^{T-1} \varepsilon(t, t+1)$$

Since the variance of returns through time is assumed constant (a simplification that isn't necessary but keeps the arithmetic neat) $var(\varepsilon(t, t + 1)) \equiv \sigma^2$, and $var\left(\sum_{t=0}^{T-1} r(t, t+1)\right) = \sigma^2 T$. This means that the cumulative returns of a portfolio will have a total expected return of μT and a standard deviation of $\sigma\sqrt{T}$. In other words, this means that the long-run risk of a portfolio grows proportionately with the square root of time.

Just Get Over the Hump

This fallacy is yet another variation of the theme that by lengthening the horizon, your client can just grow their way out of a hole. The "over the hump" fallacy is predicated on the notion that flooring a limited window during the early stages of retirement is sufficient to ensure success of a drawdown plan.[4] The idea is that the higher expected returns of a risky portfolio will eventually overcome volatility. By reference to the "less risky in the long run" fallacy, we can knock this one off pretty quickly.

Let's suppose that there is no longevity risk. Suppose further that we floor everything except for the final year. Is this a safe strategy? As we saw in the last case, the cost of protecting against underperforming relative to the risk-free rate does not decrease, but increases, over time. Consequently, for someone who was underfunded relative to their final year, capital markets pricing indicates no increased prospect of success. There is the gamble that may or may not pay off. The client may end up worse off or better off; looking forward there may be optimism but there is no greater assurance of success.

HOW TO DIG OUT OF A HOLE

Since the beginning of fourth quarter of 2007 markets have declined substantially. Due to the nature of the credit problems, fixed-income instruments issued by entities other than the federal government have offered no safe haven. The result is that most portfolios are down substantially in both their equity and fixed-income components. Client portfolios that were positioned for accumulation discovered that they were designed with symmetric risk; diversification did not provide enough protection. Many portfolios were held firm or were rebalanced into the teeth of a market[5] described as in close to a freefall.

What's done is done. Now the task is to make the best out of what remains. There is no magic bullet. Some have promoted the idea that it is best to remain fully invested for the bright day that the market snaps back. This leaves the clients in the same danger as before.[6]

What is clear is that at the aggregate level, creating a secure floor engenders confidence and enables discretionary consumption. When lifestyle is uncertain, people pull back and delay consumption decisions. Therefore, at the aggregate level, creating flooring security is stimulative to the economy. It's not your job to fix the economy, but the more people are made confident in their individual futures the quicker that consumption will recover.

Assess the Situation

The first step is to check the present value of future lifestyle needs against the current value of the portfolio. If the client is still in an overfunded position, then, not to minimize the problem, only upside has been lost and the lifestyle can be made to remain secure. On the other hand, if the client's portfolio has fallen enough to expose an underfunded lifestyle, then there are even more difficult conversations that lie ahead.

Many people fall in the precarious position between the two extremes. Has the client purchased real estate in the last five years? If so, then there is a good chance that even if they had a conforming mortgage that, if their leverage was more than 4:1, then that asset is underwater. It has been worse for retirees buying homes in the Sun Belt states of Florida, Arizona, Nevada, and California. In those states, leverage of 3:1 was not low enough to keep them above the waterline.

Of course, being underwater on an asset is not the same as having total liabilities exceeding total assets. However, the ability of their assets to generate cash flows has probably also taken a hit.

If the client still has earnings capability, then it is something to keep in mind. Delaying retirement or coming out of retirement creates options. Their willingness to work can be left as an open question until the next section. If possible calculate the present value of earnings under a few scenarios: full time, part time, one year, five years, and so on.

It will be useful to, delicately, seek answers to the following questions:

- What is the current value of the remaining portfolio?
- What is the present value of the client lifestyle?
- Are there future liabilities that can be delayed or deferred?
- Is remaining in the labor force longer than previously anticipated an option?
- Are there parts of the lifestyle that are of secondary importance?
- Is an overall simplification of lifestyle plausible?
- Are there other assets than can be monetized?

Triage

Be prepared for a triage view of the situation. There are some clients who may need to adjust their portfolios for retirement income but are basically okay. They may be unhappy about their losses and regret if they change posture and the market snaps back quickly, but their lifestyle is still fundamentally sound.

There are many who are in a precarious position and will require effort and vigilance, but with lifestyle pruning, prudent risk taking, and solid risk management should end up in a better position after a few years. Members of this group may be somewhat underfunded. If they are still in a preretirement stage, it may be possible to patch up their portfolios before they retire. Some extra risk may be warranted, but it needs to be prudent and carefully considered.

The third group finds themselves severely underfunded. Most in this group will have already retired and be unable to rejoin the labor market. This group faces a diminished lifestyle and, without a willingness to run extraordinary risk, perhaps inadvisable risk, is probably best off annuitizing into a fixed-income stream at a far lower level than they would have expected 18 months ago.

Create an Action Plan

Once the situation is assessed, it is time to put pen to paper and create plans for your clients. In each of the triage categories, be prepared for some of the options to be unpalatable for particular clients. You want to present the options along the line for which you expect greatest success, but you may need to adjust to the clients needs. For the healthy and the precarious, you will have a couple of options to go with. For the lost, there is no room for maneuver. For the lost the best result to obtain is that no more ground will be lost.

Make sure that you are well prepared. You can expect that some of the discussions will involve clients who are angry or agitated. In order to convince the clients, you need to be clear in your own mind why the proposed action plan is best.

The Healthy   On the face of it, it may seem like this would be the easiest group to deal with, but it may still be quite difficult. On the bright side, this group is still overfunded relative to their lifestyle needs and still has positive discretionary equity. The downside is that much of their discretionary equity may have evaporated. Where they perceived themselves to be comfortably well off, they may now see themselves as getting by on a budget. The facts of the situation may be at odds with their feelings about the situation.

The safest action plan for this group is to immediately transition their portfolios for retirement income. By transitioning completely their lifestyle will be immunized against further declines, they will likely be recognizing losses that can be used to partially offset income and future gains, and they will still retain some upside exposure in the event of a market turnaround.

Since clients in this category are still in an overfunded position this action plan can be undertaken either in static (Chapter 7) or active (Chapter 9) forms. Either one of these two options would be the recommended strategies.

Members of this group don't need to work longer or adjust their lifestyles to a lower level. However, any adjustments that they are willing to make can go straight to reinvigorating their upside portfolio and perhaps better conform the portfolio to their aspirations.

If such clients are unwilling to go the safest route, then all of the portfolio constructions entail assuming risk to their lifestyle. As a straw man, suppose that a client is only willing to put down half of the floor that he or she needs and keeps all the rest as upside. His or her hope clearly is to grow to meet lifestyle needs. The risk is that at some point the client may fall below the present value of remaining needs. If undertaken as a passive strategy, then the outcome of success or failure is binary. If the client is looking for a partially active strategy, where gains will be used in whole or in part to secure more of their flooring needs, then there will be a greater likelihood of partial success, but still a risk of failure. If undertaken as a fully active strategy, then the process can be managed.

The Precarious   We define the precarious as those whose remaining assets are within 20 percent of the present value of remaining lifestyle needs. The window runs from those who are underfunded by 20 percent to those whose floor can be fully funded, but they have little room for precautionary balances or upside.

This is the group for whom the options around working longer, deferring consumption, simplifying lifestyle, and monetization of other assets can have the most impact. For our purposes, we assume that the adviser has had a discussion with client about the aforementioned options. So we focus on portfolio construction:

> *Option 1: Is an annuity an option?* Although the client may not have been interested in insurance solutions a year ago, for clients now on the cusp, insurance might be a more viable option. By monetizing their mortality, they may be able to create a small amount of room for an upside portfolio. By changing their flooring type, they may be able to get comfortable with trading off a large measure of portfolio control for lifestyle security.
>
> *Option 2: Taking limited risk.* For this option you need to know the level of the lowest lifestyle that they are willing to tolerate. Typically, this would mean removing the unnecessary items and most vacation travel from the concept of flooring. These items would be

reclassified as nice but not necessary. The idea is to create a floor at their necessary lifestyle. In the static framework, one can secure the floor to this level and, ex precaution, post the rest toward upside. This generally means that in some years there will be sufficient wherewithal for the extras, but other years will be leaner. In an active framework you need to have a plan to both cover gains and willingness to cut losses. The trick is to use the volatility advantageously without being at its mercy. Know your stops and stick to them. If you manage to claw back to the start line, have the wisdom to seek a defeasance of the risks.

The client may be willing to risk a little more of their lifestyle to try to grow their way out of the hole, but it is a risk. Remember what we saw in the early part of this chapter: the cost of insuring underperformance of the risk-free rate does not cheapen over time. In short, the market is not optimistic about the prospects for success. In light of this risk the expectations of the client need to be managed. This should not be promoted as anything other than a measured and monitored risk.

What we do not advocate is either a stay-the-course strategy or a strategy of covering only the near end of retirement. Stay the course offers the hope for a turnaround against the potential for further declines. It is a risk without a plan for what to do in either the up or down cases. The idea of having a floor that will be rolled out as time passes is also not advocated. While such a plan may be a fine strategy for accumulation of a retirement floor while still working and obtaining new funds to devote to retirement, it is a fallacy to think that one can simply expect to grow into flooring needs as time passes.

The Lost   This is the group for whom there is no reasonable prospect of returning to a fully funded lifestyle. The cutbacks are expected to be more severe. Working longer and monetizing other assets may provide some relief, but there is no panacea. Some will accept the new reality and others will try to reject reality.

The one safe option is to fully monetize mortality and annuitize at the highest level possible. Presumably, even this will leave the client with a diminished lifestyle. No amount of sugarcoating will make the pill of a diminished lifestyle easier for the client to swallow.

The risky strategies are, in this case, very risky. There is no room for maneuver. There are neither reasonable static nor active strategies for digging out of the hole. The hurdle to get back to a fully funded lifestyle is insurmountable under reasonable amounts of risk. Essentially, the risk would entail either portfolios with very high beta or the use of leverage.

Neither case is considered appropriate for most retirement portfolios. While the bankruptcy laws create a call option–like profile, by any prudent expert's or prudent man's standards, these risks are unacceptably high.

Stay on Top of the Situation

Many of the options provided here have elements of active management either explicitly or implicitly inherent in them. If your practice is traditionally one with a more static focus, then, to some extent, you will need to abandon tradition for these clients. You may want to go back and reread Chapter 9 to see how to craft the plans around infrequent monitoring. But infrequent doesn't mean nonexistent.

Throughout the course of this book, I have attempted to show how retirement income portfolios differ from accumulation portfolios. I have tried to convey the idea that the simple change in portfolio construction that results from taking horizon and lifestyle needs into account can have profound changes in the probability of success in retirement. I have further tried to show that most of the changes required of portfolios are simple, scalable, and fit into current business models. I encourage you to think of ways to include a retirement income option in your business. It will benefit both you and your clients

SUMMARY

Trillions of dollars in client assets were vaporized last year. For many whose wealth declined, the recriminations are nearing their end and the planning for gaining back lost ground is beginning. Advisers need a plan to help clients to both restore their portfolios and restore trust in their advisers.

In the field of retail finance, there are many solutions that are offered for treating "sick" portfolios. Many of these proposed solutions are nothing more than the financial equivalent of folk remedies that generally offer no improvement in prospects and may make things worse. In the wake of the Panic of '08, where the credibility of financial advice is being questioned more than ever, it is time to offer clients reliability. Therefore, this chapter debunks some of the myths around long-run risk. The long run is risky. Risk increases with the time horizon. There is a vast distinction to be made between where the market tells us that the odds are in our favor and where we only have a hope that the odds are in our favor.

We also delved into practical steps for making the best of a bad situation. Lives have been ruined by a business model that for 25 years was tolerant of mistaken beliefs, and bad advice. The reputation and viability of the retail industry has not been more in doubt since the 1930s. Many of you who have read this far are worried about your future. Instead of focusing on the extremity of the related challenges faced by clients and the financial services industry, this book has been about creating a business model that is more beneficial for clients and advisers alike. I hope it is beneficial to you and your clients.

History of Theoretical Developments in Life-Cycle Planning

Many models have been developed to understand the consumption and investment plans made by individuals over their life cycle. Among the seminal works are Yaari (1965), Samuelson (1969), and Merton (1971). The common theme is that optimal solutions for investment and spending decisions are made together as part of a complete life-cycle solution. All end up showing the importance of wealth in determining consumption (as opposed to income) and the importance individuals place on reducing the volatility of consumption.

The early models often focused on the importance of wealth rather than simply income in determining consumption, the importance of consumption smoothing, and the corollary that risk-averse individuals will be willing to pay to ensure a stable and smooth consumption plan. More recent approaches extend the basic framework. The more modern approaches help understand how dissimilar individuals can be when it comes to setting their unique goals. See, for example, Thorp (2005), Horneff (2006), and Sharpe, Scott, and Watson (2007). We follow the development toward more general models of behavior, and allowance for the possibility that individual lifestyles may be prone to habit formation as in Lax (2002), which allows for minimum lifestyle preferences to ratchet upward following an increase in wealth. For our purposes, these general models have the most interest because they help us to segment client types and better understand how to map types to solutions.

THE MODEL

Too often economic models are counterproductive in the sense that their specificity makes them unhelpful for anything more useful than broad generalizations: great for classroom use but lousy for practical use. It is more useful to start with a wide class of models and distill the commonality in their solutions rather than focus on the solution to a single model. We can then more easily determine the information of practical value by synthesizing the commonalities. The HARA (Hyperbolic Absolute Risk Aversion) class of utility functions is a very broad class of behavior. It encompasses all of the standard models that are most often used in practice; the standard models are special cases of the HARA class. The generalized function allows for the different ways that risk aversion can vary with wealth.

Using a HARA framework, we show the solution to consumption and investment choices for an individual with a finite lifetime choosing between a risk-free and a risky asset. We show the case where there is a minimum level of consumption required by the individual.[1] The model can easily be adapted to allow for time-varying minima, as this seems to better reflect observed behavior.

Consider an investor with time separable preferences over consumption with the following utility:

$$U(C, t) = \delta^t \frac{(C - C_F)^\lambda}{\lambda}$$

where U = investor's utility function, δ = discount factor (impatience), C = consumption per period, and λ = risk aversion. With W = wealth, α = allocation, and r = returns on the risky and risk free assets, the investor's life-cycle maximization problem becomes the following:

$$\max E[U(C_t, C_{t+1}, \cdots, C_T)] = \max E\left[\sum_{i=0}^{T} U(C, t+i)\right]$$

$$= \max \sum_{i=0}^{T} \delta^i E\left[\frac{(C_{t+i} - C_{F,t+i})^\lambda}{\lambda}\right]$$

subject to $W_{t+i+1} = (W_{t+i} - C_{t+i}) \times (\alpha_t r + (1 - \alpha_t) r_f)$ and terminal condition $C_T = W_T$. When the lifestyle floor is constant and the risky-asset returns are distributed lognormally, Ingersoll (1987) shows that the optimal consumption plan can be written as $C_t^* = C_F + f_t^{pct} \cdot (W_t - PV(\text{Future Lifestyle Floors}))$.

The solution is that optimal consumption in each period equals the minimum consumption need plus a fraction of discretionary wealth in excess of planned lifestyle needs. In general, the value of f_t^{pct} depends upon the remaining horizon, the investor's risk aversion, the parameters of risky asset return distribution, and the risk-free rate. The variation in f_t^{pct} across specific models highlights the importance of flexibility in drawing on the portfolio of risky assets, and underscores where many of the magic-bullet products have a weakness.

The intuition of drawdown rates can be shown with simple examples. For an investor with $C_F = 0$ and log utility, the fraction depends on impatience and remaining time.

$$f_t^{Pct} = \frac{1}{1 - \delta^{T-t+1}}$$

With the addition of perfect patience ($\delta = 1$), the optimal fraction reduces to

$$f_t^{Pct} = \frac{1}{T - t + 1}$$

For this individual, discretionary wealth would be consumed at a constant rate over his/her remaining life. Minimum required distributions for IRA withdrawals follow a similar rule with $(T - t + 1)$ replaced by actuarial life expectancy. One immediate result is that only for those individuals with ascetic lifestyles, such that their needs are minimal with respect to their wealth, will a drawdown policy be optimal. For those whose lifestyle needs[2] approach or exceed their wealth, there will be a greater incentive to monetize mortality or take greater risk.

For the general case where f_t^{pct} depends on the parameter of risk aversion, the more risk averse will act more frugally early in retirement, until impatience and shortness of remaining time overcome risk aversion. With a level floor $C_{F,t} = C_{F,t+i}$, consumption is an increasing function of time. The shapes that are possible include gradual and sharp increases in consumption.

While the optimal behavior implied by all model types is a desire to separate assets into floor plus upside, each model provides very specific prescriptions about creating and drawing out of the upside portfolio.

For a specific example, Ingersoll (1987) shows optimal asset allocation to the risky asset as in the following:

$$\alpha_t^* = \frac{W_t - C_t^* - \left(\hat{W}_{t+1} \big/ (1 + r_f)\right)}{W_t - C_t^*} \alpha^P$$

The optimal investment policy implies that the flooring is locked in to meet the PV of future lifestyle needs with the risk-free asset, allocating the remaining to the risky asset.

So far, we have assumed that lifestyle needs are nominal and constant. Nominally fixed lifestyle floors yield the undesirable result that the floor becomes increasingly irrelevant as nominal consumption grows; allocations to the risky asset increase through time, a facet which is counter to observed behavior; empirical studies document a shift away from the risky assets after the onset of retirement.

RISING LIFESTYLES AND HABIT FORMATION

Since the seminal work of Abel (1990) and Constantinides (1990), habit formation has been increasingly used to explain consumption and investment decisions. These models are broad in scope and consistent with the stylized facts of empirical observation that lifestyles tend to increase with wealth but do not decrease as quickly when wealth declines.

Much of what follows is based on the work of Lax (2002) who uses a simple habit formation model to derive solutions for optimal consumption and investment strategies. The intuitive underpinning for habit-formation models is that people quickly become accustomed to betterment in their lifestyle. They are then loath to return to a lower lifestyle: They want to keep the lifestyle to which they've become accustomed. In the framework provided by Lax,

$$C_F(t) = \rho C_F(t-1) + hC(t-1)$$

where ρ and h are constants such that $\rho + h < r_f$.

The previous equation can be read as saying that the consumption floor for this period is a function of last period's floor and also last period's consumption. In general this can be interpreted as ratcheting upward in response to transitory bumps in actual consumption. A special case is where $\rho = 1$ and $h = 0$, which implies a constant nominal floor. When $\rho = 0$, the consumption floor varies and becomes what is often called Markovian.

Lax derives the following closed-form solution for his model:

$$C_F^*(t) = X(t)W(t) + Y(t)C_F(t)$$

where $X(t)$ = the rate of growth of wealth, $W(t)$ = current wealth, $Y(t)$ = the rate of growth of consumption, $C_F(t)$ = the current consumption floor. Growth rates for consumption and wealth will depend on the particular individual's path and preferences.

For the habit formation model, optimal allocations to the risky asset are given by:

$$\alpha_t^* = \alpha^P \left(1 - \left(\frac{PV_t(\mathrm{FHL})}{W(t) - C(t)} \right) \right)$$

Where, α^* = the optimal allocation to the risky asset, α^P = the previous period's optimal allocation to the risky asset, and FHL = estimated future habit level. The rate that the floor grows depends on the starting level of the floor. The phrase *high initial habit formation* refers to the case where the individual starts with a very high floor relative to wealth; *low initial habit formation* is where the individual starts with a very low floor relative to wealth. These two ends of the spectrum provide initial conditions that can lead to vastly different, and interesting, outcomes.

Initial Habit Formation: Starting High

Starting from a high consumption floor relative to wealth, little opportunity for future consumption growth remains. Simulated high initial habit formation results are presented in Figure A.1; the parameters of Lax's model with $\rho = 0.5$ and $h = 0.5$ are used. This graph shows that in the Lax model, starting from a high floor relative to wealth, the portfolio is rapidly diminished and there is little potential for lifestyle enhancement. Notice that although the floor grows with consumption as the individual becomes accustomed to higher consumption, the growth in consumption is modest.

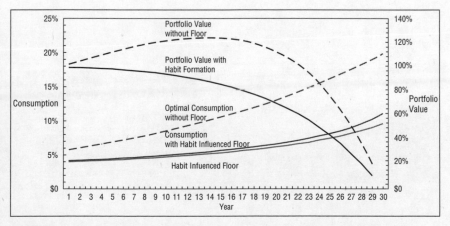

FIGURE A.1 Lax Model: Initial Habit Formation Starting from a High Floor

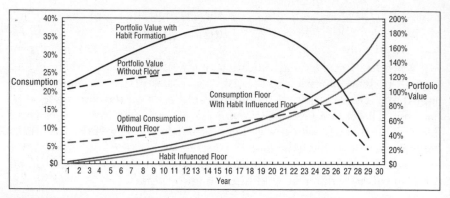

FIGURE A.2 Lax Model: Initial Habit Formation Starting from a Low Floor

Initial Habit Formation: Starting Low

Aspects of low initial habit formation simulations are presented in Figures A.2 and A.3. In this case, the investor starts with no floor but creates and adjusts the floor as his consumption rises (again with $\rho = 0.5$ and $h = 0.5$). Notice in Figure A.2 that the floor increases rapidly with consumption. In this case, the individual started with no requirement for lifestyle relative to wealth but quickly adapts, and lifestyle needs begin to rise with wealth.

In Figure A.3, the portfolio result is interesting because this case agrees with the conventional sentiment that the allocation to risky assets decreases during retirement. The graph shows that the allocations to risky assets

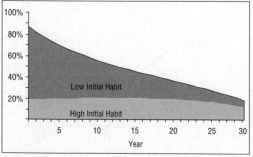

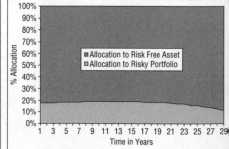

FIGURE A.3 Allocation to Risky Assets

evolve differently depending on whether the individual starts with a high or low consumption floor relative to wealth. Once retired, as flooring needs rise, the portfolio will have a lower allocation to upside and tend toward lifestyle security.

With a long horizon, the present value of future consumption needs is high. So for someone with a longer horizon this pushes up the allocation to the risk-free asset; Lax calls this the age effect. By itself this would lead to the risk-free allocation declining through time as the remaining floor shortens and the value rolls off. However, the long-horizon individual will habitually consume more than a short-horizon individual. This will result in the longer-horizon investor allocating more to the risk-free asset as the consumption habit grows. This means that while the old floors are rolling off, the future floors are rising. If the individual started with very little flooring relative to wealth, then the floor has nowhere to go but up and the allocation to risky assets will decline through time. On the other hand if the initial allocation to flooring is high enough, then the roll off of flooring will trade off fairly evenly with increases in future habit.

EMPIRICAL STUDIES OF LIFE-CYCLE BEHAVIOR

There does not appear to be a single optimal asset allocation and consumption plan that is right for everyone. This means that the products that do everything and offer themselves as *the* solution for retirement are likely to appeal to no more than a single segment, if that. However, understanding the drivers of behavior and the places where more or less flexibility is needed to accommodate individual differences is the key to success in offering solutions. We strive to offer consumption and asset allocation advice that is practical, optimal, customizable for each individual investor, and scalable across multiple individuals. The findings of a few important empirical studies relevant to this book are presented here.

Asset Allocation, Risk Tolerance, and Wealth
- Evidence that investors exhibit decreasing relative risk aversion (DRRA) can be found in Bajtelsmit (1999), using the Health and Retirement Survey.
- Using Survey of Consumer Finances (SCF) data and a panel of data from TIAA-CREF, Ameriks and Zeldes (2004) do not find any evidence supporting increased risk aversion by age alone. This is a hugely important point: age alone does not lead to a desire for gradually reducing risk; rather it is the act of retirement that is contemporaneous with the shift in behavior. The practical importance of this is that target-glide paths

are more likely to have greater success as components of postretirement portfolios than as components of preretirement portfolios.

- Carroll (2000), using the (SCF) data, points out that wealthier individuals hold a much higher proportion of risky assets and suggests evidence of decreasing relative risk aversion.
- Also using the (SCF) data, Gomes and Michaelides (2004), note that more risk-averse households prefer to invest a smaller fraction of their wealth in risky investments.

How Professionals Can Maximize the Usefulness of this Book

This book has been primarily aimed at financial professionals. The term *financial professional* covers a multitude of subtypes and specialties. For our purposes, it is probably most useful to take the following headings and expand on the most beneficial direct impact that this book can have on your practice. We categorize and consider the following types of professionals:

- Transaction-oriented salespeople
- Asset gatherers
- Insurance planners
- Financial planners
- Portfolio managers

For each group a brief definition is provided, followed by a discussion of how to bring the most value to your practice out of this book. All groups will find ways to attract rollover assets, create stickier assets, and find ways to create both opportunities for themselves and strategic value for their clients.

TRANSACTION-ORIENTED SALESPEOPLE

Transaction-oriented salespeople are what would be traditionally called "brokers." These professionals hold Series 6 or Series 7 registrations. In conjunction with their FINRA registrations, many hold insurance licenses.

For the most part, transaction-driven models preclude a deep knowledge of their client. Generally, this is a volume business and there need to be simple and scalable pitches. This is the group that derives value in the ideas and interest generation created by sell-side analysts.[1] These professionals stay up-to-date on research, companies, corporate actions, and the flows of their successful clients. Selling ability is enhanced by projecting knowledge, competence, and an ability to find a repeatable trade that will appeal to a wide variety of client types. Here's where retirement income can fit right in.

Without detailed knowledge of the client, other than age, the transaction-oriented professional can help clients build a retirement income portfolio simply by adding a table of bond strips to their repertoire (see Chapter 5). There are four main opportunities for current and future transactions:

1. *Rollover assets.* When trying to attract rollover assets from 401(k)-type plans, the advantage that an IRA account offers is the ability to customize the portfolio for the particular client's retirement. To that end, demonstrating the ability to create flooring makes clear the linkage between assets and postretirement lifestyle. Most 401(k) plans are for an indeterminate client. As such, few 401(k)s offer more than generic bond funds, which do not help the client lock in their retirement floor. Using rollover assets you can customize portfolios for client needs both scalably and tax efficiently in a way that 401(k) plans can't generally match.

2. *Accumulation plans.* While the client is still saving and accumulating assets, purchase of bond strips as either strategic purchases, that is, annual contributions earmarked for flooring; or tactical purchases, that is, rates are high ≥ buy strips now, if rates are low ≥ wait a while. Buying and adding to a position is a part of the acquisitive nature of most clients. They like to build their positions. This feeds into a client's natural acquisitiveness, but in a way that is beneficial to their retirement lifestyle.

3. *Stack-and-roll plans.* A stack and roll is a process where a liability stream that is due beyond the maximum maturity of the listed market is hedged by stacking assets at the limit of the listed market. For example, a 40-year-old client may expect to retire in 25 years at age 65, but the listed market in Treasury strips only goes out for 30 years. The client may be willing to use IRA or even rollover assets to buy strips covering the interval from 25 to 30 years out. The client, fully expecting to live more than 30 years, places multiples of what is needed at the 30-year mark (the stack) that can be sold in the future to purchase later maturing strips (rolling). As time elapses and the maturity of the listed market moves out and begins to cover more of the period where the cash flow is needed, part of the stack is sold off and rolled out to appropriately match the liability stream. For the transaction-oriented adviser, the ability to stack and roll sets up both current and future transactions.

4. *Capital markets to insurance markets.* Once accumulation ends and retirement begins, there is a marked reduction in transactions around the flooring assets. At this point it is beneficial for the client and broker to consider a partial annuitization of the portfolio. The client may be perfectly happy and comfortable with the capital markets flooring that has been accumulated, but the client would benefit from thinking about longevity. This provides an opportunity to discuss either pure longevity insurance or annuitization. Annuitization of the existing flooring to take care of the potential for longevity may also allow taking advantage of mortality credits sufficiently to boost the floor. In sum, you may earn a fee and trailer while the client may achieve a higher floor.

ASSET GATHERERS

Asset gatherers are compensated based on AUM (assets under management). They generally act as feeders to the actual investment managers. They primarily focus on directing assets toward mutual funds and separately managed accounts (SMAs). As with their brokerage brethren, they tend to possess Series 7 and Series 66 registrations.

Traditionally, asset gatherers have close relationships with their clients and with the fund managers on whom they rely. Gathering ability is enhanced by projecting knowledge of what asset managers are thinking, competence, and an ability to find asset managers and portfolio components that can be reused for a variety of client types. Retirement income fits in as a flooring sleeve in a portfolio construction. Although the compensation scheme differs for asset gatherers and transactional representatives, both benefit from approaches that stress customization that is both tailored but can be somewhat impersonal.

With a firm relationship but no detailed knowledge of the client, other than age, our goals are to draw in more assets and create stickier assets:

Rollover assets. When trying to attract rollover assets from 401(k)-type plans, having a sleeving for fixed-maturity instruments is a natural way to help the client build a floor while attracting assets that earn fees. For some gatherers, this may entail a mixed model of transaction- and fee-based revenue if specific strips are used and the fee structure does not cover individual securities.

Admittedly at this writing, there are few ("40 act") funds that are specifically designed for retirement income over a fixed window of time. One existing possibility that is still relatively new is the insurance-wrapped portfolio construct. A process of migrating from long-term bond funds to a mix of maturity targets that shorten as retirement draws near is simple and can be automated, but it is riskier than an actual floor constructed of maturing instruments.

Accumulation plans. During accumulation either a fixed or discretionary schedule for migrating assets from generic funds to specific flooring may provide both reputational enhancement and create stickier assets as it stresses the process of migration from accumulation of assets to preparation for their harvest.

Keeping AUM. For asset gatherers, the notion of insurance is often dismissed out of hand. Insurance usually means that the assets are going away. However, there are two types of insurance products that may be beneficial to consider. The first is pure longevity insurance. Both as bullets and as deferred annuities, longevity insurance is potentially cheap enough to require minimal dissipation of assets while providing the client with a tangible benefit. Generally available for about 10 cents per dollar of coverage 25 years out, longevity policies may incur minimal asset reductions while strengthening the level of trust between advisor and client. The other type of insurance to consider is the previously mentioned wrapper. In this case the assets stay under management but an insurance fee is paid guaranteeing performance of the wrapped part of the portfolio. The market for these wrappers is relatively new but the product is designed specifically for the fee-based market.

INSURANCE PLANNERS

Insurance planners sell life insurance products and solutions. As a group they are extremely well positioned for retirement income products. Insurance planners who couple their insurance licenses with a FINRA Series 7 can offer a full array of insurance products and financial products.

Requiring a slightly better appreciation for a particular client's needs and risk profile, insurance planners are well positioned to take advantage of the retirement income market. With a focus on the comprehensive needs of retirees and showing how to create a secure lifestyle, insurance planners can offer a range of products for secure retirement income. There are some first-generation insurance plus upside bundled products such as index-linked products, variable annuities, Guaranteed Minimum Income Benefits (GMIBs) and Guaranteed Minimum Withdrawal Benefits (GMWBs) that can be used for insurance-only approaches. Of course, a less constraining set of options widens the ability to appeal to a diverse client base. It has been popular for issuers to embed, rather than attach, upside potential to insurance products. It is possible that many planners who can operate in both capital markets and insurance markets will find attaching components has more appeal to clients than a single-issuer embedded bundle.

Some of the problems that insurance planners encounter include resistance to solutions that require major changes in portfolio construction,[2] are hard to reverse,[3] have a reputation for being complicated or a reputation for being expensive.[4] Even if their ultimate goal is to provide insurance products, a flexible approach will be beneficial. Rather than focusing on insurance-only solutions, insurance planners can mix a combination of capital markets products and insurance products to create a relationship with the client. An approach that initially places greater weight on capital markets and seeks to transition clients gradually, over time through education, will be more likely to yield a mutually advantageous relationship.

Generally, with a good knowledge of the client's concerns and the client's risk profile, the goal is to attract financial assets:

Assets outside of tax-advantaged accounts. While insurance products are often aimed at the low- and midmarkets, the tax deferral property of insurance contracts, particularly with mortality credits attached make them attractive to HNW and UHNW individuals. Once 401(k)s and IRAs are maxed out, flooring with discount bonds becomes a tax nightmare. With the tax deferral inherent in insurance contracts, they gain a distinct advantage over many capital markets flooring products outside of the tax umbrella of retirement accounts.

Secure flooring. Flooring needs to be secure. Insurance planners have an opportunity to sell flooring, but also flooring security. A disadvantage of capital markets products is that they don't cover longevity risk; a disadvantage of annuities is that they are not diversified across issuers. Single-contract, multiple-issuer annuities have begun to be offered by some institutions as a way around this disadvantage. Insurance planners who focus on the retirement market may find ways of selling the components of flooring security even if the bundled packages of flooring or flooring bundled with upside do not appeal to a particular client.

FINANCIAL PLANNERS

Financial planners offer comprehensive financial planning processes and are often fee only. Typically, these fee-only planners are registered with Series 7 and 66 registrations; many will also seek the Certified Financial Planner (CFP) designation and be well schooled in insurance products. This group will likely find value in Retirement Professional designations such as the proposed Retirement Income Industry Association designation of Retirement Management Professional and the like.

With a firm relationship and detailed knowledge of the client, financial planners are extremely well positioned to offer comprehensive retirement income solutions for clients including the following:

Life-cycle planning. Life-cycle planning is an important predicate to creating retirement income solutions. The planning process takes time and effort. However, it does afford both a degree of standardization and experiential expertise. The planning process itself may provide revenue opportunities, particularly for cases where the actual management of assets is not desired.

Rollover assets. When trying to attract rollover assets from 401(k)-type plans, the knowledge and ability to help clients build a floor is of value to both parties. Planners can easily scale flooring construction to many clients arbitrarily, particularly using basics like Treasury strips and annuities. Even at the minimum, knowing the year that flooring is to begin and the desired height of flooring provides a target and guide for future actions.

Accumulation plans. During accumulation, the planner is able to provide valuable information to clients such as the amount of flooring that their current portfolios afford. The planner and client are thereby able to craft a portfolio of floor and upside that makes the risks of not locking in flooring clear. Conceptually, distinguishing between flooring and upside allows the planner to help the client bifurcate flooring and upside accumulation schedules.

Allowing for either a fixed or discretionary schedule for migrating assets from generic funds to specific flooring creates a way of transitioning the clients from accumulation to retirement income in a way that is beneficial to clients and allows the planner to move multiple clients in quick succession.

Comprehensive solutions. With their greater knowledge of client needs and risks, the financial planner can offer the full range of solutions that not only create flooring and upside, but create a portfolio that is resistant to many of the typical risks of retirement portfolios and resilient in the face of market downturns.

PORTFOLIO MANAGERS

Portfolio managers usually do not face clients directly. They primarily work institutionally and manage mutual funds and exchange-traded funds (ETFs).

Most will have the FINRA Series 7 and Series 66 registrations. Surprisingly, even for those with advanced accredited degrees, the Chartered Financial Analyst (CFA) designation offered by the CFA Institute is popular.

Currently, there are few portfolio managers who construct portfolios in the retirement income space. There are what some might generously call "first-generation" retirement income portfolio constructs such as the so-called "target date funds" that are meant for retirement accumulation. However, the pickings are slim and what exists can best be described as "all hat and no cattle." The opportunities for portfolio creation in the retirement income space are boundless. The goals for portfolio managers are distinct from client-facing professionals in the sense that they want to create products that make rolling over from a fund to a directed account a less attractive option. There are efforts at development of '40 act companies for retirement income that are currently under way; it will be interesting to watch this area for developments.

With no knowledge of the clients, one may think that there are impediments to the ability of portfolio managers to address the retirement income market, but that is not the case. The areas that portfolio managers can have the greatest impact on the retirement income market are the following:

- *Accumulation to decumulation.* Opportunities abound for the creation of portfolios (closed end, open end, notes, UITs, and ETFs) designed to accumulate flooring for a period of time followed by a known and fixed term of disbursement. In spirit, these portfolios would be natural extensions of current practice for many funds that exist in the closed end and unit investment trust (UIT) areas. In practice, these would be different with either protected or guaranteed floors, depending on whether targeted to fully taxable or tax-advantaged accounts.
- *Flooring plus upside managed decumulation.* Portfolios can be created that combine upside accumulation with flooring designed to cover a fixed window of time. Myriad opportunities exist for tying to potential sources of upside and the disbursement options for the upside such as straight line with the floor, accelerated, or deferred.

Notes

Introduction

1. The term *alpha* is shorthand for implying that there are opportunities for out-performance that can be regularly and reliably discovered and sold to a retail audience.

Chapter 1

1. To take the metaphor as far as it will go, if you can run up the score high enough you don't need to worry.
2. The oldest joke in finance is that the difference between bonds and bond traders is that bonds mature.

Chapter 2

1. Hyperbolic absolute risk aversion (HARA) $\rightarrow U(C_1, C_2, \cdots, C_T) = \sum_i \beta^i (C_i - C_{\text{Floor}_i})^\lambda \div \lambda$, where C_t denotes consumption during period t, C_{Floor} denotes the individual's specified minimum lifestyle, λ denotes the individual's risk aversion, and β represents impatience.
2. To be feasible, i.e., affordable, the floor needs to lie somewhere between 0 and $W_t(1 + r_f)$, where r_f is the return on a risk-free asset.
3. Using more general but standard models of behavior that incorporate consumption floors can explain much of what is considered anomalous behavior, including a client's lack of interest in diversification, and simultaneous purchase of insurance and lottery tickets. What is happening is that inclusion of a consumption floor implies that optimal consumption takes the shape of a call option. Once the consumption floor is achieved, some amount of volatility becomes valued even by the risk averse.
4. The interesting part about the popularity of assets that act like lottery tickets isn't that they are a somehow irrational bet, but that their asymmetric payoff is so valuable that their equilibrium price is bid to where the expected payoff is below zero. Most structured products achieve their yield "enhancement" by selling protection on their relevant market so that the buyer of the structured product is enabling someone else's asymmetric upside payoff by taking the downside in exchange for some premium.
5. Throughout the book, we use the abbreviation PV(*x*) to denote the Present Value of *x*.

6. Tontines are the most straightforward example of this where the payoff is highest to the last person standing. In most cases they are illegal because they create the incentive to kill off others in the pool—in that regard, tontines are the poster child for moral hazard.
7. Accredited investors meet income and/or wealth eligibility requirements and in exchange for fewer investor protections gain access to financial products that don't generally qualify as regulated securities (e.g., exotic options and private placements).
8. We provide a working definition of natural candidates for annuities in Chapter 3.

Chapter 3

1. For something to be called *flooring,* we want to be able to tell the client that you'll get at least this much for at least that long. That long may be their uncertain lifespan.
2. There are commuting costs, wardrobe costs, and other costs that everyone incurs related to working.
3. With $\ln(x)$ denoting the natural logarithm of x, r denoting the discount rate, and i^e denoting expected inflation, the number of periods

$$N = \left(\frac{\ln\left(1 - \frac{\text{Wealth}}{\text{Lifestyle}} \left(\frac{r - i^e}{1 + i^e} \right) \right)}{\ln(1 + i^e) - \ln(1 + r)} \right).$$

This is a handy formula for figuring out a myriad of problems, such as the length of time it will take to pay off a loan if extra principal is added on to regular payments. In that case, replace the value for wealth with remaining principal and replace lifestyle with the actual payments being made.
4. The British economist J. M. Keynes is often credited with the phrase, "I'd rather be approximately correct than precisely wrong."
5. Metaphorically, a stepped-up floor that takes expected or possible inflation into account can be described as building a stairway to heaven.
6. TIPS reset the notional value monthly based on the three-month lagged, not seasonally adjusted value of the urban CPI. In the event of deflation, the notional value of TIPS is floored at $1,000. TIPS pay coupons on a semiannual basis.
7. Interest on I-bonds consists of a fixed-rate component plus an inflation-indexed component. I-bonds reset the inflation component of their interest rate semiannually based on the urban CPI.
8. The list of people suggesting that TIPS are the best way to go for most, if not all, people include some very eminent thinkers such as Zvi Bodie and William Sharpe. I agree that TIPS are very good for many people and I cautiously agree that the advice should be taken as a universal default protocol. But the willingness to buy nominal securities, reap the embedded call premium, and take a

position on future inflation is just one more aspect where there is a risk versus return trade-off.

9. The Markowitz model and the vast majority of models, including CAPM (Capital Asset Pricing Model) and most ICAPM (Intertemporal Capital Asset Pricing Model) models, *assume* that financial assets are completely separable from consumption goods. This simplifies the mathematics of the models but creates a blind spot in our ability to explain why, for example, during the housing boom the average square footage of new construction jumped so dramatically—people were buying more house than they needed for the consumption of shelter as an investment; not necessarily more houses but more house.

10. Or equivalently, find the market prices for principal strips on government securities that match the timing of flooring needs.

11. The distinction between financial assets and wealth can best be illustrated by the notion that human capital is part of wealth but until one actually goes to work and monetizes the human capital it does not add to financial assets; monetizing human capital does not change wealth, it just transforms a part of it into financial assets. In a sense, one's wealth is pretty much fixed the day learning stops.

12. Insurance companies can provide average and median conditional life spans.

13. Adding a credit adjustment to the discount rate would be appropriate for finding this PV since, as mentioned elsewhere, insurance is not risk free.

14. One advantage of fixed-window insurance products is that they remove the difficulty faced by the insurance company in pricing the extreme tail. Where insurance companies have difficulties in estimating probabilities they adjust prices to reflect the risk that they bear of misestimating probabilities.

15. In general, figure your client as average and just compare market results. However, if your client has a strong reason for PV'ing using probabilities other than those given by the mortality tables, you may want to adjust for a shorter/ longer lifespan. For example, a good friend of mine has lymphoma in remission. He has indicated a complete lack of interest in monetizing his mortality, valuing the PV of annuity flows at zero; figuring that he will be extremely lucky to make it even to age 65. In such cases, you may want to ask, "What if you live?"

16. A discount rate of 4 percent and 3 percent inflation.

17. This group is typically the hardest group for advisers to serve. The typical example is the client who has $3 million but wants to live on $300,000 per year and expects the adviser to be able to deliver in all market conditions. These are the clients who are naturally attracted to the Bernard Madoffs of the world.

Chapter 4

1. I'm still not wholly pleased or convinced about the inevitability of that mortality thing where I'm concerned, but don't let my self-delusional state affect the planning for your clients.

2. In this example, there is no death benefit. The death benefit in life annuities can be thought of as a consolation prize, but it does not change the essence of monetizing mortality.

3. Bullet Bond is another term for a zero-coupon bond. A zero coupon bond, as its name implies, does not make coupon payments; it simply pays off its notional amount on maturity. Some zeroes are born that way (e.g., OID—Original Issue Discount bonds), while others are created after issue (e.g., Principal Strips). The Principal payment is stripped from an ordinary bond—sometimes called POs— principal only. In general the stripping of a bond creates 2 pieces: the coupon strip (Interest Only or IO piece) and the principal strip (Principal Only or PO piece). It is the financial equivalent of an automotive chop shop.

4. In fact, the bond listings will usually tell you the interest rate that is implied by the price.

5. This is known as a *conditional probability*. It should be somewhat intuitive that the odds of surviving until age 90 are higher for someone who has already survived to age 65.

6. Mortality frequencies are adjusted to reflect the fact that mortality isn't what it used to be, life expectancies in the United States have been lengthening over the last 100 years. But that could change.

7. This may be an unrealistically high mortality rate, even by standards of the bubonic plague, but it compares favorably to Tom Clancy's later novels.

8. We are assuming properties consistent with an exponential probability distribution. Apparently the only creatures whose survival probabilities are independent as per the implications of the exponential distribution are certain shellfish.

9. Unless your in-laws live with you, the idea of death benefits can sound like an oxymoron.

10. *Capital markets* are the markets used by companies to obtain funds from the investment community. Capital markets include familiar stock, bond, option, and currency markets.

11. Equity-linked capital markets products are usually of much shorter duration than many of the current crop of variable annuities. The variable annuities with downside protection tend to be priced far lower by actuarial markets than capital markets. The discrepancy in pricing is of great concern to risk managers.

12. A long position in a put option pays off when the underlying security falls below a specified level. The lower the underlying security falls, the higher the payout that the owner of a simple put option receives. Buying a long put is a way to put a floor under a portfolio.

13. The liability management issue was the assumption that property damage claims are more or less independent. Unlike house fires, a hurricane has a way of flattening whole counties. In a nutshell, the insurance companies lacked proper geographic diversification.

14. Insurance contracts are not securities as defined by the U.S. Securities and Exchange Commission.

Chapter 5

1. This couple has figured out that with 401(k)s usually offering a limited menu of fund choices, the way to customize their portfolio for their own needs is to

roll over part of their 401(k) into their IRA where they can work with an adviser to direct some of the assets to meet their flooring needs.

2. A complete discussion would make for a much longer book and would lose sight of the main aim of the book, which is managing the risk of portfolios for and through retirement.

3. Usually *mass-affluent client* is defined as one having somewhere between $250,000 and $2 million in financial assets. The high-net-worth (HNW) client goes from the upper limit of mass affluent to about $10 million. The next level of client is the ultra-high-net-worth client (UHNW). Those in the UHNW category usually have little interest in retirement planning. However, estate and monument planning is a different story.

4. Even in this artificial example, there would be a slight difference in cost since the coupons are paid on a semiannual basis.

5. Sharpe was one of three codiscoverers, along with John Lintner and Jan Mossin, of what we commonly call the Capital Asset Pricing Model (CAPM). Along with Harry Markowitz and Merton Miller, William Sharpe was awarded a Nobel Prize in Economics in 1990.

6. There is a fringe view—now more widespread since the 2008 credit crisis—that municipalities have an incentive to default and seek bankruptcy payments as a way to relieve the burden of their pension obligations without resorting to taxation. It's a proposition that is doubtful but not impossible.

7. To calculate the taxable equivalent yield on a municipal security, divide the yield to maturity by $(1 - \tau)$, where τ is the marginal tax rate. For example, if the yield on a municipal is 3 percent and your marginal tax rate is 40 percent (Federal + State − Federal × State), then your taxable-equivalent yield is $3\%/(1 - 0.4) = 5\%$.

8. If any governors of high-tax states are reading this, please consider issuing long-dated zeroes direct to the retail sector as a way to fund budgets with stable retail money. That way, these retail operations will have a strong incentive to maintain residency in your state and hold until maturity. For the retail client, this would be a zero-coupon bond with no tax headaches.

Chapter 6

1. The efficient frontier can be interpreted in two equivalent ways: (1) The combination of risky assets that yields the highest expected return for a given level of risk; or equivalently, (2) the combination of risky assets that yields the lowest level of risk for a given expected return.

2. For example, suppose that a firm's research has suggested that a portfolio weight of 30 percent large-cap U.S. equity is recommended. A sleeve of products, large-cap U.S., would be created from which the adviser could choose. Within the large-cap sleeve, the adviser would be able to find a set of ETFs, index funds, and managed mutual funds that the firm feels are appropriate for that sleeve. The firm might also set limits that can be allocated to the particular sleeve (e.g., no less than 10% or more than 60% of the portfolio can be put in any single advisory sleeve). A fee-for-service broker would not be constrained

in the same way that an adviser is constrained. Advisers, in the FINRA 63, 65, 66 sense, are usually paid to manage portfolios and must conform at least minimally to "prudent man" standards.

3. For example, an individual with a present valued floor at only 30 percent of wealth may decide to keep the entire 100 percent at-risk planning to lock in the flooring in the face of a significant drop in wealth.
4. Whenever possible, these should be purchased outside of the tax-advantaged retirement accounts.
5. Whenever possible, these should be purchased outside of the tax-advantaged retirement accounts.
6. There is probably an idiot somewhere who wanted to kill their spouse for the insurance money, but bought the intended victim an annuity by mistake.
7. Flooring locked in with either a long ladder of bonds or an annuity may be changed, for example, if your client's life expectancy were to suddenly decrease and they have less need to plan for the distant future.
8. Different states have Byzantine laws regarding tax exemptions that may include reciprocity agreements with other states and the like. This book isn't the place to wade into that swamp, but I would encourage a new book on tax issues for retirement planning, written with an emphasis on the portfolio constructs contained in books with the theme contained here.
9. Complex annuities include variable annuities and all of the GM-type offshoots that combine fixed annuities with potential or guaranteed portfolio upside.

Chapter 7

1. As in "won't know, won't care."
2. In his novel *Jude the Obscure*, Thomas Hardy created a great line for describing the feelings of the main character: "the hell of conscious failure."
3. Remember that the fraction of discretionary wealth that is optimally consumed in any period is highly idiosyncratic depending on individual horizons and risk tolerances.
4. The probability of ruin discussed in Chapter 1 is the probability that a fixed withdrawal drawdown rule applied to accumulation portfolios will run out of funds too early.
5. I first heard of this rule of thumb when I asked a surgeon why he was so willing to replace the joints of elderly patients. His answer was the rule of thumb for conditional life expectancy, $(100 - age)/2$, and that he felt it was worthwhile to operate on anyone who would have more than five years of expected life remaining.
6. Many insurance firms have priced contracts with assumptions about lapse rates, that is, clients who stop paying or fail to pay in a timely fashion. Overestimation of lapse rates is a risk that many insurance companies have learned to fear.
7. Not to mention colleagues and their families.
8. To be clear, we are talking about a widening of the comfort zone as a follow-on effect of having flooring securely in place.

Chapter 8

1. In October 2008 and again in March 2009, Japan's Nikkei index was trading around where it was in 1982, at the start of the bubble that has bedeviled Japan's economy ever since.
2. Many people find alternative assets to be quite attractive on a stand-alone basis; but very few people who are attracted to alternative assets think of their management in a portfolio construct. In practice, it is extraordinarily difficult to demonstrate in a rigorous manner that alternatives as an asset class either move the efficient frontier or provide any sort of risk reduction. The so-called "endowment models" usually rely on creating a frontier using a very small set of assets, so that every asset helps. They also have a tendency to confuse the concept of illiquid with uncorrelated.
3. Wash sale rules apply on the sale of an asset at a loss in order to recognize this loss for tax purposes. The asset is bought back—or an asset that is substantially the same is purchased instead—within 30 days. In a wash sale, the IRS will disallow recognition of the loss.
4. The dollar volatility is σA, where σ is the percentage volatility and A represents the dollar value of assets in the portfolio. When rebalancing, σ will change; with taxes (or transactions costs) A will also change. The products σA target and σA postrebalancing provides a useful comparison. In the presence of taxes, it is easier to rebalance to a lower level of desired dollar volatility than a higher one.
5. In a more complex engineering approach, the assets would be pledged and the recourse would be the smaller of loan amount or value of the pledged assets. To avoid tax triggers the structure can't cross the IRS threshold, "no longer at risk," constituting a sale. The financial intermediary would short the asset for the period of the loan. Extending the loan could be at the option of the investor. Upon death the loan terminates: Short is cancelled by delivery of the original assets. Any excess would revert to the estate at a stepped-up basis.
6. Far too many financial products that are issued are essentially punts or products where the investor is essentially selling protection against market declines—that covers virtually every "enhanced yield" product ever seen. Enhanced yield implies either arbitrage or enhanced risk. Arbitrage opportunities available to institutions are infrequent; at the retail level real arbitrage opportunities are as rare as rare can be.
7. Don't wake me until I can afford a place in Tahiti.

Chapter 9

1. Many of my former colleagues would differ slightly on this, but only after the first half dozen letters.
2. In many cases Wall Street risk managers were compensated and promoted for their ability to find ways to reduce regulatory capital, that is, they were paid to help their firms find ways to convince regulators that the firm was so well managed that the regulators should allow an increase in their firm's leverage.

If that wasn't stupid enough, risk limits were often based on a business unit's revenue without regard to the leverage of the balance sheet or the liquidity necessary to unwind the risk. Risk managers who demurred from the opportunity to self-destruct were described as "not partnering with the business" or "just doesn't understand the business"; you were either on the bus or under the bus. LTCM was a watershed event and, perhaps, the last time that "we *just* didn't know" was a valid excuse. The debacle in 2007–2008 is due to a willful failure of action at the executive level; it's not that the risks weren't understood, they were just ignored.

3. For a client with whom contact is infrequent and unprofitable, this is probably most advisable, particularly if they are also highly averse to lifestyle risk. Similarly, for an individual who is an infrequent consumer of financial news, rarely trades, and is worried about lifestyle risk, then a static allocation will let you sleep at night and spend your afternoons away from a television.

4. There is a large academic literature about the efficacy of risk management techniques. Some show that particular plans may work pretty well, for example, Cesari and Cremonini (2003), and impart only a small average drag on the higher expected returns. Many show what market conditions favor which particular technique—which kind of misses the point since you don't know beforehand what face the market is about to show you.

5. Quite often rather than use a normal distribution and its implication that greater than two standard deviation events can happen roughly 5 percent of the time, risk managers will use Chebychev's inequality which tells us that at most two standard deviation events can happen 25 percent of the time. In general, Chebychev's inequality tells us that n standard deviation events can happen at most $1/n^2$ of the time.

6. In national security, there is a saying "never plan defenses based on what you think the enemy will do, but plan based on what the enemy is capable of doing." The Maginot Line, constructed on an expectation of a replay of World War I, is a great example of this maxim going unheeded.

7. From $100 \rightarrow 90$ is a 10 percent move, from $90 \rightarrow 80$ is an 11.1 percent move, $80 \rightarrow 70$ is a 12.5 percent move, and so on.

8. This can be set up to ease the workload as a rolling rebalance across clients or as all clients simultaneously.

9. In other words in a static allocation we would put 70 percent into flooring and 30 percent in discretionary wealth.

10. It is common to refer to the quantity (1/Maximum drop) as the multiplier. A multiplier of 1 corresponds to a static allocation, for any multiplier > 1 periodic rebalancing is necessary.

11. If firms wanted to optimize CPPI notes for expected usefulness to clients, they would offer them as protected notes with m being inversely related to tenor. At the short end, go big or go home with $T = 1$ year or less and $m = 20$. At the long end, where the real goals are to ratchet the floor while keeping participation, they would better serve clients using a much lower m ideally between 1.5 and 2. Unfortunately, most of the CPPI notes are constructed to

generate margin rather than results: An intermediate tenor too short dated to be useful to retirees, but having a multiplier that is too high for the tenor of the note.

12. They are defined at the end of this chapter. But the short introduction is that a buy/write is a long position in a stock plus a short position in an out-of-the-money call. The client agrees to sell off exposure to upside in exchange for receiving call premium.

13. The precise rules are somewhat Byzantine, but the important point is that the vast majority of principal guaranteed notes are subject to ordinary income taxation.

Chapter 10

1. In the first step of the transition, the basic flooring is put in. The basic transition flooring being a capital markets construct, is built to a finite endpoint. It is only in the final step of the transition that the flooring is secured for longevity, either by augmenting the capital markets floor with a deferred annuity or by replacing all of the flooring with some form of immediate annuity.

2. I offer little advice to advisers who want to know what to do with the clients hoping for the miracle bequest that never comes. The best I can offer is the reality of "Here's where your floor is now, if the money arrives we can raise the floor, but until it shows up we work with what we have."

3. Sometimes the word "complexity" is used as shorthand to express a vague discomfort that can't be articulated, but take it for what it means—not today.

4. Throughout the autumn of 2008, the country was in the midst of a profound financial crisis and the government was preparing a stimulus package. Both consumption and GDP felt the impact of the crisis. Imagine how much lower of a stimulus package would be required if the clay-footed titans of Wall Street had focused on retirement income rather than jamming hedge fund and enhanced-yield paper into the retail space. Individuals who are secure about their income are more prone to discretionary consumption. With lifestyle security, retirees and near retirees would not have watched their lifetime savings halved and would not have felt compelled to shut their wallets so tightly.

5. Let me contradict myself here to satisfy a nit that has been picked. There are some things that can be done before age 35 for a client who focused on retirement security from an early age. You can stack fixed-income securities 30 years out. If they're 30 years old, the stack would mature when they are still working. Once they hit 35, you can begin to roll the stack that you have already created.

6. This is true on both theoretical and practical levels. On the theoretical level, a floor is a level below which utility is undefined—meaning do anything to avoid breaching the floor. The Markowitz and most other pre-Merton MPT models ignore the concept of a floor. On the practical level, if the floor isn't secure, then it isn't a floor.

7. Typically the fixed-income component relies on a handful of bond funds with varying focus.

Chapter 11

1. Private information about life expectancy, state-specific bankruptcy laws, and so on.
2. Previous experiences can matter as do inertia, cognitive dissonance, and the like.

Chapter 12

1. Ironically, the notion of exclusivity and limited access is the fertilizer that crooks such as Bernard Madoff use to lure registered and overseas investors into unregulated entities, where it is easier to steal client funds and avoid easy detection. Theft is the ultimate high-margin offering. The victims of such frauds often fail to report the frauds with an embarrassment related to a twist on a familiar question: "If you're so rich, why aren't you smart?"
2. Many of the alternative assets were sold on the premise that they were uncorrelated with other investments. Quite often both buyers and sellers made the mistake of confusing illiquid for uncorrelated and mistaking a convenient organizational structure for a separate asset class.
3. To drive the intuition of brittleness of optimized systems versus resilient systems, consider the difference between a stick-and-rudder airplane to a B2 bomber. The optimization that allows an ungainly craft like a B2 to fly is too complicated for the pilot to act as a, well, pilot. If the B2's computers fail then the crew knows that it is a good time to test the rescue parachutes attached to their seats. In contrast, a stick-and-rudder plane is resilient to most mechanical problems—short of structural failure—because it is made to be simple enough to be flown by the barely trained.

Chapter 13

1. A friend of mine, with an MBA from the University of Chicago, once lamented that his middle-class upbringing made him prone to stay in a job that made him miserable rather than strike out on his own and suffer a potential, albeit temporary, period before success would ensue.
2. If longevity insurance as a pure play is unavailable, then a deferred annuity can be used.
3. See, for example, Milevsky and Young (2002).
4. The anecdotal information was presented by an insurance executive at the Managing Retirement Income Conference in Boston, February 2009.
5. Institutional plan administrators have far too often been happy to manage simple funds until retirement and then have the assets either annuitize or roll away. The views of administrators can be summed up with a comment made by the head of retirement at a major Wall Street firm who said to me, "Why should I change my way of doing things? Who cares if 70 percent of the assets roll away on retirement? I've been in this business for 20 years and even with the roll-away assets, my net assets have gone up every year." Administrators

have an incentive to clip an administrative coupon and do little else. This attitude partially explains why it has been such a struggle to push retirement income to advisory practice. Most retirement income initiatives are located within the retirement divisions of financial firms. The retirement divisions are chock-full of administrators. The incentive within such units is to serve plan sponsors and put money to bed at low administrative expense. They are administrators; neither transaction based nor client-service based.

6. Insurance professionals sometimes wince when I describe these contractual relationships as yielding a degree of control over assets. Although they agree that the constraints are in place, they dislike the terminology. They prefer to describe the process as creating more freedom in the assets that aren't annuitized.

7. The underfunded clients are almost always the ones with the unreasonable expectations about portfolio returns.

8. It is easy to be cynical and think that enhanced returns and enhanced solutions are euphemisms for enhanced profit margin for the financial firm. However, the high net worth may have some real needs for collaring concentrated positions or some real desires to take a few speculative gambles.

9. One interesting quirk relates to static versus active strategies for risk management. If a structured note (static strategy) is created that guarantees a minimum value at or above 70 percent of principal, then the entire note becomes subject to taxation as ordinary income, even if the note is comprised of roughly 30 percent equity. In other words, the note ends up converting a capital gains asset (the 30 percent that is comprised of equity) into an ordinary income asset. Most notes with guarantees are subject to ordinary income treatment. On the other hand in a portfolio that is actively risk managed, the assets will bifurcate into their component types. This remains true for most active strategies that protect the portfolio in exactly the same way as certain guaranteed structured notes.

10. I haven't seen any evidence that tilting portfolios toward alternatives enhances long-run performance; with the higher fee structures, the contrary is true. Certainly those marketers of alternatives, unimpeded by conscience, would love for you to use them for all of your clients. That said, there are clients who seek—and even demand—alternatives.

11. If the client needs a fixed annuity, inflation protection is always preferred. It can't always be afforded but it is always preferred.

12. In informal conversation with those who structure fixed-income ladders, the lowest they want to go for putting a ladder together is $3 million notional.

13. If longevity insurance as a pure play is unavailable, then a deferred annuity can be used.

14. This doesn't advocate that clients be told what's good for them. However, a changed focus can be disorienting and mortality is never an enjoyable contemplative topic, unless it's about someone else. Most people would rather contemplate winning the lottery, which is unlikely to ever occur rather than contemplate their own mortality, which is somewhat more likely.

15. See Chapter 6 for examples of accumulation specifically for retirement.

16. $r = 5\%$.

Chapter 14

1. I live in a very small but highly diverse town. I have neighbors who make more than 10 times the national average per year but live such a lavish lifestyle that they have no savings—none. Others, with roughly the same income for whom frugality is the norm, save over 30 percent of their income per year. At the other end of the income spectrum, the story is the same. Lavishness and frugality are not absolutes but relative. Patience and impatience concerning consumption are unlikely to change after retirement. Neither lavishness nor frugality are moral characteristics, they are human characteristics.
2. There is repudiation risk even in government securities. For example, the Soviets repudiated, that is, refused to pay, the debt incurred by the Czarist and Kerensky regimes. Governments not only own the printing presses, but they also have unique ability to repudiate their debts and eliminate legal recourse.
3. The beneficiary can usually be changed but the name of the insured cannot.
4. There are some bonds that never mature—they are known by the terms *perpetual* and more archaically *consol*. Consol derives from the way that they were created in the early 1800s in England: After the Napoleonic wars, the English sought better control of the aggregated debt issued by all of the different agencies and ministries. They simply did not know how much they owed. Therefore they decided to call in all debt, tally it up, and reissue as consolidated (hence *consol*) obligations which were issued as perpetual debt.
5. The distribution of mortalities is skewed, meaning the average is not the same as the midpoint. A few people living a lot longer than expected can pull the average up even if the typical person dies before the expected date. Life expectancies at birth are usually skewed downward by those who die at a very young age. On the other hand, the conditional life expectancies of those who have already survived to 65 are skewed upward by those who live to extreme old age.
6. Ratings can change and mergers can reduce diversification. One of the benefits of an advisor is that they can and do monitor changes in holdings that may go unnoticed by individuals.
7. Selling an insurance annuity back to the issuer is a process known as *surrendering the annuity*.

Chapter 15

1. A word coined by comedian Stephen Colbert denoting statements offered as fact and with great vehemence, but which are neither verified nor falsifiable.
2. See Bodie (1995).
3. At-the-money puts and calls are not of equal value because the value depends on the terminal distribution, not the starting point. With a one-year horizon and a risk-free rate of 3 percent, the strike price at which puts and calls would price equally would be where the strike was above the current spot price by $e^{.03}$.
4. The usual approach is to lock in flooring from ages 65 to 75 with the hope that someday, before age 75, the floor can be extended to cover the later years.

5. There is a saying that "if you are the type to stand firm while others are in a state of panic, then perhaps you have misjudged the situation."
6. Even when markets appear to be on the mend, exogenous events can intervene. The downswing from the tech bubble seemed largely behind us by Labor Day 2001. The headline in the *New York Times* on September 11, 2001, showed the mayor doing a meet and greet, reflecting that September 10 was a slow news day. Premarket indicators on September 11 looked as bright as was the weather in New York that day, right up until 8:46 A.M.

Appendix A

1. Some authors describe the minimum level of consumption as subsistence, but since it is a subjective notion of subsistence, we use the terms consumption floor and lifestyle floor synonymously.
2. This can be interpreted to include planned bequests.

Appendix B

1. The relevant fact about sell-side analysts is that, aside from their abysmal records, they help to keep money in motion, flowing to the idea of the day.
2. Some refer to this problem as a manifestation of cognitive dissonance. That is, there is a sense that such a major change casts aspersions on the previous portfolio that it was flawed. Correlating to the first problem is a second problem where the question is why now, why not yesterday or tomorrow?
3. While some have argued that reversible annuities can be made less costly, that is doubtful. The act of surrendering an annuity, on average, conveys information about the annuitant's private information regarding life expectancy—those whose life expectancy shortens will be more likely to seek to surrender annuities.
4. The reputations may be somewhat undeserved, but it would be foolish to deny that the reputational difficulties exist.

accumulation portfolio An accumulation portfolio is a portfolio that takes the portfolio objective as maximizing expected return for a given level of risk. This approach works best for those whose use of the portfolio for funding consumption is sufficiently far in the future that it is sensible to act as if the investor never expects to need to liquidate assets to fund consumption.

annuity (nominal) A level stream of payments over either a fixed term or indefinite period of time. Most of the traditional annuities pay for the lifetime of the holder; in that regard, indefinite annuities couple mortality credits with a perpetual bond. The probabilities of your survival over future dates make annuities less costly than perpetual debt.

annuity (real) An annuity where the stream of payments over either a fixed term or indefinite period of time rises or falls with some measure of prices. The annuity's flows adjust in order to provide cash flows that have the same purchasing power in all periods.

at the money When the price of an underlying asset equals the strike price of an option written on it. For example, if ABC shares are trading at $100 per share (sometimes the current price is called the spot price, implying purchase on the spot), then any option written on ABC shares with a strike price of $100 would be at the money (sometimes referred to as "at the Money, spot").

at the money, forward Similar to at the money, but this means at the money with respect to the forward price of the asset. For options traders, the forward price and the distribution around the forward price is a common way of thinking about an option's valuation and hedging.

balance sheet (corporate) A corporate balance sheet is a double-entry design for displaying assets on one side and the sum of liabilities and owners equity on the other. Owner's equity plays the role of the balancing amount. When assets meet or exceed liabilities the firm is said to be solvent. There are strict accounting rules that govern construction of corporate balance sheets. Some of these rules are useful for standardizing the content. However, the accounting rules can obscure the true value of the entity.

balance sheet (economic) An economic balance sheet is a double-entry design for displaying assets on one side and the sum of liabilities and owner's equity on the other. When trying to find a market value for an entity, an economic balance sheet is a valuable tool. This type of balance sheet attempts to value the entity as a portfolio of assets, some of which are not tangible or otherwise ineligible for corporate accounting. For example, a physician's practice would show corporate assets of the historical cost of the building, examination table, and the various examination doohickeys. Whereas the economic balance sheet would display current market values of the same assets plus the discounted value of the patients expected to continue after a change in ownership. The economic balance sheet would show a different value of the firm than a corporate balance sheet.

balance sheet (retiree) The retiree balance sheet is an economic balance sheet that is designed to value assets and liabilities that are both tangible and intangible at proper market values.

bottom-up estimates A process of estimating amounts by beginning at the level of greatest detail; an attempt to estimate using a precise list of the items and amounts required. See *top-down estimates*.

capital market line The line represents the highest expected return that can be obtained by varying combinations of risky portfolios with riskless assets. As a graphical representation, it is the line that starts at the risk-free rate, slopes upward, and is the highest sloping of all possible lines touching a single point on the efficient frontier.

capital markets wealth A measure of current financial assets plus the PV of future contributions to the base of financial assets.

constant proportion portfolio insurance (CPPI) Constant proportion portfolio insurance is a risk management method for dynamically rebalancing a portfolio to keep constant the proportionate risk of falling below a minimum amount. CPPI is a useful method for dynamically allocating assets that allows for enhancing expected yield by coupling with enhanced vigilance to ensure that some specified minimum level portfolio value is preserved.

constant relative risk aversion (CRRA) Clients exhibiting CRRA behavior do not change their behavior toward risk as their wealth changes; they will be equally willing to risk the same proportion of their wealth as their wealth rises or falls.

consumption floor The minimum amount of funding needed per period to satisfy the client's subjective minimum consumption needs. The amount needed depends on the lifestyle that the client minimally feels it necessary to maintain. Generally, this is used synonymously with the notion of a lifestyle floor.

CPPI notes CPPI notes are structured notes based on CPPI methodology that provide principal protection and upside exposure.

credit risk The risk that a counterparty will renege or be unable to pay a contractually obligated amount owed to a creditor.

cushion See *portfolio cushion*.

decreasing relative risk aversion (DRRA) Decreasing relative risk aversion is the type of risk-averse behavior that most people exhibit. Clients exhibiting DRRA behavior will be more willing to risk a proportion of their wealth as their wealth rises. Conversely, during retirement, when wealth is being consumed, DRRA behavior is consistent with increased risk aversion.

discretionary wealth Akin to the notion of owner's equity in corporate balance sheets, discretionary wealth is the balancing amount found by calculating assets minus liabilities within the client balance sheet.

diversification Diversification is the act of moving one's eggs into multiple baskets. Diversification spreads the risk around in attempt to reduce the influence of any element of a particular risk. Diversification may reduce risk, but it is only under special circumstances that diversification eliminates risk. As many have recently rediscovered, diversified portfolios reduce the specific risk of a particular asset, but they still contain risk related to the overall condition of financial markets.

dynamic allocations An allocation of funds to investments where the proportions are changed by design is known as a dynamic allocation. The two main types of dynamic allocations are discretionary and formulaic. Discretionary allocations are changed based on a flexible but defined standard. Formulaic allocations change based on rules that are preset. See *static allocations*.

floor See *consumption floor*.

GMxx An umbrella term meant to capture all of the variations and permutations in the guaranteed minimum product world, including but not limited to GMAB, GMIB, GMWB products.

guaranteed minimum accumulation benefit (GMAB) Such benefits add a feature to variable annuities by embedding guarantees on performance of the subaccount over some horizon. Roughly Annuity + Fund + Long in the money put.

guaranteed minimum income benefit (GMIB) Such benefits extend variable annuities by embedding guarantees on payments regardless of the performance of the subaccount once payment starts. Roughly Annuity + Fund + Long forward starting put.

guaranteed minimum withdrawal benefit (GMWB) Such benefits extend variable annuities by embedding guarantees on payments that cannot fall once payment starts. Roughly Annuity + Fund + Long forward starting lookback put.

human capital The present value of future earnings.

income statement Display of income from all sources and expenses paid out.

insurance-wrapped portfolios Relatively new idea that attempts to detach the management of the insurance from the management of the underlying assets. The idea is to allow advisers to keep assets under management with the insurance funding the only part that "goes away."

lifestyle floor See *consumption floor*.

market risk The probability that changes in the market value of assets held in a client's portfolio could adversely affect the value of the portfolio. For a long position the risk is a reduction in price.

Modern Portfolio Theory An umbrella term that usually refers narrowly to the work of Harry Markowitz (1952, 1959) with its emphasis on diversification. Diversification is very important but it is not sufficient for client portfolios.

money in motion Wealth that has recently changed hands and has yet to find a home. Money in motion is commonly associated with divorces, rollovers, sale of a business, and inheritance. Having an approach for attempting to gather money in motion is always part of the adviser's repertoire.

moneyness The amount by which an option is in the money, at the money, or out of the money.

onboarding An admittedly awful bit of jargon referring to the process of bringing in a new client and integrating the client relationship into the business practices of the advisor.

point of smoothest transition   The point in time or age of the client when the allocation to fixed-income securities is closest to that client's proposed allocation to flooring in a retirement income portfolio is known as the point of smoothest transition.

portfolio cushion   The difference between the current value of the portfolio and the present value of flooring. The cushion measures the maximum losses that the portfolio could sustain before the losses would impinge on the ability to purchase the lifestyle floor.

present value (PV)   The value as of today for something that will not occur until a future date. For example, it is the value that would be placed on receiving $100 one year from today. At the personal level, the present value that *you* would place on receiving $100 a year from today depends on your rate of impatience and the risk of the prospect. In aggregate, the market value of receiving $100 one year from today is observable by reference to the one-year rate of interest.

risk pooling   An insurance term for achieving well-behaved risks; pooling allows risk to be spread across a spectrum of individuals.

risk sharing   See *risk pooling*.

risk transference   Risk transference allows the risk of an event to be completely transferred to another party. Typical risk-transference instruments include option instruments like puts and calls.

sleeving   The practice of grouping products, by type, for menu-driven use in portfolio construction templates. Quite frequently, large advisory firms will guide their advisers about how to allocate assets among product types, rather than particular products. Instead of suggesting an *x* percent allocation to a particular asset, the firm will recommend that the advisers allocate *x* percent within a particular product type (sleeve), thus giving the adviser a small degree of freedom among approved products, managers, and funds within that sleeve. For example, within equity, there may be a recommended allocation for large-cap equity; inside the large-cap equity sleeve there will be a list of approved large-cap funds that the adviser is permitted to recommend.

social capital   The present value of all cash flows arising as part of the social compact and not a direct quid pro quo. Social Security income benefits and other transfer payments are included in this category.

stack and roll   The process of hedging an exposure that is longer dated than the traded market. In this case the hedge is "stacked" up at the furthest liquid point. As time moves on, the region beyond the stack becomes liquid enough to "roll" part of the stack out to the part of the timeline that has become tradable.

static allocations   An allocation of funds to investments where the proportions remain fixed from inception to maturity is known as a static allocation. This includes allocations that are rebalanced periodically to remain on a static target. See *dynamic allocations*.

top-down estimates   A process of estimating amounts by beginning at a very high level; an attempt to estimate starting with an approximation of where you think you might end up before adding detail. See *bottom-up estimates*.

Treasury Inflation-Protected Securities (TIPS) Treasury securities where the notional value (face amount) off of which coupon payments are calculated is adjusted for inflation. TIPS reset the notional value monthly based on the three-month lagged, not seasonally adjusted value of the urban CPI. In the event of deflation, the notional value of TIPS is floored at $1,000. TIPS pay coupons on a semiannual basis

variable annuities Annuities with embedded mutual funds. Generally, they offer a wide array of fund choices. Payout is typically a minimum value plus a percentage of the attached subaccount (fund).

References

Abel, Andrew B. 1990. "Asset Prices Under Habit Formation and Catching Up with the Joneses." *America Economic Review Papers and Proceedings* 80: 38–42.

Ameriks, John, and Stephen D. Zeldes. 2004. "How Do Household Portfolio Shares Vary with Age?" SSRN Working Paper.

Ando, A., and F. Modigliani. 1963. "The 'Life Cycle' Hypothesis of Savings: Aggregate Implications and Tests." *American Economic Review* 53, no. 1: 55–84.

Arrow, K. J., and G. Debreu. 1954. "Existence of Equilibrium for a Competitive Economy." *Econometrica* 22, no. 3 (July): 265–290.

Backus, D. K., A. W. Gregory, and C. I. Telmer. 1993. "Accounting for Forward Rates in Markets for Foreign Currency." *Journal of Finance* 48: 1887–1908.

Bajtelsmit, V. L. 1999. "Evidence of Risk Aversion in the Health and Retirement Study." Proceedings of the Risk Theory Society.

Basak, S. 2002. "A Comparitive Study of Portfolio Insurance." *Journal of Economic Dynamics and Control* 26: 1217–1241.

Black, F., and R. Jones. 1986. "Simplifying Portfolio Insurance." *Journal of Portfolio Management* 14, no. 1: 48–51.

Bodie, Z. 1995. "On the Risk of Stocks in the Long Run." *Financial Analysts Journal* 51, no. 3 (May–June): 18–22.

———. 2003. "Lifecycle Investing in Theory and in Practice." *Financial Analyst Journal* 59, no. 1 (January–February): 24–29.

Breeden, Douglas T. 1979. "An Intertemporal Asset Pricing Model with Stochastic Consumption and Investment Opportunities." *Journal of Financial Economics* 7, no. 3: 265–296.

Brunnermeier, Markus K., and Stefan Nagel. 2006, December. "Do Wealth Fluctuations Generate Time-Varying Risk Aversion? Micro-Evidence on Individuals' Asset Allocation." SSRN Working Paper.

Carroll, Christopher, D. 2000, July. "Portfolios of the Rich." NBER Working Paper.

Campbell, John Y., and John H. Cochrane. 1999. "By Force of Habit: A Consumption-Based Explanation of Aggregate Stock-Market Behavior." *Journal of Political Economy* 107: 205–252.

Cesari R., and D. Cremonini D. 2003. "Benchmarking Portfolio Insurance and Technical Analysis: A Monte-Carlo Comparison of Dynamic Strategies of Asset Allocation." *Journal of Economic Dynamics and Control* 27: 987–1011.

Constantinides, George M. 1990. "Habit Formation: A Resolution of the Equity Premium Puzzle." *Journal of Political Economy* 98: 519–543.

Duffie, D., W. Fleming, H. M. Soner, and T. Zariphopoulou. 1997. "Hedging in Incomplete Markets with HARA Utility." *Journal of Economic Dynamics and Control* 21: 753–782.

Dybvig, P. 1995. "Dusenberry's Ratcheting of Consumption: Optimal Dynamic Consumption and Investment Given Intolerance for any Decline in Standard of Living." *Review of Economic Studies* 62: 211–287.

Friedman M. 1957. *A Theory of the Consumption Function.*" Princeton, N.J.: Princeton University Press.

Gale, William G., and John K. Scholz. 1994. "Intergenerational Transfers and the Accumulation of Wealth." *Journal of Economic Perspectives* 8, no. 4: 145–160.

Gomes, Francisco, and Michaelides, Alexander. 2004. "Optimal Life Cycle Asset Allocation: Understanding the Empirical Evidence." SSRN Working Paper.

Horneff, W. J., R. Maurer, O. S. Mitchell, and I. Duis. 2006. "Optimizing the Retirement Portfolio: Asset Allocation, Annuitization and Risk Aversion." NBER Working Paper 12392.

Ingersoll, J. E. 1987. *Theory of Financial Decision Making.* London: Rowan-Littlefield, Savage.

Kingston, G., and S. Thorp. 2005. "Annuitization and Asset Allocation with HARA Utility." *Journal of Pension Economics and Finance* 4, no. 3: 225–248.

Lax, Yoel. 2002. "Habit Formation and Lifetime Portfolio Selection." SSRN Working Paper.

Markowitz, H. 1952. "Portfolio Selection." *Journal of Finance* 7, no. 1 (March): 77–91.

———. 1959. *Portfolio Selection, Efficient Diversification of Investments.* New York: John Wiley & Sons.

Merton, R. C. 1969. "Lifetime Portfolio Selection Under Uncertainty: The Continuous Time Case." *Review of Economics and Statistics* 51, no. 3: 239–246.

———. 1971. "Optimum Consumption and Portfolio Rules in a Continuous-Time Model." *Journal of Economic Theory* 3: 373–413.

———. 1973. "The Intertemporal Capital-Asset Pricing Model." *Econometrica* 41: 867–887.

———. 1992. *Continuous-Time Finance.* Malden, Mass.: Blackwell.

Milevsky, M. A. 1998. "Optimal Asset Allocation Towards the End of Life." *Journal of Risk and Insurance* 65, no. 3: 401–426.

———. 2001. "Optimal Annuitization Policies: Analysis of the Options." *North American Actuarial Journal* 5, no. 1. 57–69.

Milevsky, M. A., and V. R. Young. 2002. "Optimal Asset Allocation and the Option to Delay Annuitization: It's Not Now or Never." Discussion Paper PI-211, Pensions Institute, Birbeck College, University of London.

Richard, S. F. 1975. "Optimal Consumption, Portfolio and Life Insurance Rules for an Uncertain Lived Individual in a Continuous Time Model." *Journal of Financial Economics* 2: 187–203.

Samuelson, P. 1963. "Risk and Uncertainty: A Fallacy of Large Numbers." *Scientia* 98: 108–113.

————. 1969. "Lifetime Portfolio Selection by Dynamic Programming." *Review of Economics and Statistics* 51: 239–246.

Sharpe, W., J. S. Scott, and J. G. Watson. 2007. "Efficient Retirement Financial Strategies." Pension Research Council Working Paper Series, 1–29.

Thorp, S. 2005. "Risk Management in Superannuation." Ph.D. Dissertation, University of New South Wales, Australia.

Wachter, J. 2000. "Habit Formation and the Cross-Section of Asset Returns." Unpublished paper, Harvard University.

Yaari, M. E. 1965, "Uncertain Lifetime, Life Insurance and the Theory of the Consumer." *Review of Economic Studies* 32 (April): 137–150.

Index